CATTLE, WOMEN, AND WELLS

CATTLE, WOMEN, AND WELLS

Managing Household Survival in the Sahel

CAMILLA TOULMIN

CLARENDON PRESS · OXFORD
1992

Oxford University Press, Walton Street, Oxford OX2 6DP

Oxford New York Toronto
Delhi Bombay Calcutta Madras Karachi
Petaling Jaya Singapore Hong Kong Tokyo
Nairobi Dar es Salaam Cape Town
Melbourne Auckland
and associated companies in
Berlin Ibadan

Oxford is a trade mark of Oxford University Press

Published in the United States
by Oxford University Press, New York

British Library Cataloguing in Publication Data
Data available

Library of Congress Cataloging in Publication Data
Toulmin, Camilla.
Cattle, Women, and Wells: Managing Household Survival in the Sahel / Camilla Toulmin.
Includes bibliographical references and index.
1. Bambara (African people)—Agriculture. 2. Bambara (African
people)—Domestic animals. 3. Bambara (African people)—Social
conditions. 4. Agriculture—Economic aspects—Mali—Kala.
5. Cattle—Economic aspects—Mali—Kala. 6. Human ecology—Mali—
Kala. 7. Kala (Mali)—Economic conditions. 8. Kala (Mali)—Social
conditions. I. Title.
DT551.45.B35T68 1992 338.1'096623—dc20 92-926
ISBN 0-19-829006-3

Typeset by Best-set Typesetter Ltd., Hong Kong
Printed and bound in
Great Britain by Biddles Ltd,
Guildford & King's Lynn

Acknowledgements

This book describes the findings of a two-year period of field-work in a group of Bambara villages in central Mali. Carried out as part of the research programme undertaken by the International Livestock Centre for Africa (ILCA), the field-work lasted from April 1980 to March 1982. During this period, the two researchers were permanently resident in the villages, apart from a few short breaks. It is a tribute to the inhabitants of Kala, Markabougou, Dofinena, and neighbouring communities that we were so happily settled there and, when away from them, were impatient to return. On the few occasions when I have been able to visit Kala since leaving in 1982, I feel the same sense of excitement and anticipation about returning, to find out what has been happening and to pick up, albeit briefly, the threads of a familiar existence amongst friends and neighbours. This book is therefore dedicated to the villagers of Kala, in acknowledgement of their patience and enthusiasm for explaining how, what, and why they do the things they do. The two years spent there were not only highly enjoyable but also very valuable to me for understanding better the common structures and values demonstrated by human society in very different settings.

Financial support during the period of field-work and subsequent thesis writing was provided by the International Livestock Centre for Africa and the United Nations Association International Service. Thanks are due to both organizations, and particularly to Stephen Sandford of ILCA who encouraged me to pursue my studies and get my thesis finished and published. I owe much gratitude to Duncan Fulton, with whom I did the field-work in Mali and who must share the credit for many of the ideas developed here. Our four observers Karounga Coulibaly, Sidiki Diarra, Abdurahman Djire, and Baba Konate showed great stoicism, despite the rigours of life in a small bush village and to them I am grateful. Similarly, life would not have been possible without the hard work of Bintou Coulibaly, who cooked and fetched water for us throughout our stay in the village. We also received much help from all the staff of ILCA Mali and in particular from Peter de Leeuw, Jeremy Swift, Pierre Gosseye, and Ahmadou Dagno. Other researchers working in Mali have provided me with much useful material and ideas, for which I am grateful, in particular Sara Randall, Mary Martin, Samba Soumare, Mike Winter, and Ced Hesse. I must also thank my supervisor Judith Heyer at Somerville College, Oxford who was a great source of support and advice during the preparation of this material for my doctorate in 1986.

Since presenting the thesis, several people have helped me greatly in getting this book into publishable form. Jean Drèze of the London School of Economics provided many comments on the original thesis, my uncle Roger Toulmin carried out a detailed editing job to amend and clarify the text, while colleagues at the International Institute for Environment and Development (IIED) and the Overseas Development Institute (ODI) have provided valued support and comment on many of the ideas discussed here. Simon Rietbergen, Caroline Livermore, and Nicole Kenton have been particularly helpful in tidying up the final text, for which I am very grateful.

I would also like to thank my husband Mark and three children Luke, Agnes, and William for much encouragement, and occasional distraction, during the time needed to prepare this book for publication.

C.T.

IIED, London
July 1991.

Contents

List of Figures

List of Maps

List of Tables

Abbreviations

BFM   Bush-field millet, the longer cycle *sanyo*.

CTW   Hand-weeding labour, weighted according to time of input and also weighted for sex and age of the worker.

FCFA   The franc of the Banque Centrale des États de l'Afrique de l'Ouest, part of the Franc Zone, a monetary system tied to the French franc and supported by the French government. There is a fixed exchange rate of 50 FCFA to 1 French franc. In 1981, at the time of field-work, 1,000 FCFA was approximately equal to £2.

HWD   Hand-weeding labour, weighted by sex and age of the worker.

ILCA   The International Livestock Centre for Africa, one of the International Agricultural Research Centres, has its head-quarters in Addis Ababa, Ethiopia and one of its country research programmes based in Mali.

MN   A measure of the manure available to the farming household, calculated using a 'manuring index'.

MVP   The marginal value product, the value in terms of extra output produced by one extra unit of a given input.

NPV   The Net Present Value associated with the flow of returns stemming from a given investment, calculated by discounting returns in future years.

PNB   The proportion of land newly cut within the bush field.

PTD   Plough-team days of work.

RAIN   The dummy variable used to weight differentially bush fields according to whether they caught rain from a late storm in 1981.

SOIL   The dummy variable used to weight differentially bush fields according to whether they had particularly hard laterite soils.

SWI   The dummy variable used to weight differentially bush fields in which sowing was carried out particularly early in 1980.

TLU   Tropical livestock units, a measure used for aggregating animals of different species, age, and sex according to their fodder requirements. A camel is taken as 1 TLU, sahelian cattle are usually taken as 0.7 TLU, while each sheep and goat is taken as 0.12 TLU.

VFM   Village-field millet, the shorter cycle *souna*.

1

INTRODUCTION

The aim of this study has been to try to understand the choices open to farmers in a sahelian village called Kala, in central Mali. Lying a long day's walk to the north of the great River Niger as it flows past the town of Ségou, this community of Bambara farmers maintains a fierce allegiance to their glorious pre-colonial past. At the same time, modern civilization has intruded greatly into peoples' lives and ways of doing things, bringing some gifts in the form of ploughs, medicines, and bicycles, but also bringing changing values and—as the old men complain—making things no longer as they ought to be. The climate has been less even-handed in its gifts. While rainfall has always fluctuated from year to year and from place to place, the past twenty years have witnessed lower and more erratic rainfall than previous decades. Farmers have had to change substantially the way that they farm, the crops they grow, and the plans they make, in order to adapt to a drier climate. This book documents some of that process of change and the continuing uncertainty faced by farmers regarding future sahelian rainfall trends.

Life in this drought-prone region of West Africa can be harsh and full of risk—to health, to crops, to one's herd of cattle. Yet there are also opportunities open to the hard-working, the audacious, and the lucky which bring considerable returns. This book presents the choices facing different farm households and the factors that limit such choices. Decisions must be made about how much time to spend on different activities, which crops to grow, how much to invest in cattle and other assets, how best to manage the large and diverse work-force within the household, and a host of related questions. Constrained by time and other resources, people have to balance up the benefits from different courses of action.

Kala is a village of some 550 people lying on the northern edge of the savannah farming zone of West Africa. Settled for several centuries, its southern flank faces the more densely populated region around Ségou town while northwards there lie a few small villages scattered amongst the vast pasture lands that stretch up towards the border with Mauretania and the desert beyond. Kala maintains a dual inheritance stemming from its southern links with cultivation and trade combined with looser alliances northwards from whence come herders bringing dusty flocks of black sheep, camel trains, and herds of pale-skinned cattle.

This mixture of resources, linkages, and opportunities presents an array

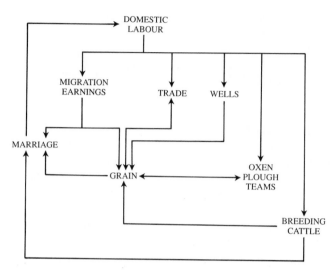

F IG. 1.1. Production, investment, and household development in Kala

of choices facing farmers in Kala. Yet households are not equal in their ability to take up such opportunities. In the following chapters, some of the constraints on successful performance at individual and household levels will be examined to get a clearer picture of how and why some people are better able to survive and prosper in this tough environment.

THE PRODUCTION SYSTEM OF KALA

The main elements of the production system of Kala are shown in Fig. 1.1. Many of the elements are interlinked either through conversion, as when grain is sold to purchase cattle, or through production links, as when domestic labour is used to water and care for cattle and oxen plough teams.

Grain, mainly in the form of bulrush millet, is at the centre of the farming system. The Bambara consider themselves cultivators, first and foremost, despite the considerable livestock holdings that they now have. Millet cooked in its various forms is the staple food for these farming families and it is millet porridge that is spilt on family altars, at sowing and harvest time, to ensure the spirits are kept in good temper.

Grain is the product of domestic labour combined with oxen plough teams and the manure acquired from breeding cattle and from water–manure exchanges. The millet production system and the relative importance of these different inputs are the subject of Chapters 4 to 6. Grain may also be reinvested in these assets, as when several sacks of grain are bartered for a young heifer or bull, or where a blacksmith is hired to dig a well. Grain is used to finance a trading business and to pay for marriage costs. Payment in grain is also made to hire Fulani herders on contract to guard and pasture the cattle during the farming season, when the Bambara spend all their days in the field. But most importantly, the production and storage of a big millet harvest provides the household with a certain strength and flexibility by ensuring that the family has enough to eat until the next harvest.

Domestic labour is used to maintain and expand the household's economic base, by cultivating millet, digging wells, developing an active trading venture, training and managing the oxen plough team, and watering the cattle herd. Domestic labour is also involved in migration, providing cash earnings for many households to pay their taxes and marriage costs.

Wells, oxen plough teams, and breeding cattle are the main physical investments made by farmers in Kala. They each play a major role within the production of millet, while breeding cattle additionally serve as the household's bank account. Cattle can be sold in years of poor harvest to buy grain, and are of especial value in helping finance marriage costs. The costs and returns from these three assets are examined in Chapters 7 to 11.

Marriage is one of the main rites for men and women in Kala. For men, it marks the possibility of establishing a growing source of labour and influence within their own household and the village. Having a wife confers status on a man and provides him with greater comforts than a bachelor can hope for. For women, marriage should provide a secure position where, with hard work and successful child-rearing, they will achieve a respected old age. As they grow old, they will hope to be surrounded by daughters-in-law to ease their burden of work, and a horde of grand- and great-grand-children to tease and mock their toothlessness. Marriage and child-rearing do not always bring such happy and successful outcomes, as will be seen in Chapters 12 to 14.

Three related themes underlie the analysis presented in the following chapters. These themes are at the centre of household strategies and decision-making in farming communities like Kala: the role of risk, the long time-frame within which decisions are made, and the close linkages between economic performance and household size and organization.

Risk

Risk affects most areas of life for farmers in Kala, whether it be in the variability of harvests from year to year, in the number of calves born to their herd, or in the illness and death of family members. However, the distribution of such risk is not random, nor are all households equally vulnerable. Household size and wealth moderate the impact of risk on both the individual and the domestic group as a whole.

Risk stems from several sources, the most important of which are climatic and demographic. As Chapter 2 will show, rainfall in this area is low and highly variable in its volume and distribution within the short rainy season. As a result, harvests of the two millet varieties and the returns from different activities vary greatly from year to year. Demographic risk takes the form of high child mortality, low adult life-expectancy, and wide variation between couples in their ability to produce and rear children. Little can be done to reduce these risks; instead, a variety of strategies and institutions have evolved to guard farmers from the worst effects of crop-related or demographic risks. These strategies include the cultivation of two millet varieties of different cycle length, and the storage of surplus in the form of livestock holdings. Institutions such as the large extended household reduce the risk faced by the individual, while the establishment of marriage alliances between households in different settlements provides a form of social insurance against disaster in times of localized harvest failure.

The long time-frame

The second theme pursued by the study relates to the need for a long-term analysis of production and investment decision-making. Studies of resource allocation by farmers are often based on a single year's crop-production data from which conclusions are drawn and recommendations made about optimal cropping strategies. Little account is taken of the great variability in productivity from year to year, although this is of great importance in a semi-arid region like the Sahel. To investigate such variations ideally would require farm-production data over a run of many years, which is rarely available. This study uses data collected over two years which, although it obviously cannot represent the range of expected returns over the long run, is an improvement on a single year's data. Results gained from an analysis of these farm-production data are used to assess the parameters within which farmers must make longer-term investment decisions. The results provide a range of returns for alternative uses of funds between farmers and between seasons. The investment analysis also considers the extent to which the asset-holdings of farmers in Kala can be thought of as constituting a 'portfolio'. With such a 'portfolio' approach to investment, farmers invest in a variety of assets in order to reduce their overall exposure to risk and to balance expected returns against their need for liquidity.

Marriage is a particularly long-term investment. While the woman's labour and services provide some immediate returns for the heavy wedding costs, many of the benefits will accrue over the following 30 years or more. Much care is taken over the choice of girl to bring into the family as a wife, as the consequences of such choices will be with the family for decades to come. As described in Chapter 13, families rely heavily on existing ties of marriage and exchange of women that have developed over many generations with particular households in this and neighbouring villages. In this way, the household head hopes to ensure that marriages endure and are free of conflict.

Returns to investment in the longer term must also be understood in relation to shifts in economic, environmental, and institutional factors. Changes in these factors help explain how the composition of asset holdings in Kala has altered over time. For example, longer-term returns for digging a well are highly vulnerable to trends in rainfall, the carrying capacity of pastures, and the local balance of power between the Bambara and other groups in the region. The main reason why farmers in Kala dig wells is to attract herds to come and water there in the dry season, in exchange for the dung deposited by the animals on the field. However, when rainfall is poor, the millet crop may be damaged by the heavy use of manure, so that little or no return on the well investment is gained. The effects of these broader economic, environmental, and institutional factors on investment strategies are examined in more detail in Chapter 11.

Linkages

The third main theme of the study concerns the interrelations between economic performance and the organization and management of the household. Farmers differ greatly in their access to resources and in particular to supplies of labour, the overwhelming proportion of which is supplied by their own household members. In this labour-scarce economy, the establishment and maintenance of a large domestic group is given a high priority. Households invest considerable resources in marriage in order to ensure themselves a future labour supply from the production of legitimate offspring.

Questions to do with marriage and household organization have tended to be ignored in economic analyses of peasant-farmer behaviour or dealt with as exogenous cultural factors. Our study, however, brings domestic investment into the centre of the analysis and shows the rationale behind high fertility and the maintenance of large and complex households among the Bambara. Demographic issues are of such importance in this case-study because:

(i) the extreme vulnerability of the single individual in this environment means that there are great advantages from pooling risks in large domestic groups within which production and child-bearing take place;

(ii) the very limited development of a market in agricultural labour implies that households must rely almost exclusively on their own members to provide their farm work-force; and

(iii) there are no insurance markets or assets which could provide the individual either with the means to protect him/herself from risk or a secure income in old age.

BACKGROUND TO THE STUDY AND COLLECTION OF DATA

Most of the material presented in this book comes from two years' fieldwork in a group of Bambara farming villages in central Mali. This work was carried out between April 1980 and March 1982 by a social anthropologist and the author.[1] It formed part of a larger research programme being conducted by the International Livestock Centre for Africa (ILCA) in the semi-arid zones of Mali. The aim of the broader study was to gather comparative data on household production, labour use, and budgets from a range of pastoral and agro-pastoral societies in the Malian Sahel. The agro-pastoral Bambara farming villages of Kala and its neighbours, described here, provided a case-study at one end of the spectrum of production systems investigated by ILCA researchers. Other studies covered Fulani herding and rice-growing communities in the inland Niger Delta, the Fulani and Rimaibe herders and millet farmers of the Gourma region of eastern Mali, and a pastoral Tuareg group on the edge of the Niger Delta. Results from these other studies have been presented elsewhere (Swift, 1985).

Two years after the main field-work was completed, a three-week visit to Mali in October 1984 allowed the author to pursue a number of issues which had arisen as a result of the data analysis and to investigate at first-hand subsequent developments in Kala. This was of particular value given the very large increase in the number of private wells dug in 1983 and the consequences of this for continued equilibrium between crop and pasture productivity. The extremely poor rainfall of 1984 and consequent failure of the village-field millet harvest provided a sad but useful basis for discussion with farmers about future crop and investment strategies.

A short visit in September 1988, in the course of the wettest rainy season for decades, demonstrated the resilience and great productivity of soils and crops when rain falls well. The millet fields were thick with plants and the heads of millet grain twice as long and as thick as any seen in previous years. Cattle were sleek and well filled-out, the pastures

---

[1] The research was written up in preliminary form in D. Fulton and C. Toulmin (1982), 'A socio-economic study of an agro-pastoral system in central Mali', Report to the International Livestock Centre for Africa (Addis Ababa, Ethiopia).

still green, and everyone in the village could barely suppress their joy. Granaries could be restocked, taxes paid, new clothes bought, and investments made in new ploughs and cattle. Sadly the rainfall and harvests of 1989 and 1990 have returned to less impressive proportions and pest damage from grasshoppers and the millet-head miner moth has become increasingly important.

Choice of research site

The choice of area and villages to be studied was determined by several factors. Since this study was to contribute towards a comparison of different production systems by providing material from a sedentary farming community, it had to be carried out in an area of rainfed farming where the population derived the greatest and most steady part of its income from crops. It was decided to choose a group of villages not too distant from ILCA's research station at Niono (see Map 1), given the need for year-round access and support for the research team. However, villages close to Niono were avoided, due to this town's position in the large irrigation scheme of the Office du Niger. To minimize the impact of this giant project on the communities to be studied and to find an area more representative of the Sahel as a whole, an area was chosen to the south-west of Niono. To the east of Niono, the inland Niger Delta with its extensive floodplains exerts a great influence on patterns of livestock production, while to the north agriculture becomes steadily more marginal and pastoral herding systems predominate with the decline in expected rainfall.

Two villages some 80–100 km (a two or three hours' drive) south-west of Niono were taken as the research site—Kala and Dofinena. The two villages differ considerably in size, access to water, soil type, and historical background. Neither of them can be said to be a 'typical' village for the area, just as no household within either village can be considered a 'typical' household. Kala is a large settlement for the region with over 500 inhabitants, in comparison with less than 200 in Dofinena. Kala is also a wealthier village with its extensive manured village fields, its easy access to subterranean water, and its large cattle holdings. It represents a relatively successful community in this marginal farming zone, and despite the vagaries of climate many households can expect, over a period of several years, to produce grain in excess of the household's subsistence needs which can be invested in a variety of physical and domestic assets. There are several other villages similar in size and farming system to Kala in this region, strung out along the same latitude, benefiting from a low population density, good water supplies and regular visits from transhumant pastoralists who bring their herds to manure farmers' land in exchange for access to water in the dry season. Dofinena, with its smaller size, harder clay soils and poor water-supplies represents a more marginal community, containing a large number of small households who must supplement agricultural output with earnings from migration, trade, and handicrafts in order to provide sufficient food for their needs. Many young men from Dofinena spend long periods away from the village earning money in the main towns of Ségou and Bamako, in contrast with households in Kala for whom migration is very largely confined to the dry season.[2]

The village of Kala became the primary research site; the villagers built a house there for the researchers and their three assistants and this was their main place of residence during the two years of field-work. Regular visits were made to Dofinena where a fourth assistant was based. Other settlements in the neighbourhood were also visited on a less regular basis in order to build up a picture of different production strategies and constraints and the pattern of trading and social links existing between villages in the region.

Data collection and methods

Permanent residence by the researchers in the study villages was of fundamental importance in deciding how and what sorts of data would be collected. The advantages of being present during the two years of study were that:

(i) the researchers could continuously check upon the collection of data by the research assistants through their own enquiries and through visits to different households during the day;

(ii) residence in the village implied learning the Bambara language. Being able to understand and use the language meant that the researchers could both follow conversations and carry out their own interviews. The latter were especially valuable in cases where sensitive subjects were under discussion when only the informant and researcher were present;

(iii) by limiting the amount of data sought, by collecting much of these data ourselves, and by being permanently in the villages, it was hoped that we could make better sense of the material obtained, thus avoiding one drawback of large research studies using questionnaires and many research assistants. By acquiring sufficient background information, we were better able to put the data into its socio-economic context;

(iv) a further advantage found by being present all the time was that questions could be asked at appropriate times rather than always being brought up in formal interviews. Thus, for example, costs of marriage come up naturally for discussion when negotiations are being undertaken or a wedding is in preparation. At this juncture, questions could also be

---

[2] For further details on the differences between these villages, see Fulton and Toulmin.

put about the relative costs incurred by other households, by marriages involving other villages and so on. Information on these issues was less reliable when the subject was brought up 'cold'.

The method of collecting data took a variety of forms depending on what was being measured. The approach adopted by the two researchers itself evolved over the period of field-work. It was originally intended that a questionnaire be used, covering labour use and household-budget data. This questionnaire, similar in format to those used by Norman (1972), Delgado (1979), and others, was to be administered on a twice-weekly basis to all households in the village. After an initial assessment of the situation, it was decided to abandon the questionnaires completely and to adopt a variety of less formal techniques. Reasons for deciding against the questionnaire method included the following:

(i) households in Kala are very large, averaging more than 18 people, making it very difficult to get information either from a single household informant or from the numerous individuals concerned;

(ii) the Bambara are very reluctant to discuss the affairs of other household members with outsiders, particularly where such information would throw light on internal tensions and conflicts within the domestic group;

(iii) there was considerable suspicion about the motives of the researchers, of ILCA, and of information being written down. While many villagers came to accept that research was a valid form of activity, there were always a few who imagined a complex web of motives behind the researchers' presence in the village;

(iv) there are particular problems in expecting older people to give information to young research assistants, given that according to social convention the latter should be their subordinates and should not pester them with questions.

It was thought better to concentrate on collecting good quality data on a limited number of factors to be considered in detail in the subsequent analysis, rather than to accumulate a large quantity of material of low quality on a wide range of subjects. A further consideration was not to overload the village population with too many visits and questions during their busy working day. This was necessary not only to maintain good relations with the villagers but also to avoid the tendency of those being questioned saying anything in order to end the interview rapidly.

Types of data collected

Labour data A major objective of the research was to collect data on labour inputs into millet cultivation which could be used in a subsequent analysis of returns to crop production. Several approaches to collecting these data, and the form in which they would be sought, were considered before settling on the method described below. As noted earlier, an initial step was to abandon the use of comprehensive questionnaire methods covering all labour use, by hour, and income and expenditure data for each household member. Having monitored the first few days of the cultivation season, it was decided to note the presence or absence of different household members on a half-daily basis in the household's fields. This was felt to be a reasonable compromise between the potentially greater accuracy obtained by asking for hour-by-hour use of labour time and the heavier burden of questioning which this would imply, particularly for those households containing a large number of members. It was also felt that to use hours to measure labour inputs would give too precise a picture of actual labour use, given the many other problems in weighting and aggregating work inputs.

In the farming season, almost all household labour is devoted to the cultivation of its field, from first light until the sun goes down. This demand on household members' time forms part of the contract within these complex domestic groups, examined in greater detail in Chapters 2 and 12 to 14. Thus, it was only for exceptional reasons, such as a child's illness or preparations for a wedding, that someone was absent from the field. There was also a common pattern in terms of the hour at which men and women would leave for the fields. Men go soon after dawn while women had to prepare food before their departure and would reach the field between 9 and 10 o'clock in the morning.

Data on labour use was collected by the three research assistants in Kala and by the single assistant in Dofinena. These data consisted of noting which household members were present in the field on the half-day concerned, the reasons for any absences, whether any non-household labour was present, where such labour came from and its cost, and the farming operations being performed. In the case of Kala, allocation of households to different assistants was based on which households had adjacent bush fields. This was to allow the assistants to visit their households each day while they were out at work. This daily round of field visits formed the pattern of work amongst the research team during the farming season, each of the two researchers joining one of the three assistants to carry out the round together. This meant that problems associated with asking for and recording information could be discussed as they arose. Other obvious advantages from spending so much time out in the fields were that the researchers could monitor crop performance in the different fields, they were able to ask questions about varying cultivation practices and were seen to be serious in wanting to understand how the Bambara cultivate their millet.

In the dry season, most people pursue a number of different tasks; for example, men fetch firewood to sell, plait fibres to make ropes, and go hunting while women spin cotton, wash clothes, and prepare food. During these months, the assistants noted down the main activities of different individuals so that a check could be kept on various income-earning activities.

Field size Bush and village fields were measured using two different techniques. Most bush fields are large rectangular areas, their even shape the result of plough-team use, and averaging over 28 ha in size. These were measured by pacing the sides of the fields. In addition, the proportion of land that had been taken in and abandoned each year was measured to calculate the average age of the field. The presence of other crops, such as a patch of groundnuts or a few stands of *dah* (*Hibiscus* species) was noted. Village-field holdings, by contrast, consist of several plots of irregular shape. Household land is interspersed with fields allocated to women and to Fulani herders. An aerial survey of the village fields was carried out using ILCA's light aircraft in November 1980, an ideal time of year as the harvest was just complete and the lines of field boundaries were still clearly visible. A few weeks later these would have disappeared under the pressure of livestock grazing the millet stubble. These photos were used to calculate field areas, the dimensions of which were subsequently checked on the ground. New village fields, cut in 1981, were measured by foot and compass on the ground during the 1981 rainy season.

Fields of groundnuts and other crops belonging to the household were measured on the ground using paces and a compass. Estimated sizes of fields allocated to women and to herders were calculated from the aerial photographs.

Crop output The main measure of crop output was taken after the millet had been stored in the household granary. A tape-measure was used to get several estimates of the circumference of these cylindrical structures, before taking the depth to which each was filled. The width of the straw and mud wall had also to be measured. These volumetric measures were converted into weights using an estimated density for millet grain. Output from the bush and village fields is usually stored in separate granaries since different millet varieties are grown in each. The estimated weight of stored grain was then checked against the number of journeys taken by cart to carry this millet from the threshing ground to the granary. With an average of 250–300 kg per load, this check allowed us to be sure that substantial amounts of grain had not been hidden from us.

Millet devoted to other uses before reaching the household granary had also to be measured. On average this comprised 15 per cent of the total estimated harvest. Grain taken for early consumption by the household, due to the granary being empty, was assessed by noting when cutting of the crop began and the number of baskets harvested each day. Threshing payments were made in those cases where a mechanical thresher (usually a lorry or tractor) was used, a certain number of sacks being paid, depending on the size of the harvest. Payments to visiting harvesters could be gained by monitoring the use of non-household labour for this purpose and knowing that each couple of days' work would be paid for by a basket of millet spears. Illicit transfers of grain by women to their own stores were also monitored, these taking place at the threshing ground when the millet was winnowed, an operation at which only women are allowed to be present.

The advantage of being permanently in the villages was brought out clearly when trying to measure household grain production. First, it allowed the researchers to monitor early consumption of grain and estimate how much went in this form. Many households were not keen on discussing their resort to cutting fresh millet for daily food needs, as it reflected poorly on the household's ability to feed itself over the year. Second, the author, as a woman, was encouraged to work on the winnowing and thus could note the quantities of grain given to visiting women for their part in this work and to 'wages' assessed and taken by women belonging to the household whose millet was being winnowed. These latter payments varied from 50 kg to 1,000 kg per woman, representing a substantial loss to the household granary in certain cases. The relative importance of this source of income for women is described in greater depth in Chapters 2 and 13.

Output of other crops was also measured but, as will be seen in the following chapter, they are of negligible importance in comparison with millet.

Household budgets As will be seen in Chapter 2, the large Bambara household exhibits a distinct structure whereby certain sources of income and kinds of expenditure are the responsibility of the joint household budget, while others belong to the individual. It was decided, initially, to concentrate on the joint household budget, noting sales and purchases of grain, livestock, farm equipment and labour, and expenditures involved in preparing and celebrating a wedding. We wanted in particular to get data on the size of grain flows, how much was used in barter transactions, which households were buying and selling grain, into what forms of investment surplus grain is put, and the ways in which households feed themselves in years of poor harvest. Data on the household budget was collected both by formal interview every few months and by informal observations and questioning by the research team. Thus, for example, when a grain trader arrived in the village we all kept our eyes open to see who was selling grain. This was made easier by the fact that the large fig tree next to the researchers' house also acted as the regular stopping-place for visiting traders. Monitoring of grain sales was made more difficult, however, by the villagers' desire for secrecy on this subject. This was partly due to strong social pressures against such sales—grain that leaves the village being no longer available to help out others in need—and partly the result of the government's supposed monopoly on all grain transactions in the couple of months after harvest. During this period, quotas of grain were meant to be delivered to the Office des Produits Agricoles du Mali (OPAM), the government agency concerned, at a fixed low price. While OPAM's quota system in this area was not fully effective during the two years of study, nevertheless considerable care was taken by traders to avoid being seen, such as by travelling at night. Privatization of the grain trade and withdrawal by the government from this and other areas of control have come about with Mali's programme of structural adjustment and reform. Hence, OPAM no longer has the power to enforce grain quotas.

In the case of individual budgets, it became clear that it would prove impossible to monitor the income and expenditure of all individuals without becoming very intrusive. Thus, it was decided to follow a few cases, with whom the researchers were most familiar, in order to get estimated income and expenditure for different kinds of people, such as retired or working women, or those in large as opposed to small households. In particular, it was felt important to find out which individuals had substantial livestock holdings, as these were evidence of considerable sources of income.

Other data   A household survey was undertaken at the start of the field-work, detailing household composition and the relationships between different members. For married women, their natal household was also sought to show the pattern of intermarriages existing between households and villages. As time went on, the original household survey was adjusted to take account of births, deaths, and marriages and of people who had been missed out in the original survey. For example, many households had one or two members who were not mentioned at the time of the first survey. Typically these would be either children from other households currently living and working in the surveyed household, or children born within the household but living elsewhere. A genealogical survey was carried out in this and all neighbouring villages, which obtained much detail on the pattern of marriages between households over the previous three or four generations. This survey also investigated the fate of households which had apparently disappeared, leaving behind only a few female relatives with that family name.

Asset ownership was surveyed at a number of points during the field-work to note changes in holdings and to make some measures more precise. Some assets posed far greater problems than others for measurement. It was clear how many wells or ploughs were owned by a household, as these could be observed by the researchers and were not the object of unease. Cattle holdings were the main asset for which there were considerable problems, such as knowing how many were owned either at the household level or by individuals. Getting data on this matter was left for many months, the villagers having a marked suspicion of any questions on these points because of the envy such holdings of cattle incite and the association of cattle counting with tax payments. It was not until the rainy season of 1981 that a clear idea of who owned which cattle was obtained, more than 12 months after field-work began. This information was obtained as a by-product of a survey of milking practices during which the author cycled to the rainy-season cattle camp for the morning and evening milking in order to measure levels of offtake. Since individual owners would visit the camp themselves in order to collect their milk, it was relatively simple to monitor cattle ownership in this way. Changes in cattle ownership were monitored through the budget survey.

Daily rainfall was measured at Kala with the use of three gauges and at Dofinena with a single gauge. For Kala, these were placed in different places, more than a kilometre apart, in order to examine localized variability in rainfall.

Tables All tabulated material throughout this book is based on field data unless otherwise noted.

Other research in Kala

Several supplementary studies were done in Kala and neighbouring villages during and after the period of research described here. Of particular value as far as the arguments in this book are concerned was the demographic survey carried out among the Bambara population of the *Arrondissements* of Doura and Monimpebougou in April and May 1981, the results of which are presented in Randall (1984), and A. Hill (1985). Agronomic research and a variety of field trials were carried out to test the effects of chemical fertilizer on millet yields, and to allow the village to experiment with new varieties of millet and cowpea (Wilson *et al.*, 1983). An animal production team started monitoring small stock and cattle performance from November 1981 (Wilson *et al.*, 1983). Ecological research was also carried out in 1981, focusing in particular on the evolution of grass and bush cover over time as land is abandoned following cultivation (Cissé and Hiernaux, 1984).

When the two researchers left Mali in 1982, ILCA continued its research programme in these villages. From May 1982 to September 1983, a nutrition study was carried out aimed at detecting seasonal variations in food intake and disease incidence (Martin, 1984). From the 1983 rainy season, there has been a programme of research into work-oxen nutrition and the introduction of forage cultivation. The continued presence of these researchers for some years in the region has enabled the author to keep in touch with events in these villages and to monitor crucial variables such as rainfall distribution within the year. However, restructuring of research priorities with the ILCA programme led to the discontinuation of all research activity at the end of 1988.

PART I

THE VILLAGE SETTING

2

BACKGROUND TO THE VILLAGE OF KALA

Kala is a Bambara farming village lying some 60 km north of Ségou in the southern sahelian zone of central Mali (see Map 1). The Bambara are the largest ethnic group in the Ségou Region and are also the dominant population in Mali as a whole. While agriculture plays a major role in shaping household and community organization, other activities are also of economic importance; livestock-keeping, trade, urban migration, crafts, hunting, and gathering all contribute to household incomes. Kala is a relatively large village for the area, with its population of over 500 people, living in 29 households, or *gwa*. With an average size of more than 18 persons, these domestic groups are unusually large and it will be shown later (Chapter 14) that considerable production and demographic benefits are gained from the risk-spreading which this form of social organization permits.

The village is a tight cluster of mud-brick houses gathered in a gentle depression in the plain which extends beyond the village for many kilometres in each direction. Each household lives in a compound bounded by several others and surrounding a courtyard in which the household's granaries stand, animals are tethered, and equipment is stored. A couple of carefully tended saplings provide a little shade and a wooden shelter is used to store bundles of cowpea hay and cut grass to be fed to the stock. In one corner of the compound lies the kitchen, the focus for the daily round of food preparations and next to the cooking hut stand the ranks of mortars and pestles which women use twice daily to transform calabashes of dusty grain into sweet-smelling bowls of millet porridge. Around the settlement lie fields on whose manured surfaces the millet grows so tall and thick that the village is hidden for several months a year. Dotted among these fields are more than forty wells at which drinking water is drawn and livestock are watered. Beyond the village fields, which ring the settlement to a distance of a kilometre or more, the open countryside is reached. This has a light covering of bush and tree growth and at ground level a sward of annual grasses, vegetation which results from the impact of several centuries' use. To the west lies the cattle camp used during the rainy season to keep the herds away from ripening crops, while some 3–5 km to the north, south, and east lie the settlement's bush fields, vast areas of land, roughly cleared as the fields shift outwards over the years.

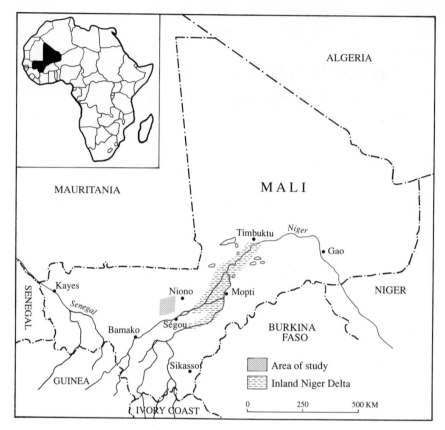

MAP 1. Mali

Though to the south the density of settlement starts to rise as one moves towards higher rainfall zones and the nearest village is only 5 km away, to the east and west a three to five hour's walk (15–25 km) is needed to bring people to their neighbours. Northwards there is little permanent settlement, although occasional tumuli can be seen marking the sites of long-abandoned villages.

PATTERNS OF SETTLEMENT

The north bank of the River Niger is lightly settled with an average population density of less than 10 persons per sq. km, in comparison with more than 30 persons per sq. km in areas to the south and west, where rainfall levels are higher. The population density around Kala is very low when compared with other parts of the West African savannah-sahel region where similar farm and household studies have been carried out.

For example, P. Hill's Hausa village on the edge of the Kano Close-Settled Zone lies in a region of more than 200 persons per sq. km (1972), as is also the case for the Hausa studied by Norman (1972), Watts (1983), and Sutter (1982). Of research done in Mali, Lewis's (1978) work in a Bambara village to the south of Ségou takes one into a region of between 20 and 40 people per sq. km and even in Pollet and Winter's (1971) study in north-west Mali the density is over 20 persons per sq. km.

The abundance of land in the region surrounding Kala is of fundamental importance in understanding the pattern of farming and the nature of constraints on expanding production, which are here posed largely by a household's access to labour and plough-team inputs with which extra land can be brought into cultivation.

People live mainly in villages rather than scattered in isolated homesteads. Defensive considerations dictated the evolution of a fortified, walled settlement within which people and animals could shelter from raiding parties. These nucleated settlements continue to exist, particularly in the area around Kala, because water is difficult to find and a permanent new village cannot be established until a supply of drinking water is assured. Farming hamlets spring up periodically in otherwise uninhabited parts of the bush, certain families splitting off from the village to farm a site over 5 to 10 years, moving back to the home village at the end of each harvest. These hamlets may in time form the basis for a new village if water can be found. The setting up of temporary hamlets allows farmers to use a much larger area of land than is available in the vicinity of the village. Departure to a hamlet is also a means by which tension between village members can be defused, parties to a conflict being able to distance themselves for a period without losing their rights within the village community.

Other ethnic groups—Fulani and Maure

The north bank is settled by a number of different ethnic groups: farming villages are settled by Bambara, Soninke, and sedentarized Fulani and Maure, while temporary herding camps harbour the remaining Fulani and Maure populations with their stock. The region was originally settled by the Soninke who dispersed throughout the north, west, and central Mali following the fall of the empire of Ghana in the thirteenth century. Fulani and Maure herding groups have used the area on a migratory basis for many centuries. Towards the middle of the seventeenth century, the Bambara started to move towards the north from an origin in the south of Mali, establishing their capital at Ségou around 1670 and settling throughout the region. The Fulani were used as herding labour by the Bambara rulers of Ségou, to care for the cattle being kept on the extensive pasturelands of the north bank.

The past few decades have seen considerable migration into the zone by different herding groups, movement which was formerly kept under tight check by the French administration which required a *laissez-passer* and the payment of taxes before animals could be taken from one *Cercle* to another. The descent of ex-slave Maures (*harratin*—many of whom were originally captured from among the Bambara) from southern Mauritania into more southerly farming zones where they can escape the close attentions of their former masters has been particularly noteworthy. Both Fulani and Maure herding populations pursue a transhumant existence based around a farming hamlet in the north where they plant millet and pasture their herds in the rainy season and from which they depart after the harvest in January. They then travel south to pass the dry season camped around Bambara villages, watering their stock at the wells, exchanging stock and milk for food grains, and taking advantage of their proximity to the major livestock markets of Ségou and Niono.

Relations between the different groups are variable. In general, the Bambara and Maure populations get along well, in part because the latter have no intention of settling in the district. Much greater tension exists between Bambara and Fulani groups and this revolves around a number of issues. Firstly, many Fulani families are long-time residents of this zone, some claiming to pre-date the Bambara settlement of the region. However, control of the land resides with the Bambara who exercise it at village level by stipulating the conditions under which incomers are allowed to farm land in the village's territory. The Fulani justifiably resent their dependence for access to farming land on the decisions made by the Bambara village council. Many Bambara villages refuse to allow the Fulani permanent settlement rights, fearing damage to crops from their herds and the creation of a neighbouring community not totally under Bambara authority, whose size and wealth could grow to rival that of the Bambara host village. Secondly, Fulani are used as hired contract herders for the care of Bambara village cattle. Relations between herder and herd owner are fraught with conflicting interests, particularly over the share of milk taken by the herder and the consequences for calf survival. Thirdly, the Fulani are strongly associated with the expansion of Islamic Tukolor power in the mid-nineteenth century which established an ardent, proselytizing theocratic state through much of the western Sudan, which conquered the Bambara state of Ségou in 1861. Historical enmity continues to play its part in accentuating the opposition of interests between the two groups felt in other spheres.

VILLAGE HISTORY

The settlement of Kala probably dates from the establishment of the Bambara state at Ségou in the late seventeenth century. The Ségou

Empire was based on control of trade in grain, salt, gold, and cloth along the River Niger and the receipt of tribute from subject peoples, in the form of commodities—grain and honey—and levies of fighting men. Warfare was carried out by the *fama*, or ruler of Ségou against neighbouring states, to expand the empire and to seize the assets of rival powers. It was also used to dominate and subordinate communities within the empire's main sphere of influence who refused to accept the *fama*'s authority. The benefits of raiding were shared amongst the ruler and his chiefs: grain, slaves, gold, cowries, cattle, and horses were the main treasures to be gained and were used to reward loyalty.

With the establishment of a centre of military power at Ségou, the *fama* sought to protect the state and its wealth from attack on its northern frontier by settling a ring of fortified villages some 60 to 80 km from the river. The enclosed region was used for the pasturing of cattle and horses belonging to the *fama*, both very valuable assets in the pre-colonial economy. Kala was one of these military outposts, built to counter the threat of attack from the rival Bambara kingdom of Kaarta, to the northwest, and from Maure raiding parties seeking cattle and people to be taken as slaves. These villages were defensive settlements, surrounded by a mud wall, pierced by a single gate. Guns could be fired through narrow slits in the walls. Granaries and wells lay within the village while livestock could be brought inside the wall in case of siege. It is only since the end of the nineteenth century that these tight village clusters have slowly allowed themselves to unravel beyond the limits of the defensive wall with the growth in population and desire for greater domestic space.

The Bambara kingdom of Ségou fell, in 1861, to the Tukolor, led by El Hadj Umar, the head of the Islamic jihad movement, whose objective was to found a large theocratic state in the western Sudan. The Tukolor never controlled much of the north bank of the River Niger, however, and throughout the 30 years that they held Ségou town, opposing Bambara forces conducted a persistent guerilla campaign against their military and trading columns.

Hostility between the Bambara and Tukolor was skilfully used by the French in their attempts to weaken the latter's power, and French supplies of arms to the Bambara contributed to the final downfall and flight of Tukolor forces in 1890 when the French army captured Ségou. Hostility between the Bambara and the Tukolor continues to this day and helps account for the generally poor relations between many Bambara and Fulani communities.

The colonial impact

Once in control of Ségou, the French sought to exercise power over the region, instituting taxation and trying to develop avenues of profitable economic activity, such as cotton, indigo, and groundnut production. The early years of colonial administration were marked by their desire to show themselves firm in the face of possible opposition. An occasional show of force was welcomed to demonstrate the colonial army's strength, as the case of Kala demonstrates. In 1895, when colonial officers came to the village to carry out a census and levy taxes, an incident occurred during which shots were fired by both sides. As a result, the officer in charge retreated from the village and called for reinforcements from Ségou, which arrived the next day. The village chief, his brothers and sons were taken and imprisoned, never to be seen again, the granaries burned, and the village razed. The remaining population was forced to take refuge in neighbouring settlements. One old woman in her eighties during the field-work period remembered being carried away to Kango, a nearby village and spending several years of her childhood there. After three years, and many visits by the villagers to visit the *Commandant de Cercle* at Ségou, they were allowed to re-establish their community on the old site.

The impact made by the French colonial administration and the policies followed varied from one region to another. Certain policies affected all regions, such as the levying of taxes, military conscription, and the abolition of slavery. Others were of greater or lesser importance depending on proximity to markets and administrative centres. The Ségou Region was seen by the French as a potentially very prosperous zone, producing cotton, grain, indigo, and groundnuts. But the north bank of the River Niger was always considered the most disadvantaged part of the region, having poor water supplies, and a population ravaged by disease, drought, and locusts. The French left this unpromising region largely to itself, apart from levying taxes, while concentrating on the promotion of agricultural improvements in the higher potential areas further south.

For villages on the north bank, the main effects of the French administration were payment of the poll tax, forced labour duties, and military conscription.

Taxation was levied on all those over eight years old and was set at 3.50 francs in the *Cercle* of Ségou for much of the colonial period, equivalent at 1910 prices to 15–25 kg of millet. The tax rate for north-bank villages was questioned by several colonial officials who contrasted the poverty of this area with the better-off areas to the south of Ségou town. While in the early 1890s much tax was paid in commodities ranging from millet, cattle, sheep, horses, and rice to blankets, wool, cotton, and cowries, by the turn of the century, most tax receipts were in coin, introduced to replace the traditional cowrie shell.

Forced labour took two forms. The first involved each taxable person performing 9 to 12 days' work around the village, usually clearing and maintaining roads to neighbouring settlements. The second involved each village sending a number of young men to provide labour for public works projects in the *Cercle*, such as the building of houses and offices in Ségou town and clearing land for the construction of the Office du Niger irrigation scheme. The second form of labour service aroused particular dislike among villagers, especially when it took young men away from the fields at a time when the household badly needed their labour. Forced labour was not finally abolished until 1945 and all men over 60 in Kala have their tales of the hardship and indignity involved. One crabbed and bent old man in his eighties in Kala described being on cooking duties to cater for the labour gang brought to Ségou to build houses for the administration in the 1930s and being made to dance and sing to keep the work-force amused.

Military conscription began in 1912 and accelerated through the First World War years, with an estimated 200,000 men from the French West African territories taken to fight in Europe by 1918. After a lull in the 1920s, conscription was again increased in the 1930s and in 1939–40 80,000 men were sent to fight in Europe (Suret-Canale, 1961). All sahelian villages have their share of *anciens combattants* from two world wars and the Indo-China conflict of the 1950s. At least five men, aged over 55 by the 1970s, were taken from Kala to fight in the French army, all of whom had the good fortune to return. For one, however, this was only after six years as a prisoner of war in Germany, growing sugar-beet by day and subject to bombing by the allied forces at night. Two of these *anciens combattants* received a military pension for some years after their return and they were both among the first to purchase ox-drawn ploughs in the early 1950s.

From the end of the 1920s and through the 1930s, reports of the Ségou region, and of the north bank in particular, are dominated by the effects of the Depression and the succession of years during which locusts devastated harvests. From 1928 onwards, farmers faced a fall in purchasing power and a growing inability to find the money needed to pay taxes. This was the result of the falling prices offered by the trading houses in Ségou for the products brought for sale by farmers—groundnuts, kapok, and shea-nut butter.

Millet harvests were very poor throughout the 1930s because of the waves of locusts that would descend in the wet season and at harvest time. Villagers were encouraged to grow subterranean crops, such as manioc and Bambara earthnuts, which could withstand the plague. However, the north bank is mentioned year after year as suffering from this plague and it was not until 1940 that the locusts stayed away.

Faced with poor harvests, a lack of buyers for their traditional produce and the need to pay taxes, many villagers resorted to sales of livestock which had been badly depleted by regular outbreaks of rinderpest and pneumonia, and gold which was brought in for sale at Ségou in large quantities. The *Commandant* at Ségou noted that in 1933 and 1934 an unprecedented 1.2 million francs worth of gold was sold to get money for taxes. When these reserves were exhausted, able-bodied men travelled to work in the groundnut areas of Senegal to earn cash. Elderly men in Kala can still recite the list of villages through which they passed on foot on the month-long walk to Senegal.

Further pressure was put on the population at this time with the setting up of grain reserves at the canton headquarters under the auspices of the Société Indigène de Prévoyance, ostensibly to act as a famine reserve. Each taxable person was required to contribute from 50 to 75 kg of grain to this store from 1930 onwards. This aroused much hostility, given the poor harvests and the joint holding of grain stocks by households. There was also the suspicion that these communal stores would be mismanaged, a suspicion amply justified by the poor storage conditions, high losses incurred, and the requisitioning of these stores in 1941 by the administration to feed troops in Senegal. Grain levies were continued throughout the war years to provide for the troops.

In the 1930s, the Société Indigène de Prévoyance set up credit schemes to supply animal-drawn carts and equipment to farmers. Oxen-drawn ploughs were given special prominence as they helped increase yields of groundnuts. A farmer was expected to repay the cost of a pair of oxen over three years and of a plough over five years. Take-up of these new technologies was rapid, with the number of ploughs in the Ségou region growing from 35 in 1929 to 1,375 in 1937, and 2,053 in 1940 (Rapports Économiques, 1936, 1937, 1940). However, farmers in Kala were reluctant to take up loans to pay for equipment, feeling uncertain of their ability to repay the debt at the due date, and fearing the wrath of the colonial administration should they fail to do so. It was not until 1950 that the first plough was purchased by a villager from Kala, and this as with subsequent purchases was bought outright with earnings from migration or livestock sales.

The Office du Niger irrigation scheme was the major public works project carried out in Mali during the colonial period. Originally conceived in 1919, it was not until 1928 that work began by diverting water from the River Niger into an ancient dry northern branch of the river. From this, a network of canals was planned to irrigate 1.2 million ha of land growing cotton and rice and allowing the resettlement of 1.5 million people. However, work was much slower than planned. By 1952, only 19,000 ha had been irrigated and the Office was facing severe difficulties in finding people to settle and farm on the scheme (Suret-Canale, 1961). It was anticipated that the attractions of irrigated agriculture would draw in much of the population farming in the dryland zones around. However, the local population was not willing to move from their traditional communities to become tenant farmers for the Office and the administration had to recruit forcibly two or three families from each village in the surrounding region. These families had to stay and farm within the scheme for a certain number of years before being allowed to return to their home village. Two households were taken from Kala in the 1940s to settle in the eastern part of the scheme around Kolongotomo, one of which returned after the seven years demanded while the other stayed. The returning household is now amongst the richest in Kala despite returning destitute from the Office. The large deficit in the number of tenant farmers required by the Office was only finally made up by moving large numbers of people from the heavily populated Mossi plateau of Burkina Faso in the 1940s and 1950s. The Office continues to exert some influence on the region of Kala, as a source of earnings for young men from rice harvesting and as an alternative zone for pasturing animals in the dry season for transhumant pastoralists who might otherwise visit Kala. Additionally, the sugar-cane estate on the Office, some 40 km east of Kala provides seasonal employment for a few migrants, though the work is disliked greatly. The sugar refinery is also an illicit source of industrial alcohol that occasionally makes its way to the village, where it is bought in thimbleful glasses by some old men. However, the main commercial and migration links are with the old Bambara capital Ségou, rather than Niono and the Office du Niger.

POLITICAL AND ADMINISTRATIVE STRUCTURE OF MALI

Mali is divided into seven administrative *Régions*, each composed of from five to eight *Cercles* which are further subdivided into *Arrondissements*. Each village has a chief, whose position is hereditary, and this chief is responsible to the *Chef d'Arrondissement* for ensuring that taxes are paid. The *chef-lieu d'Arrondissement* usually has a clinic, a school, and a representative of SCAER, the Société du Crédit Agricole et de l'Équipement Rurale which acts as the agricultural extension agency through which fertilizers and other inputs are occasionally available. SCAER is also often given responsibility for assessing and collecting the grain contributions to be made by each village to OPAM, the Office des Produits Agricoles du Mali, which until 1982 was involved in the channelling of grain quotas, purchased at a fixed government price from every village. This agency had been set up in the 1960s to try to reduce the role of and profits made by private grain traders and speculators, by giving an assured price to farmers while keeping down urban food prices. Increasingly, however, OPAM operated to obtain cheap grain from farmers, extracted at times by force, to be sold at subsidized prices to government employees in part payment of salaries.

Kala is some 30 km west from Doura, the *chef-lieu d'Arrondissement*, the journey to which takes the best part of a day on foot. The villagers consider this distance to be a blessing since it assures them a certain protection from the attentions of the Malian administration. Neither the school nor the clinic are valued by those from Kala, who when ill prefer to go to the hospitals at Markala or Ségou, despite these being further away.

Education

The population of Kala is almost entirely illiterate, with no children currently going to school. Villagers refuse to send their children to school as they need their labour for farming and they fear that children once sent will never return to work on the land. They also know that a few years of schooling do not ensure the school-leaver finds a job; even those who have completed ten years' schooling have difficulty in getting employment. One partially crippled man in the chief's household did several years at school in the 1940s when the chief was obliged to send a son to the School for Chiefs' Sons at Ségou. However, he can no longer remember how to read and write. Another man in his early fifties has taught himself to read and write with the help of an *ancien combattant*, now dead, who had learned the alphabet while serving in the French army. In 1988, this man received training in adult-literacy teaching and the village has now built a schoolroom to hold reading classes. An ex-soldier in his seventies is the only villager who speaks a little French, having learned this during his years in a German prisoner of war camp. Given Kala's strongly pagan tradition, there is no Koranic schooling.

Thus, the villagers of Kala along with most other communities in this region live within an entirely oral culture, passing their knowledge of past events and of farming skills by word of mouth, from one generation to another. The villagers recognize the weakness of their position as illiterates when faced by the national administration, knowing that it is easy to pull the wool over the eyes of a man who can neither read nor write.

Communications

Roads in this region consist of dusty tracks through the bush, not always passable by motor traffic after a heavy rainstorm. These tracks link one village with its neighbour and were originally travelled on foot or on horseback, but have now been widened so that a donkey-cart can pass. Lorry and car traffic is extremely rare, being restricted to the occasional passage of a long-distance grain trader trying to avoid the major routes or to the trucks that arrive at harvest-time to thresh the villagers' millet for a fee. Kala and its neighbouring communities depend for the carriage of goods and persons on less rapid and sophisticated forms of transport.

Donkey-carts are the main means by which goods are taken to market at Ségou and are used by itinerant traders whose tracks criss-cross the countryside. Bicycles are used by young men to visit neighbouring villages to carry messages and pursue their affairs. Older men travel on foot or horseback and women walk. Despite the rudimentary nature of transport and communications in the region, people travel a great deal, particularly in the dry season. Villages keep in close contact with each other and news travels fast; after a death, for example, friends and relatives are brought from a wide area to pay tribute at a funeral service that will succeed the death within less than 24 hours.

Trade

The West African savannah has long been a trading region of great importance, its cities having grown up on the exchange of gold, slaves, and kola from the south against livestock, salt, and cloth from the north. Ségou, which was at the centre of a great empire in the eighteenth and nineteenth centuries, remains one of the major market towns of Mali, drawing in produce, livestock, and customers from a wide stretch of countryside around. Villagers from the north bank of the River Niger use Ségou as their main source for the supply of manufactured goods and village shopkeepers visit the market town every two or three weeks. Other villagers tend to visit Ségou once a year to carry out special purchases, say before a wedding.

Apart from the few village shops and the occasional visit to Ségou market, village people buy the other goods they need from travelling traders, or *dioula*, who have a regular circuit of villages which they visit every month or so. They usually operate between two towns, such as Nyamina and Niono, 150 km apart, trading a variety of goods (hardware, cloth, spices) for cash and millet. On arrival at one end of their route, the grain is sold and a new stock of commodities purchased before setting off again in the reverse direction. The passage of donkey-carts is especially common in the few months following the harvest from January to March when several traders may visit the village each day in search of grain to buy. The growth in the network of grain buyers throughout the region has been greatly aided by the introduction of the donkey-drawn cart, which with a couple of animals can carry more than 500 kg. Village grain prices are now closely related to those in the major market towns because of the activities of these traders and the knowledge about prices gained by villagers on their visits to Ségou. Local grain-deficit households complain that they must now compete for millet supplies with a large number of outside traders and that this has inevitably raised village grain prices.

Villagers sell most of their grain locally to visiting grain traders, to food-deficit households or to herders in exchange for a heifer or young ox. Grain is also used to pay for locally provided services such as blacksmithing.

VILLAGE AND LINEAGE

The village is one of the basic units of Bambara society. Each village is made up of a number of different households, or *gwa*, some of which will be members of the founding lineage while others are later arrivals. In the case of Kala, three lineages make up the original inhabitants of the village, and these account for 17 of the 29 households currently present. Most of the other households joined the village, seeking protection, during the disturbed period of the late nineteenth century when different villages who supported rival claimants to power in this region raided and pillaged their neighbours.

Lineage for the Bambara is akin to our idea of a clan. Every legitimate Bambara man, woman, and child belongs to a lineage which has its own clan name (*jamu*), its own history, its own illustrious forebears, and its own particular taboos and established alliances with other lineages. Marriage takes place between those of different lineage (described in detail in Chapter 13). A person's clan name is an important label which defines his or her identity *vis-à-vis* others and is used in the ritual exchange of greetings gone through every day. Women keep their clanname when they marry. Each lineage is usually represented by several households in any village, since over time the original household will have grown and split into a number of separate units. Other household members may have moved away to neighbouring settlements but the eldest male of the family remains the head of all these groups and will be consulted on the most important issues.

The Bambara household

The Bambara household or *gwa* (meaning a hearth) is the basic unit of production and consumption, farming a common field and eating from a single granary. Table 2.1 shows the distribution of households according to structure and demonstrates the expected tendency for larger households to be more complex in composition. These domestic groups are much larger than those found in many other studies from West Africa, where the extended household has been under increasing pressure to dissolve into its nuclear components. As can be seen from the table, two-thirds of the households in Kala contain 85 per cent of the population living in complex domestic groups, the largest of which contained nearly 60 people.

The main focus for common household activity is the joint cultivation of its fields and care of the livestock and equipment needed to perform

TABLE 2.1. *Mean household size by type, Kala, 1981*

	Households			
	No.	% of total	Mean size	% of total population
Complex households[a]	19	66	23.8 (12.9)	85.6
Simple households[b]	10	34	7.6 (3.8)	14.4
VILLAGE TOTAL	29	100	18.2	100.0

[a] Complex households are those containing more than one married man.
[b] Simple households contain either a single married man or unmarried men with a widowed mother.

Note: Figures in brackets refer to the standard deviation.

this successfully. Work at the joint household level is termed *foroba* activity, meaning literally 'big field', in contrast to the efforts of individuals to earn a private income in their spare time. *Suroforo* is used to describe the latter activities, meaning 'night field', and refers to the private fields formerly cultivated by individuals late in the evening once work on the *foroba* had finished for the day.

The household demands from its members that they work every day except Monday for the common estate from the first sowing of millet in June until the grain is finally stored in January. Monday is market day at Ségou and also the traditional day of rest. During the dry season, labour is also needed to water and feed the animals, to dig and maintain the household wells and to prepare land for the next farming season. Women have domestic tasks to do throughout the year, such as cooking and fetching water, but where there are several women in the household they can arrange among themselves for each to have some time free to visit relatives in other villages. In return for their labour, household members receive certain benefits; these consist typically of food throughout the year and payment of taxes, while male members also expect that the household will organize and finance part of the costs of their marriage.

Within the household, however, there are several other levels at which property is owned and certain production and consumption activities carried out, termed *suroforo* as noted above.

Each married woman has her own granary which she fills from the harvest of her individual fields and from winnowing earnings and gifts of millet received at harvest time. Millet from her granary is used both as a source of income which she spends on the needs of herself and her children and as a supply of additional food for herself, her husband, and her children. Retired women control considerable quantities of grain, their granaries often holding more than 1,000 kg of millet and these stores feed her offspring should the household granary be empty. In addition, these granaries are the basis on which women accumulate wealth for themselves and their children, which passes to the woman's sons on her death, rather than becoming the joint property of the whole household.

Men within the household who share a common mother form the second pole around which various productive and investment activities are carried out. Commonly, a woman's sons will help her to cultivate a field, for example by ploughing her groundnut plot and helping weed it on days when they do not have to work on the joint estate. They benefit from this work if not immediately, then on their mother's death, when they inherit the wealth she has accumulated by her different activities. During the groundnut boom of the 1950s and 1960s, these subgroups of men also became involved in farming separate fields of their own with this crop, investing the profits in cattle. Many of the cattle and the complexities of ownership of these animals stem from this period when groundnuts were being grown and their profits invested at three different levels: at the household level, at the level of fraternal groups within the household, and at the level of the individual man or woman. Groundnuts are hardly grown now, due to the decline in rainfall, so that this source of income and accumulation is effectively non-existent.

Individuals themselves are involved in certain activities on and off the farm described later in this chapter, the income from which satisfies personal needs, such as clothing, shoes, and petty expenses such as sugar, tobacco, and kola-nut.

Changing poles of production within the household   There has been a change over time in the relative importance of different poles around which production and accumulation takes place within the Bambara household. In the past, men as well as women farmed substantial *suroforo* millet fields, alongside those of the joint household. Typically, men were free from household work by mid-afternoon each day and would also have Friday free for their own interests. While women still have grain plots of their own, men have almost entirely abandoned farming except that done for the *foroba* joint household; they no longer have the late afternoons and Fridays free but must continue to work for the household during this time. This move away from individual farm production towards a pooling of labour and other resources dates from the early 1960s and is probably the result of declining yields of groundnuts, the crop providing the main source of income for individuals and subgroups of men within the household; the growth of investment in oxen plough teams, donkey-carts, and wells requiring a major capital outlay that could only be raised by pooled resources at the household level; and a shift in social values whereby production by men outside the context of the joint household was increasingly seen as divisive and likely to lead to the household's competitive destruction.

Caste groups—nobles, slaves, and blacksmiths

Bambara society is traditionally made up of three social classes or castes: the noble (*horon*) who fought and farmed, the slave (*jon*) who worked for his master, and the blacksmith-griot (*nyamakala*) who worked with metal, wood, and leather, made pots, and sang the nobles' praises. In village society, these castes are still identifiably separate. Despite the formal abolition of slavery in 1905, ex-slave households are still known as such and they maintain systems of marriage alliance separate from those of nobles. Ex-slave families tend to intermarry because, while a noble family is eager to take a woman from these households in marriage, it is very hard for the ex-slave household to gain a woman for marriage in exchange. Thus, rather than lose all their women in unreciprocated exchanges, they prefer to marry among themselves. Outside the field of marriage, however, no trace of slavery remains in terms of the relationship between ex-slave and master household; the latter is unable for instance to demand any labour service from the former.

The *nyamakalaw* are made up of several occupational groups of which the blacksmith (*numu*) is the most important. Blacksmith men work in wood and metal and have retained an important position within rural Bambara society since they manufacture and repair the ploughs, carts, and hoes used in agricultural production.

Age-groups and the village ton

All men and women in the village are classified into a system of age-groups. For men, this is based on the date of circumcision, an event that takes place when a boy is about 14 years old. It is a major rite which marks the passage from child to adulthood. All men who are circumcised at the same date form a single age-group and within this group each member has a special relationship of equality, trust, and mutual help with the others which cuts across divisions based on lineage or household wealth. Circumcision ceremonies take place every three to four years, thus each age-group spans those born within a three to four year period. For women, the age-group to which they belong depends upon their date of marriage, those marrying in a single year forming a mutual help association who aid their fellow members in cotton-spinning and pounding millet.

The *ton*, or village youth association, is a work-group based on five or six male age-groups spanning the years from 14 to 30. This group is available for hire by households in Kala and in neighbouring villages and will perform particular tasks in farming and in house construction. In Kala, unlike many other villages, the *ton* does not do weeding or other cultivation work for households—though it can be hired to clear land for new bush fields. Its other main occupation is brick-making in the early part of the dry season. The *ton* is paid for its work and every household must send those in the appropriate age-range when there is work to be done, the *ton*'s earnings being used to hold a three-day festival, during which it provides porridge and meat for the whole village. At threshing time, the *ton* is divided between the two wards of the village when hand-threshing of the millet is to be done.

RECENT POLITICAL AND ECONOMIC DEVELOPMENTS IN MALI

Following Mali's Independence in 1960 and the installation, by the first President, Modibo Keita, of a government committed to socialist principles, legislation was enacted giving free access to land and water resources for all. This decree was intended to break the local monopoly on resource exploitation held by powerful chiefs. The extent to which this legislation has been effective and the consequences of its enactment differ from one area to another. In the case of Kala, free access to resources has been interpreted in a partial manner to include only members of the Bambara village, excluding Bambara settlers from elsewhere and Fulani families resident in the zone. Both of the latter groups are only given conditional and often temporary access to land and water that lie within Kala's territory. The villagers are usually supported in this interpretation of the legislation by the local administration when disputes occur over rights to farm land or dig wells. Judgment in such cases is still partly based on the traditional concept of the village chief's power to decide how resources within the village's territory will be allocated. The relative size of gifts made by the two disputants also plays its part in deciding the case.

The result of this legislation for Kala has been that all households in the village can dig private wells, the water from which is exchanged against dung with visiting livestock-keepers. This dung ensures high yields of the short-cycle millet variety grown on the settlement's village fields. Households in Kala have found it relatively easy to get a well dug, using their own or hired labour, due to the shallow depth at which water is found and the soft sandstone through which the shaft is dug. In some neighbouring villages, by contrast, the chieftaincy has remained sufficiently strong to continue to control the digging of wells by village households, despite the change in the law. In these cases, wells are dug, maintained, and owned by the community as a whole. However, these

are usually villages where water is hard to reach and where most households would be unable individually to finance the cost of digging a well.

The socialist government of Modibo Keita was overthrown in 1968 by a
military coup, the leaders of which were in power until March 1991 when
President Moussa Traoré was overthrown by a *coup d'état*. Elections and
a return to a democratically elected government have been promised by
the new leaders.

The government has retained some measure of control over the
economy, particularly in the marketing and distribution of certain commodities, but in general there has been a freeing of economic activity in
comparison with the period from 1960 to 1968. Having taken Mali out of
the French monetary system, known as the CFA zone, in 1962, the Keita
regime re-entered the system in 1967 by which time the Malian franc had
halved in value. In 1984, Mali was fully reabsorbed into the system and
adopted the CFA currency in use in much of francophone West Africa.
As part of the franc zone, Mali benefits from a stable exchange rate at
fixed parity with the French franc. This is achieved by monetary support
from the French exchequer to the Malian government's account, giving
France substantial leverage over economic and political decision-making.
French government transfers also go some way to reducing the chronic
imbalance in Mali's foreign trade. Exports, consisting mainly of cattle,
cotton, dried fish, and groundnuts, account for less than 50 per cent of
the value of imported goods in most years, leaving a large trade deficit.
This is met by a combination of transfers, loans, and foreign aid receipts.
The government also suffers from a chronic inability to finance the cost of
its personnel and services. Until very recently, it has been government
policy to guarantee a job to all graduates emerging from the education
system. The payment of salaries to all its employees is a heavy charge on
the government's limited resources and has reduced the sums available
for operational expenses. Thus, for example, extension agents rarely have
transport or fuel available with which to carry out their duties.

In a village like Kala, despite its distance from the main economic and
political centres, the progress of the country through Independence, the
socialist period of Modibo Keita, and the subsequent military regimes,
has been followed with interest by villagers. The demands made by
succeeding regimes remain very similar whatever their complexion.
Villagers call the present administration *fama*, the term used to describe
the kings of the pre-colonial state of Ségou. *Fama* is one who can demand
obedience from the *fantan*, or powerless, as the Bambara villagers describe themselves. However, these villagers are not totally without power.
The main weapon in the Bambara peasant's arsenal is his capacity to
grow surplus grain, needed by the government to feed the politically
sensitive urban dwellers, bureaucracy, and armed forces. An escalating
list of taxes and dues to be paid by farmers on livestock, carts, ploughs,

and rifles is used as one means to keep grain flowing onto urban markets. The government purchasing agency, OPAM, until recently also channelled grain from village to town. Since 1982, grain marketing has been freed from many of its restrictions and grain reaches town mainly because farmers need cash rather than because it has been requisitioned by government buying agents.

The 1970s and 1980s have seen a prolonged period of drought, with rainfall in some years at very low levels, as happened in 1973 and 1984. Mali has been one of the worst-hit states in West Africa because so little of its land lies in the area normally enjoying more than 1,000 mm of rainfall. Livestock losses in the early 1970s were especially high with an estimated fall in the cattle population from 5.4 m. in 1969–71 to 3.7 m. in 1973–4. Kala and many of its neighbours on the north bank seem to have weathered the 1973 drought without too much difficulty. The worst years of 1972 and 1973 came after a long series of years in which rainfall had been well above average (see Fig. 3.1). Consequently, people had sufficient stocks to pass most of this time without hardship, although the final months saw most people collecting wild fruit and grains in the bush to supplement their dwindling stores of food. Fruit from the *bere* shrub (*Boscia senegalensis*) was of especial importance at this time as a famine food and remains crucial to certain grain-deficit households in more normal years. Villagers also built up their cattle herds during this period, as grain prices rose while livestock prices plummeted. Herders would even try to pledge the unborn calf of a pregnant cow in exchange for a small quantity of millet. The recent drought years of 1983–4 throughout the Sahel have had a similarly devastating impact on harvests and livestock populations as in the early 1970s. In 1984, almost all the villages on the north bank of the Niger suffered varying degrees of harvest failure. By October of that year, many men and women had left the villages to go in search of work and food in urban areas. Villagers were preoccupied with thoughts of how to feed their families over the year to come.

By happy contrast, when I visited Kala in late September of 1988, the rains had been very heavy and had brought an exceptional harvest for all villages throughout the region. The village was full of people, starting the long period of harvest, and an atmosphere of relief and gaiety was strongly present.

Since the 1973 drought, farmers in Kala have been shifting their resources out of long- and towards shorter-cycle crops, that take only 60 to 80 days from sowing until ready to harvest, and groundnuts have lost their role as the main cash crop. The reallocation of land, labour, and investment resources between alternative lines of production forms the subject of Chapters 5 to 10, which deal with returns to factors in farm production and the returns from investment in different assets.

3

CLIMATE, CULTIVATION, AND HOUSEHOLD INCOME

THE PHYSICAL SETTING

Climate

Kala lies in the southern part of the sahelian zone which stretches across Africa from Senegal and Mauritania in the west to the Red Sea coast in the east between the 13th and the 17th parallels. The climate is characterized by a single rainy season from June to September followed by eight to nine months without rain. Temperatures throughout the year are high, with a mean of 28 °C. The heat of the sun for most of the year means that evaporation rates are very high and humidity low, except for the central weeks of the wet season. Even then, the common occurrence of several weeks without rain can bring a dusty heat similar to that of the long dry season.

Map 2 shows the general pattern of rainfall distribution in Mali and the decline in rainfall as one moves northwards. This map, based on the average rainfall recorded at different meteorological stations over 30 to 50 years, gives mean precipitation in any one year. However, variability is very high and increases as the region becomes drier, so that producers in the more northerly zones experience not only lower absolute levels but also more variability of rainfall. This variability occurs not only in the total received from year to year and its distribution within the rainy season, but also in its distribution in space, with neighbouring villages often receiving widely different amounts of rain in any given year.

Table 3.1 presents data from three rainfall stations which lie relatively close to the village of Kala—Ségou to the south, Sokolo to the north, and Markala to the east. As may be seem from this table and Map 2, Kala's geographical position would lead one to expect a long-term average rainfall of around 600 mm per annum. Table 3.2 shows that the actual rainfall received by Kala in the five years from 1980–4 averaged only 375 mm per annum. Current levels are thus less than two-thirds of the expected long-term average. It seems from the pattern found elsewhere that this trend towards lower rainfall began at the end of the 1960s. All rainfall stations in the Sahel have recorded rainfall significantly below the long-term mean (where this is calculated over 40 years or more), during the last 15 years. Little agreement has been reached by scientists on

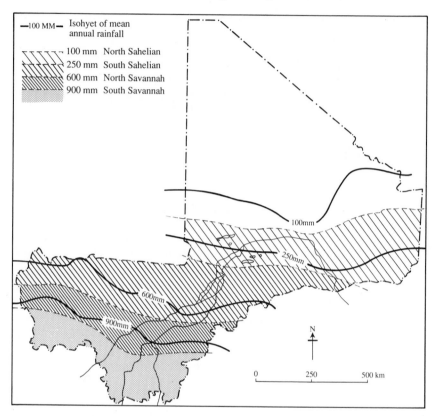

MAP 2. The distribution of mean annual rainfall in Mali

Source: Wilson, R.T. et al, 1983.

Note: Rainfall data presented here are based on the period 1921–76. Current isohyets are 50–100 km to the south of those shown on this map.

TABLE 3.1. *Rainfall of neighbouring stations*

	Ségou	Markala	Sokolo
Geographical position	13°40′	13°68′	14°73′
No. of years of data	52	25	40
Mean annual rainfall (mm)	676	628	500
Standard deviation	122	180	141
Coefficient of variation	18%	29%	28%

Note: The high coefficient of variation for Markala is due to the relatively short period for which data is available and to its proximity to the large irrigated areas of the Office du Niger, the effect of which is to provoke a high degree of variation in rainfall patterns.

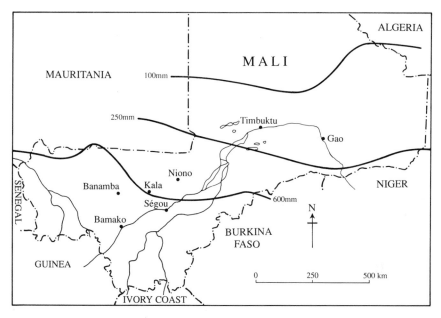

MAP 3. South and central Mali
Source: Wilson, R.T. et al, 1983.
Note: Rainfall data from selected stations, 1920–76.

whether the last 15 years represent a marked break with previous rainfall patterns (Lamb, 1982; Farmer and Wigley, 1985). Certainly, periods of several years with lower than average rainfall occurred in the past, as may be seen from Fig. 3.1, which gives the amount of rain falling at Ségou from 1921 to 1980. The relatively good rainfall of 1988 led some to hope that the cycle of poor rainy seasons had broken at last, but both 1989 and 1990 have shown such hopes to be misplaced.

As each dry year succeeds the next, however, the present low rainfall period becomes increasingly untypical in terms of the length of time it has continued. Ecologists and geographers disagree about the likely causes of the drought years of 1968–73 and of the low rainfall which has followed it. These climatic events have been variously attributed to sun-spot activity, over-grazing by animals in the Sahel, deforestation in coastal areas, such as the Ivory Coast, and the effect on tropical fronts of changes in ocean temperatures. There is a growing consensus that global warming is starting to play an important role in sahelian weather systems, although there is still some debate about the size and direction of possible changes. Current thinking predicts a slight rise in rainfall received, but a fall in available soil moisture, due to higher temperatures and increased rainfall

TABLE 3.2. *Rainfall, Kala, 1980–1984* (in millimetres)

Month	1980	1981	1982	1983	1984	Mean	Standard deviation
April	—	—	46.7	4.9	—	10.3	20.5
May	—	71.2	—	7.5	16.9	19.1	29.9
June	51.8	41.8	33.8	52.0	28.2	41.5	10.6
July	95.6	94.9	138.1	125.6	54.1	101.7	32.6
August	162.9	127.9	170.8	161.0	68.3	138.2	42.4
September	74.3	38.6	41.9	41.8	60.6	51.4	15.5
October	20.1	—	9.7	—	36.5	13.3	15.4
ANNUAL TOTALS:	404.7	374.4	441.0	392.8	264.6	375.5	66.6

Source: Field data.

runoff (IPCC, 1990). Whatever the actual cause of the present low rainfall, its existence is without question. Farmers and herders have had to adjust themselves to a drop in the expected volume and length of the rainy season and will continue to do so until they have evidence of a shift towards more favourable conditions.

One reason for the relatively high average rainfall figures for the last 50 years or so, when compared with the recent experience, is the existence of 15 to 20 well-watered years from the early 1950s to the end of the 1960s. During these years, rainfall was 20–30 per cent higher on average than in preceding and subsequent periods and its volume from one year to the next was less variable. Fig. 3.1 shows this favourable sequence of years using data from Ségou. During these years livestock numbers expanded greatly and farming spread further and further north. This period of good rainfall coincided in the case of Kala with the adoption of oxen-drawn ploughs and rapid growth in groundnut cultivation. A favourable climate enabled farmers to earn a steady surplus from this cash crop which was used for investment in new equipment and in the development of cattle holdings. The last ten years have seen the steady abandonment of groundnut cultivation in Kala, due to the shortening of the rainy season and its increasing variability, and to a downward shift in the relative price of groundnuts to grain. The occasional plots now farmed rarely yield more than the seed used for sowing and in some cases even the seed is lost.

Soils and vegetation

The north bank region is made up of an extensive plain with light sand and gravel soils. Fossilized river valleys, former branches of the River

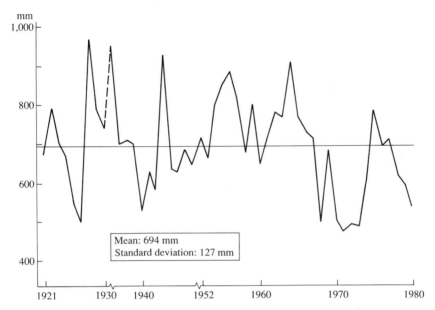

Fig. 3.1. Annual rainfall at Ségou, 1921–1980 (8 years' missing data)

Niger, cross the region providing long stretches of clay along the ancient riverbeds. Moving towards the north, soils become progressively sandier as one enters a region of ancient dunes. Kala, on the southern edge of these old dunes, has lighter soils than villages further to the south. The land is generally flat, with few hills or rocky outcrops, so that runoff is limited and erosion localized. Soil quality is an important determinant of crop performance because light sands will usually give a harvest even in years of very low rainfall whereas clays require higher and more continual rainfall if the millet is not to wither and die.

The north bank is a lightly wooded area, the main species of tree being the baobab (*Adansonia digitaria*), the kapok-tree (*Bombax costatum*), the *dugara* (*Cordyla pinnata*), the *gwele* (*Prosopis africana*), and a number of bushy trees such as *Guiera senegalensis*, *Pterocarpus lucens*, and *Combretum* species. Particular trees are valued highly for their products: the baobab for example provides leaves for sauce, fruit for eating, fibres for rope-making, and shade for resting under during the day, while its hollow trunk stores water through much of the dry season providing a reservoir of drinking water. The fruits of several trees are used in times of food shortage. Of these the *bere* (*Boscia senegalensis*) is of greatest importance, being eaten every day for several months of the dry season by those in greatest need.

The effects of nearly twenty years of poor rainfall could be seen on the tree population around Kala. Many species no longer produce blossom or fruit and are rapidly disappearing from the region; the desiccated, bare skeletons of kapok, *dugura*, and *gwele* are eventually felled and taken for timber. The work of blacksmiths and herders also takes its toll from the tree population. The former use *dugura* and *gwele* for mortars; the latter cut branches from certain species in the dry season to provide the flock with fresh leaves, a practice which if carried to excess will cause the death of the tree.

Trees and shrubs intermix with grasses, most of which are annuals. The regular cultivation and fallowing of land by farmers in this region produces a particular evolution and composition of vegetation as the fallow ages. Farmed for four or five years before being abandoned, the fallowed land provides much of the grazing used by village herds. The main annuals found are those typical of the southern sahelian zone: *Schoenefeldia gracilis*, *Diheteropogon hagerupii*, *Cenchrus biflorus*, and *Zornia glochidiata*. Perennial grasses, such as *Andropogon gayanus*, are found only in a few low-lying areas and are in retreat throughout this region, due to the persistence of low rainfall. The Bambara have names for each kind of grass and know them for their particular qualities as pasture, thatching material, sweeping brushes, and famine foods. *Wuluku* (or 'dog's tail') is collected by women to make a brush for sweeping out their houses, men search for the tall perennial, *wa*, to build large granaries, and wild rice *komalo* is cut from drying ponds before the millet harvest begins.

Water

Subterranean sources form the major supply of water for human and livestock needs for most of the year. In some places, water is easy to find at 10 to 15 m whereas in others wells must be dug to 45 m or more before an assured supply is reached. These differences can be attributed to the local pattern of rock strata and their water-holding capacities. Villages like Kala benefit from a layer of hard laterite which catches rainfall over a wide area and concentrates this water in the saucer-like depression in which the village lies. Wells of 15 to 25 m depth are dug to tap this supply.

Surface water is used mainly by livestock during the rainy season, but in villages where there are only a few deep wells, pond water also supplies the bulk of human drinking-water for several months of the year. Although particular ponds are usually set aside for different purposes— drinking-water, washing-water, etc.—villages relying on pond water tend to have a high incidence of guinea-worm infection (transmitted through drinking polluted water) which can debilitate the labour-force during much of the farming season.

TABLE 3.3. *Area of various crops, Kala, 1980 and 1981* (in hectares)

	Millet[a]			Groundnuts		Fonio		Total	
	Bush-field		Village-field		ha	%	ha	%	ha	%
	ha	%	ha	%						
1980	621.4	72.1	165.1	19.1	70.4	8.2	5.0	0.6	861.9	100
1981	641.6	71.5	221.7	24.7	26.1	2.9	8.0	0.9	897.4	100

[a] Cowpeas are intersown with both varieties of millet and are found at a density of 5–10% in comparison with millet stands.

Crops

The crops grown on the north bank of the River Niger are those commonly found throughout the West African sahel and savannah regions. The staple grain is provided by bulrush millet (*Pennisetum typhoides*) of which a number of varieties exist of varying cycle length, the longer-cycle varieties being replaced by shorter-cycle millets as one moves further north. Millet fields are intersown with cowpea (*Vigna unguiculata*), producing grain for human consumption and leaves for fodder. Sorghum (*Sorghum bicolor*) is only grown in a few areas towards the south where soils are heavier and rainfall more reliable.

Groundnuts (*Arachis hypogaea*) used to be grown throughout this region, but have retreated further south over the last 10 to 15 years and now, as already mentioned, occupy a marginal position within the farming system. Bambara earthnuts (*Vouandzou subterranea*) have long been grown in this region, as their name implies. They have a short cycle and are of particular value in providing something to eat during the hungry season, before the millet has ripened. Producing their nuts underground, this crop was of great importance during the 1930s when locusts annually devastated grain-fields. Minor crops include *fonio* (*Digitaria exilis*), *dah* (*Hibiscus* species), maize (*Zea mays*), tobacco, manioc, and assorted vegetables, grown in tiny patches within the village lands. The relative importance of areas under the main crops in Kala is shown in Table 3.3.

Livestock

The main domestic livestock kept are cattle, sheep, goats, horses, donkeys, dogs, and chickens. Cattle are kept for their milk, dung, and offspring, for draught purposes, and as marketable assets. Sheep and goats may serve many of the same purposes and are the main capital asset owned by individual men and women. Horses were once essential as mounts for military purposes, providing the speedy transport needed for raiding and for pursuit of an enemy. Now horses are relatively less important but are still highly valued, remaining the main form of transport for elderly men. A beautiful, well-kept horse conveys prestige on the owner, and old men spend much time cutting fresh grass to fatten their horses. Certain horses are well known within the region and considered exceptional animals, typically belonging to a trader or *marabout* diviner, who can afford to give a daily ration of grain. Donkeys formerly belonged mainly to herding groups of Maure and Fulani and to itinerant traders, but are now common in Bambara settlements following the introduction and widespread adoption of donkey-drawn carts. Dogs, used to guard the fields from incursion by livestock, are found everywhere in noisy and argumentative packs. Chickens are similarly widespread, providing the most commonly consumed source of meat.

The region supports a variety of wild game, hunted for their meat and skins, such as antelope, boar, ostrich, and guinea-fowl. Wild bees are also managed for their honey.

THE ECONOMY OF VILLAGE AND HOUSEHOLD

Land use

Fig. 3.2 shows the three land-use zones around the village of Kala, the external limit being pushed outwards as bush fields move further from the village. Within and beyond zone C, cattle are pastured and bush products harvested. All land in zone A is permanently cultivated and, in the case of Kala, this zone has been progressively extending outwards over recent years, as households expand the area farmed with short-cycle village-field millet. Zone B is of varying width and consists of old bush fallows that are used for shifting plots of groundnuts and fonio, many of them farmed by individual men and women.

Table 3.3 shows the proportion of total cultivated area devoted to different crops by all groups within the village—Bambara households, individuals within these households (typically retired men and women of all ages), and Fulani herding families. The relative importance of different crops for each of these three groups is shown in Table 3.4, from which it may be seen that bush-field land is only cultivated at the *foroba* household level. This is in contrast to village-field land, where three-quarters is under household cultivation, the remainder being almost equally divided between fields belonging to individual Bambara and to Fulani herders. The two millet varieties account for over 95 per cent of land cultivated at the household level, of which the long-cycle bush-field millet takes up nearly 80 per cent.

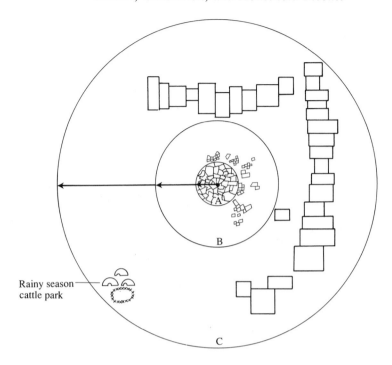

Rainy season cattle park

ZONE A: VILLAGE FIELDS (radius 1–1.5 km)
Crops grown are:
   Souna, short-cycle millet (h, i)
   Cowpeas for fodder   (h)
   Maize, sorghum   (i)
   Peanuts, vegetables,   (i)
   and tobacco.   (i)

ZONE B: OLD BUSH FALLOWS (radius 3–4 km)
Crops grown are:
   Peanuts   (h, i)
   Bambara earthnuts   (h)
   Fonio   (h, i)

ZONE C: BUSH FIELDS (radius 7–8 km)
Crops grown are:
   Sanyo, long-cycle millet (h)
   Cowpeas for grain   (h)
   Peanuts   (h, i)
   Bambara earthnuts   (h)
   Calabash and *dah*.   (h)

Note: (h)=crops grown by the household for its own needs;
   (i)=crops grown by individuals, both men and women, in their free time.

FIG. 3.2. Land-use zones around the village of Kala

The Village Setting

TABLE 3.4. *Percentage of crop area by type of cultivator, Kala, 1981*

Type of cultivator	Millet		Groundnuts	Fonio
	Bush-field	Village-field		
Household	100	75	71	19
Individual	0	13	29	81
Fulani herders	0	12	0	0
TOTAL AREA (ha)	641.6	221.7	26.1	8

TABLE 3.5. *Mean size of household bush and village fields, Kala, 1980 and 1981* (in hectares)

	Bush fields (n = 28)	Village fields (n = 29)
1980	22.2	4.3
	(14.5)	(3.2)
1981	22.9	5.7
	(15.0)	(3.6)

Note: Figures in brackets refer to the standard deviation.

Average bush- and village-field sizes for households in Kala are presented in Table 3.5, which shows the large size and wide variation in holdings. As will be seen in Chapter 5, field size is closely related to the size of the household.

Livestock ownership

The total livestock population belonging to the Bambara population in mid-1981 comprised 602 cattle, 246 sheep, 452 goats, 19 horses, 45 donkeys, and several hundred dogs and chickens. Table 3.6 shows the distribution of livestock between households in Kala, the mean household owning 20.8 cattle, 24.1 small stock, 0.65 horses, and 1.55 donkeys. Livestock holdings are far from equally distributed, the smallest and poorest households owning at best a couple of small stock and a donkey. At the other extreme are several of the largest households which own a cattle herd and small stock holdings both of over 50 head. There is a close positive relationship between household size and livestock wealth which may be seen from Table 3.6, with the largest households having not only the largest number of animals but also more animals per person. This relationship results from the economic and demographic advantages

TABLE 3.6. *Distribution of cattle, sheep, and goats by household, Kala, mid-1981*

	Livestock-holding class					Village mean
	>40	21–40	11–20	1–10	0	
Cattle:						
No. of households	5	4	1	16	3	29
Mean household size	31.1	22.0	11.5	9.7	4.0	14.6
Mean holding	78.4	31.3	20.0	4.1	0	20.8
Sheep:						
No. of households	—	4	6	8	11	29
Mean household size	—	29.5	17.7	13.2	8.5	14.6
Mean holding	—	30.3	18.5	4.3	0	8.5
Goats:						
No. of households	4	6	3	10	6	29
Mean household size	31.8	17.6	15.0	10.9	5.8	14.6
Mean holding	54.5	27.8	13.7	5.6	0	15.6

accruing to large domestic groups which allow them to generate a larger surplus, part of which is stored in animal form. An investigation of the form taken by such advantages is presented in later chapters.

The Bambara of Kala do not herd their own livestock. Instead, they are entrusted to hired herders, usually from the Fulani ethnic group. Cattle are grouped into several herding units, containing from 50 to 120 head and put into the charge of a herder. This allows the Bambara to concentrate on farming during the short rainy season, which has advantages in the form of the high yield gained per worker in farming when compared with the cost of hiring herding labour. In addition, the Bambara place a high value on their traditional specialization as millet farmers which limits their desire to undertake herding duties themselves. However, as described in more detail in Chapter 10, the use of hired herders raises a number of problems for the care of livestock, in particular the conflict of interests between herd owner and herder about the level of milk taken from cows with a calf at foot. A camp is set up in the rainy season away from the bush fields where cattle and their herders pass the night. Once the village fields are harvested, herds are kraaled on the village fields at night in order to manure the land.

Sheep and goats are tethered in the compound at night and taken out by a hired herder during the day while the village fields contain crops. After the crops are stored, cattle, sheep, and goats are left to wander freely during the day. Horses and donkeys are tethered in the courtyard for most of the time and food is brought to them: hay is cut in the bush for them and both species also receive some grain, bran, and cowpea hay when available.

Ownership of other assets

Livestock play a central role in the accumulation and storage of wealth amongst Bambara households in Kala. However, there are also other capital assets of great importance for the productivity of the household's farming operations and dry season activities. Table 3.7 presents the distribution of these assets amongst the 29 village households. Investment by a household in digging a well is aimed primarily at attracting visiting herds in the dry season, during which period well-water is exchanged for the animals' dung. By this means the well owner can fertilize an increasing area of short-cycle village-field millet. Oxen plough teams are used to cultivate both varieties of millet. Donkey-carts carry equipment out to the field, bring the harvest back from the threshing ground, transport people and firewood, and are essential in operating a trading business.

Of those households with very few assets, two own none of the above three assets. One household owns neither a plough team nor a donkey-cart, and one owns neither a well nor a donkey-cart. At the other extreme, of the five households with two wells, four have two or more donkey-carts, and three of these also farm with three or more plough teams, these being amongst the largest and wealthiest households in the village.

Grain production and use

Millet and cattle form the two main outputs from the farm sector. Their relative importance is shown in Table 3.11, from which it is seen that together they account on average for three-quarters of incomes earned at the household level. Table 3.8 presents data on the mean harvest size per household for 1980 and 1981. The high coefficient of variation can be explained by the large difference in household size within the village and the correlation between size of household, area cultivated, and final harvest. The production analysis in Chapters 5 and 6 investigates the factors determining levels of grain productivity in greater detail.

While the figures in Table 3.8 represent estimated total harvest size for each variety, the actual quantity finally stored in the household granary is often significantly less. On average, stored grain represented only 85 per cent of the harvest in 1980, the balance being used for several purposes, noted in Chapter 1, such as pre-harvest consumption and payment of wages for harvesting, threshing, and winnowing labour.

Flows of millet from the household granary, following the 1980 harvest, are shown in Table 3.9. This data covers 26 households in Kala from

TABLE 3.7. *Distribution of capital assets among 29 households in Kala, 1981*

Assets	No. of households
Wells:	
None	7
1	17
2	5
Plough teams:	
None	3
1–2	19
3 or more	7
Donkey-carts:	
None	5
1	19
2 or more	5

TABLE 3.8. *Mean harvest size per household, Kala, 1980 and 1981* (in kilograms of threshed grain)

	Bush-field millet	Village-field millet
1980	4,988 (n = 27)	4,058 (n = 29)
	(3,656)	(3,007)
1981	5,179 (n = 28)	5,707 (n = 29)
	(4,116)	(4,063)

Note: Figures in brackets refer to the standard deviation.

which data was obtainable. Three cases were omitted due to the great difficulty we experienced in getting any information about income and expenditure. One of the three was the largest household in the village, containing nearly 60 people and considerable internal subdivisions, which contributed to difficulties in gaining accurate information.

The remaining two households were both very small and substantially short of grain. In the first case, all members were absent for many months of the dry season. The second was supported in large part by the private income of the elderly man (from another household) who had inherited in marriage the widowed mother of the young household head. In all three cases, the personal difficulties faced by household members due to food shortages and internal tensions meant that there was great unwillingness to discuss questions to do with sales, sources of income, the structure of responsibilities within the household, and how to make ends meet.

TABLE 3.9. *Flows of millet from the household granary, for 26 households in Kala, 1981*

Millet stored in granary after harvest in 1981	192,220 kg
Outflows (% of total stored) to:	
Exchange against condiments	4.8
Cash sales	4.4
Exchange against livestock	2.3
Fulani herder fees	3.2
Other labour hire (weeding, harvesting)	1.0
Blacksmith fees	0.8
Food exchange, e.g. rice	0.3
TOTAL out of granary	16.8
Inflows (% of total stored) from:	
Millet purchases	0.6
Receipt of millet wages	0.5
Received in exchange for livestock	0.1
TOTAL into granary	1.2
Overall millet balance:	164,000 kg
as a percentage of stored grain after the harvest	85.4

Note: Data in this table excludes 3 households for whom budget information could not be obtained for reasons discussed elsewhere.

For the remaining 26 households, millet available for domestic consumption represented 85.4 per cent of stored grain, mean outflows of 32,000 kg greatly exceeding mean inflows of 2,300 kg. Sales of millet for cash formed only one-quarter of all transactions involving millet, demonstrating the great importance of grain as a means of payment within the village economy. However, there was also considerable variation in the share of stored millet going to different destinations, with several grain surplus households selling more than 30 per cent of stored millet. As may be seen, much millet is used to purchase condiments, a daily allocation of grain being exchanged against peppers, meat, dried fish, and salt with which to enliven the diet. Payment of wages, particularly for hired Fulani herding labour, is another important category of expenditure.

Table 3.10 presents the distribution of grain available for consumption between households in Kala following the various inflows and outflows of millet described above. The data is shown in the form of the number of days during which all household members could be fed at normal levels of consumption. This is based on the calculation of total consumption units for each household in terms of adult male equivalents (using the weights shown under Table 14.1). Each adult male equivalent is taken as requir-

TABLE 3.10. *Distribution of households by number of days grain available for consumption after 1980 harvest, 26 households in Kala*

No. of days grain available	Households		
	No.	%	Mean size
>400	4	15	14.3
350–400	3	12	17.3
300–350	4	15	11.8
250–300	6	23	25.0
200–250	7	27	18.0
<200	2	8	14.5

ing a daily ration of one measure of millet, the amount normally set aside per man, equal to about 1.5 kg of threshed grain or a little over 1 kg of millet flour. It may be seen from this table that over half the households in Kala had less than 300 days of millet supplied by the 1980 harvest, once all flows of grain had been taken into account. This number of days represents the period between the storage of the village-field millet in November of one year and the earliest date in September of the following year at which the new village-field crop can be eaten. Thus, those with fewer than 300 days' supply had to make some adjustment to levels of consumption, for example by several people leaving for much of the dry season, or turn to other sources of supply. In one case, substantial grain stocks from previous years were held and these were run down. For other households, women's stores of grain were of particular significance, enabling many a deficit household to conserve its stocks during the dry season by making women responsible for feeding the restricted nuclear family unit of man, woman, and children for certain meals of the day.

Dry-season activities

In the dry season, the household makes limited demands upon its members, allowing them time to pursue their own income-earning activities. Each man and woman has a variety of income sources; the former being involved in crafts, petty trade, collecting firewood, and weaving and the latter in spinning cotton, hair-dressing, and cloth dyeing. Few men of working age can earn more than 15,000 FCFA a year, given the many constraints on their time. This sum is devoted to buying personal items such as tobacco, kola-nut, clothing, and shoes. Women of working age tend to have a larger income, derived from their private fields, winnowing

TABLE 3.11. *Household income derived from different sources, 26 households in Kala, 1981*

Sources of income	Mean value per household (FCFA)	Mean percentage by household
Crop sales	86,420	47.2 (31.7)
Livestock sales	46,075	27.6 (27.3)
Migration earnings	14,470	22.1 (27.6)
Trading profits	6,410	3.1 (7.8)
TOTAL	153,375	100.0

Note: Figures in brackets refer to the standard deviation.

TABLE 3.12. *Household expenditure by category, 26 households in Kala, 1981*

Category of expenditure	Mean value per household (FCFA)	Mean percentage by household
Livestock purchase	31,925	19.1 (18.0)
Sauce/condiments	28,675	17.8 (14.6)
Marriage	25,425	13.3 (19.1)
Labour hire	24,690	13.8 (10.5)
Equipment	14,920	13.6 (12.1)
Taxes	13,600	10.9 (7.1)
Food	10,050	10.9 (14.8)
Other	620	0.5 (2.7)
TOTAL	149,905	100.0

Note: Figures in brackets refer to the standard deviation.

earnings, and from the millet which they appropriate after the threshing. However, their responsibility for food provision is greater than that of men and half or more of the 500 kg or so that they control will probably end up in meals cooked for their family or in purchase of sauce condiments. The remainder is sold to buy cotton, cloth, shoes, and soap, and for services such as hair-dressing.

Retired men and women have considerably greater resources at their disposal, due to their no longer being needed to work in the household, field, or kitchen. Typically, they can earn incomes in excess of 50,000 FCFA a year, trade providing the major source for men while grain from private fields and from winnowing work are principal sources for women. A few retired folk also regularly fatten a sheep or goat over several months, using bran, cotton-seed, and hay to earn a net margin of

7–10,000 FCFA per animal. The magnitude of private income sources for retired women in particular helps explain the great demand amongst men to marry recently widowed women where there is no obvious candidate to inherit her. The returns from marriage to women of different ages and status are described in much greater detail in Chapter 13.

Household income and expenditure

Tables 3.11 and 3.12 show the breakdown of income and expenditure at the household level for 26 cases in Kala for the twelve-month period from December 1980 to November 1981. These data refer to the *foroba* budget, that is the joint budget of the domestic group as a whole, thus excluding incomes and expenditures of individuals. It is only concerned with transactions undertaken by the household, such as sales of livestock or exchanges of grain for some commodity, and thus represents the total level of involvement in market transactions by the household rather than total income and expenditure. The latter would include subsistence income derived from crops and livestock and the change in value of stocks over the period concerned. As noted earlier, three households were omitted from the budget study because of the difficulty faced in obtaining data. Overall, grain provided nearly half, and livestock over one-quarter, of the resources used in cash and barter transactions by the 26 households. Migration earnings made up nearly a quarter with trade providing a relatively low share of income. However, the high coefficients of variation for each of these items demonstrates the high variability in transaction patterns between households. Of particular note is the high proportion of income stemming from migration for the smallest households; four out of five households for which more than 50 per cent of income came from this source contained 10 members or less, compared with the village mean of more than 18. Trading profits are very important for those households with a permanent trading business; the five businesses covered by the budget survey provided on average 27.5 per cent of household cash income.

As far as expenditure is concerned, there is also considerable variation in the relative importance of different items, the least variable categories being labour hire, tax payments, and condiment purchase. The amount of money spent on marriage depends on whether a wedding is to be celebrated that year. While mean expenditure per household on marriage over the 12 months of the budget study was 25,000 FCFA, those households actually involved spent up to 200,000 FCFA per wedding. The costs of marriage and the strain which this puts on household resources are discussed in Chapter 13. Money spent on food purchases, predominantly millet, depends on whether the household has had the need and the means to purchase grain.

TABLE 3.13. *Distribution of households by size of total involvement in market transactions, 26 households in Kala, 1981*

'Income' class (in FCFA)	Households	
	No.	Mean size (AEs)
<50,000	3	5.5
50,000–100,000	8	12.3
100,000–200,000	8	10.5
200,000–300,000	3	27.5
300,000–400,000	4	22.2

Note: Household size has been measured here in adult equivalents (AEs), taking those over 15 years of age as equal to 1.0, those of 15 and younger as 0.5 units.

Table 3.13 shows the distribution of incomes between households in relation to household size. As expected, the general trend is for income to increase with household size, though the pattern is modified by the following:

(i) the degree of involvement in transactions by the household depends on the special circumstances of that year, such as whether a marriage is in preparation or whether an old work ox is exchanged for a new. All households with cash outlays over 200,000 FCFA were involved in wedding preparations and several of the smaller households with relatively high cash incomes had to buy new oxen during the period that data was collected;

(ii) as household size grows, the range of expenses for which the household is responsible tends to diminish. The largest households usually produce a regular millet surplus which means that their members are granted a degree of autonomy over their time and income which is not possible in the smaller grain-deficit households. The more distant kin ties between men in larger households and internal differentiation, due to unequal holdings of cattle between different groups of 'brothers', both tend to produce less pooling of resources than in smaller, more cohesive domestic groups.

PART II

FARM PRODUCTION

4

THE FARMING SYSTEM

Millet is by far the most important crop, occupying more than 90 per cent of cultivated land; it is both a subsistence crop for households in Kala and a cash crop for sale to grain merchants and to others within the local economy, such as blacksmiths.

Two millet varieties are cultivated in Kala: a long-cycle millet, taking 120 days from sowing to harvest, is grown on large, shifting fields in the bush while a shorter-cycle, 60 to 80 day millet is grown on manured plots around the village. Farmers cultivate two millets of different cycle length in order to reduce the risk of total crop failure, it being very unlikely that both varieties will fail in a single year.

FACTORS OF PRODUCTION

Land

The low population density on land around Kala means that farming land is relatively abundant for the Bambara, needing only to be cleared and manured to be ready for cultivation. There are, however, certain limits set to this availability by lack of water, differences in soil quality, and institutional factors that control access to land.

Access to a good water-supply is one of the main factors behind settlement patterns on the north bank of the River Niger and much good farming land is untouched because water cannot be tapped easily. Recently, the use of donkey- and ox-drawn carts to transport drinking-water in the farming and harvesting seasons has greatly expanded the area in which fields may be cultivated.

Soils in this region vary from light sands on stabilized dunes to heavier clays in depressions and old river valleys. In some places, the earth has a lateritic crust, in others the soil is composed of a gravelly material. Farmers classify soils according to characteristics of texture and colour and know the relative merits of each under different rainfall conditions. Clays and gravels are said to produce high yields under conditions of regular and heavy rainfall, such as those of the 1950s and early 1960s, but to perform badly in years of low and poorly distributed rain, as in more recent years. Lighter sands are currently much in demand since they can be relied on to produce a yield in years when rain has been patchy, the lightness of the soil permitting a more extensive root system to develop so that the plant can tap water at a greater depth. Although the soils of Kala are mainly sandy, harder clays are present to the south of the village, an area where many households had their bush fields until recently. These fields have now been abandoned and farmers have moved towards the north of the village on to lighter soils and away from the main wet-season cattle routes. Similarly, most of the new village fields are being cut to the north and east to avoid gravelly soils.

Institutional factors, however, limit access to land. Custom demands that anyone wishing to farm land within a village's territory must apply to the village council for consent before starting to clear a field. The Malian administration largely supports the traditional rights of villages in this respect, although this runs counter to the position embodied in the proclamation at Independence, giving free access to land and water resources to all, as described in Chapter 2. A village holds its power over rights to farmland within its territory because it was the original settlers of the village that established an agreement with the spirits of the area that would permit them to farm unhindered. This covenant between local spirits and farmers is renewed at the start of each rainy season by a sacrifice made at the *daasiri*, a sacred grove of trees close to the settlement. While Bambara newcomers are usually granted land, the village council often demands that immigrant households settle definitively in the village and become part of the community. This is to maintain control over strangers by absorbing them into the social life and linkages within the village. Villagers also want to prevent strangers coming and farming their land, taking their harvest back to their home village and leaving the host village with greater constraints for expanding bush fields in the future. The reluctance of many village councils to host the large number of immigrant households currently looking for sandier soils on which to farm is based on the belief that these immigrants are not interested in long-term settlement.

Access to farm land is less readily given by Bambara communities for the settlement of Fulani groups within the village's territory. The Bambara of Kala are not alone in wanting to restrict Fulani residents to those employed in herding village cattle, allowing them access to land for as long as they are contract herders but withdrawing their rights to farm land once the contract is finished. Several Fulani complained that while farm land was abundant overall, they faced a shortage, due to the Bambara having acquired effective control over this resource.

There is no market in land, no sale or purchase of this resource taking place. Renting or loaning land is also very uncommon; the only case in which land had been loaned involved households that were absent for several years in a farming hamlet, during which time they had been unable to farm their village fields. Consequently, they lent their land to other households to farm for the years that they were away.

Access to land is thus controlled not through its price but by the need to get the consent of that group which controls rights to land in that area. This control is enforced by both legal and ideological means; for example, an incomer who has not gained the villagers' consent and who has therefore not made the appropriate sacrifice to the local spirits, is believed to risk total crop failure as a consequence.

Labour

Labour input into crop production during the farming season comes predominantly from the household's own labour-force. However, labour from outside the household, while not very significant for the village as a whole, can make a crucial impact on an individual household's total labour supply.

Household labour   Farming is done by both men and women, although there is some specialization of work within the field, women for instance very rarely being involved in handling the plough team. Women arrive at the field later and leave earlier than men since they must carry out their household duties and prepare food in the early morning and evening. No households in this or in neighbouring villages have adopted the practice of releasing women from the household's farm labour-force, as has happened in villages close to market towns. In the latter, there are trading activities that are more profitable to them and their families than their continued participation in farming.

The age at which children start working and at which people retire depends on the wealth, size, and age structure of the household concerned, early retirement being more likely in richer, larger households where there are a number of young workers to take the place of older ones. Women tend to stop work earlier than men, at around 45 years of age, this usually coinciding with the entry into the household of the woman's first daughter-in-law. Most men retire from the household field at around 55 years but it may be later than this where the remaining work-force is composed of adolescents and women. Children start going to the field from an early age, helping their mothers by caring for smaller infants. Boys and girls start to work properly at 12–14 years of age, often being used to lead the oxen as they plough and guarding them as they graze during rest periods.

The worker index   For the purposes of the analysis in this and subsequent chapters, a weighted index of labour was calculated in order to aggregate the contribution of different types of labour—according to age and sex—to the household's farm work-force. The index excludes those members of the household who were very rarely in the field, such as the

young head of one household who ran a trading business throughout the
rainy season and only visited the field for a few hours once every two or
three weeks. The following weights were taken to construct the worker
index:

adult men aged 16–45 years   = 1.0
men aged over 45 years   = 0.8
women aged 15–45 years   = 0.6
boys and girls aged 12–15 years = 0.7

The weights try to take two factors into account: the length of time
spent in the field by each age and sex group and the speed and efficiency
of work done by each kind of labour. They are based on observation of
working patterns and on discussion with farmers. Necessarily, they represent only an approximation of the true value of different kinds of
labour, the overall worker index suffering from the common problem of
aggregating a non-homogeneous variable.

During the short cultivation season, men leave the village at or soon
after dawn and remain in the field until dusk. They are usually accompanied by boys and girls in the 12–15 year age group. While this gives a
10–12 hour period away from the village, the number of hours actually
worked generally lies between 7 and 9, a short rest after the mid-morning
meal and a longer break in the early afternoon giving some respite.
Married women and older girls have household duties to perform and
must cook food before setting off to the field, arriving there between 9
and 10 a.m. and leaving between 4 and 5 p.m. Thus, their hours of work
in the field are shorter than men's, averaging four to five hours. As noted
already, the hours worked and pattern of labour-use during the short
cultivation season are remarkably similar between households.

Adult men aged 16–45 years of age were taken as the standard, valued
at 1.0, against which to measure the work input of other age and sex
groups. Working capacity tended to decline with increased age, with men
in the last 10 years of their working life (i.e. over 45 years) significantly
less productive than their younger brothers and sons. Women worked
relatively hard when in the field, though somewhat more slowly than
young adult men. Boys and girls in the 12–15 year age-group had less
stamina than adult men and women but, given their long hours in the
field, they were weighted slightly above adult women. The contribution of
these young workers was especially important where, by their leading and
caring for work-oxen, they freed an older man for other farm work.

Observations about the length of working day and intensity of work
effort were made as a result of being permanently resident in the village
and visiting farmers at work in the fields on a very regular basis. A good
idea of the relative working speeds of different age and sex groups could
be obtained from the way in which weeding work is carried out. House-

TABLE 4.1. *Distribution of households by size of work-force, for 29 households in Kala, 1981*

No. of workers	No. of households
1–4	9
5–8	12
9–12	2
13–16	4
17–20	1
>20	1

hold members form a single work-group and each takes a line of millet to weed. The group moves forward together to cover a distance of 50 m or so, those reaching this point first then turning back down the lines of slower workers who have still to finish. Frequent monitoring of this operation helped in generating the system of weights shown earlier. In addition, discussion with farmers confirmed the relative values ascribed to different kinds of workers, field size always being expanded where an adult man had joined the labour-force, though little or no increase would be made for the addition of a new wife or youngster.

Table 4.1 presents data on the distribution of households by the number of workers present in the household work-force in 1981. From this may be seen the very wide variation in size of household work-force with the average around 7.5 workers, the smallest households having fewer than 4 workers while the largest household in the village had more than 20 workers.

Non-household labour   Data on the importance of non-household labour for cultivation of the two millet varieties is presented in Table 4.2. The very short growing season in villages like Kala and the very limited labour-market mean that the scale of the household's involvement in farming is closely determined by the amount of labour that the household itself can mobilize from mid-June to mid-September. While there is little farm labour available for hire on a regular basis, several households gained a significant amount of their farm labour from non-household sources and all cattle-owning households in Kala employed hired labour to care for their animals. The different sources of labour and their cost will be looked at here.

The only form of hired farm labour of any significance in Kala comes from other households in the village or from neighbouring villages, and there is commonly a close tie of kinship between the worker being hired and the hiring household. A household without enough grain will loan

one worker to another household in exchange for grain at the rate of
three measures of millet a day (4.5 kg) which, with the cost of providing
this worker with food, comes to around 5 kg of millet per day. This hired
worker is often a teenage boy who can be used by the hiring household to
lead and care for the work-oxen, freeing an older worker to hoe. In some
cases, the hired worker spends the entire cultivation season with the
hiring household, although he will normally return to help his own family
sow and weed their village fields, since these operations must be done
promptly to ensure a reasonable harvest. In other cases, a few days' work
are performed to repay a debt incurred—such as the receipt of grain or
hire of an oxen plough team—or to earn grain to supplement household
millet stocks. No household was involved in selling labour in both the
farming seasons studied, indicating that this is an occasional strategy of
last resort rather than a regular source of income for the poorest households. In Kala, no households actively went in search of workers to
hire for the rainy season; instead, they gained this labour from several
millet-deficit households in this and neighbouring villages, including two
immigrant households farming for their first year at Kala.

Ton labour provided by the Village Youth Association is rarely used
for work during the farming season at Kala; in the two years studied, the
ton was hired on only one occasion, to weed the fields of the visiting
blacksmith. Although scheduled to work for one household towards the
end of the farming season in 1980, the early end to the rains and drying
out of the earth meant that this work was cancelled, it being thought that
further weeding would do little to raise yields by this late stage. The very
limited role of *ton* labour for farming in Kala is in strong contrast to the
role played by the *ton* in other villages in the region, where it allows
certain households to cultivate a field much larger than would have been
possible using household labour alone, as well as acting as a redistributive labour pool[1] providing free labour to the poorest and least able
households.

Help from relatives and friends is provided either in the form of freely
given labour by those households which have already finished weeding
their own fields or through the medium of reciprocal work-groups, or
dama teams, made up of a small number of young men from different
households who take it in turn to go and weed each other's field. Neither
of these labour transfers is of great importance, because of the small
number of days involved and—given that they take place towards the end
of the weeding season—because the actual value to the crop of a day's
work at this late stage is much less than at the start of the farming season.
However, this labour is free; labour exchanges reinforce ties of mutual

---

[1] Various forms of labour pooling are described in many West African farming systems as
is the possibility of hiring a communal work-group by which means a household can expand
the area it cultivates.

TABLE 4.2. *Non-household labour input into millet production, for 29 households in Kala*

	1980	1981
Bush-field millet:		
No. of receiving households	16	20
Average man-days received/household	12.3	16.5
Non-household labour as a percentage of total labour input, all households	4.0	7.2
No. of households for whom percentage greater than 10%	2	5
Village-field millet:		
No. of receiving households	3	7
Average man-days received/household	3.0	5.5
Non-household labour as a percentage of total labour input, all households	4.2	6.9
No. of households for whom percentage greater than 10%	—	2

support between households and individuals and they help the recipients finish weeding their fields one or two days earlier than would otherwise have been the case.

Hired herding labour is used by all households in Kala for the care of their cattle which allows the villagers to concentrate on farming during the short rainy season. This hired labour, paid in milk and grain, is provided by Fulani households. The terms of herding contracts and the peculiar problems associated with care of livestock by hired labour are described in detail in Chapter 10.

Table 4.2 provides data on the role of non-household labour for the two millet varieties in both years. From this may be seen that there is a much lower number of households receiving labour from outside the household for village-field work than for the bush field. This, as explained earlier, is due to the tendency for hired labourers to return to their own households during work on the village fields as well as the fact that much freely given labour comes at the end of the bush-field weeding season, long after the village fields have been weeded (see Fig. 4.1 for the sequence of farming operations). For those households using hired labour for village-field work, this represented much the same proportion of total labour input as for the bush field.

Capital

Kala's farmers have two main forms of capital for use in cultivation: tools and draught animals, and manure. The first contribute to an expansion in

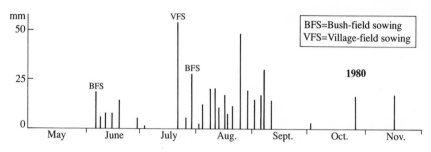

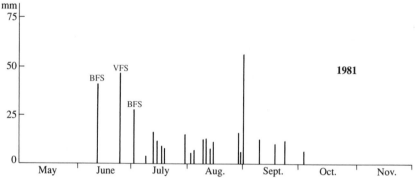

FIG. 4.1. Rainfall distribution within the farming season, 1980 and 1981.
BFS = Bush-field sowing; VFS = Village-field sowing.

area cultivated per worker and the second to an intensification of production on existing village field areas. The distribution of capital assets between households in Kala was presented and discussed in the previous chapter (see Table 3.8). Forms of land improvement other than dung are minimal, and restricted to the rudimentary clearing given to bush fields before they are brought into cultivation, which consists of chopping down some of the larger trees. This work takes place during the long dry season and requires between 10 and 15 mornings' work per hectare. The village *ton* is often hired for this task, contributing in 1981 more than 40 per cent of input to this work. However, the cost of this work is low because it is out of season.

Equipment is made up both of tools directly used in farming, such as hoes, axes, ploughs, etc., and of tools that indirectly contribute substantially to the household's ability to farm effectively, in particular animal-drawn carts for transporting seed and drinking water from the village to the field. All of this equipment is available from local blacksmiths.

Dung for the manuring of village fields is obtained from the ownership of animals, particularly cattle, and from the private ownership of a well with which the household can establish manure–water contracts with visiting livestock owners. These contracts described in more detail in

Chapter 8, are made during the dry season between Fulani and Maure pastoralists and a Bambara farm household. They permit the herder to water his animals at the farmer's well in exchange for these animals passing the night on the farmer's fields, thereby renewing and augmenting the fertility of the land. A large number of households in Kala have now dug wells that enable them to gain access to more dung to supplement what they can get from their own animals and this has allowed them to expand the production of short-cycle village-field millet.

The market for capital services is extremely imperfect. A household without its own plough team may be able to borrow this equipment for a few days to undertake essential tasks, such as ridging of village-field land, but considerable time must be spent going in search of a team and it is usually not available at the optimal time since its owner will want first call on its services. No farmer has a supply of plough-team equipment or cattle in excess of his own household's requirements and available for hire on a regular basis. Most plough teams which are hired come either from a close relative or from a neighbouring Fulani herder's household who will lend a plough team in exchange for labour to weed his field. Only three households out of the 29 were without permanent access to an oxen plough team in 1980 and 1981. The distribution of plough-team ownership and the consequences of not owning a plough team are discussed in Chapter 9.

Dung is only acquired by those who have animals of their own or who can establish manure–water contracts with visiting livestock keepers. Manure is not bought or sold for cash or any other commodity, since it is to water and grazing around the village that visiting herders require access. Refuse from the rubbish pits around the settlement is also used as a fertilizer but only by the poorest households and by women seeking to raise the yields of their small grain plots.[2]

THE BUSH FIELD

Bush fields are sown with a long-cycle millet variety, *sanyo*, which takes around 120 days to mature, in contrast with the 60–80 day millet, *souna*, which is grown on manured village fields. Bush fields are large shifting areas that have undergone some clearing during the dry season, when all but a few useful trees are chopped down, bushes are cleared, and stubble and debris burned on site. Every year a new strip of land is added to the bush field and a strip of the oldest land left behind in fallow, making each field a patchwork of land cleared at different dates. Land is farmed for four to six years before being abandoned, the farmer judging by the

[2] Women gain this commodity in return for their work supplying drinking-water to the donkey and keeping the courtyard swept daily.

TABLE 4.3. *Bush-field area: Mean field size per household and per worker* (in hectares)

Mean field size	1980 (n = 28)	1981 (n = 28)
per household	22.2 (14.5)	22.9 (15.0)
per worker	2.91 (0.80)	3.05 (0.63)

Notes: In 1980, one household abandoned its bush field after two weeks' work due to a quarrel between the two brothers. In 1981, another household was unable to farm its bush field because of its small size and lack of a plough team.

Figures in brackets refer to the standard deviation.

millet crop's performance whether the land is ready to be left fallow, his judgement supported by the spread of certain plants—such as *fogofogo* (*Calotropis procera*)—that indicate that the land is becoming over-worked. Placed side-by-side, the large rectangular bush fields extend slowly outwards from the village keeping roughly in step with neighbouring fields in order to minimize the frontier that each maintains with the bush. This frontier must be guarded against incursion by wild animals and cattle that will nibble at the newly germinated plants and trample the ripening crop in their search for food.

Each household in the village has a single bush field, the product of which is stored in a single household granary. This is however a fairly recent development; indeed, in 1980, one household still practised a division of its bush-field harvest into four parts, each going to a separate granary, one for each of the three subgroups within the large household and one for the joint needs of the household. The decline in 'private' forms of production and the trend towards increasing crop production at the wider household level in Kala were noted in Chapters 2 and 3.

Area cultivated

Data on bush-field size is presented in Table 4.3, from which may be seen the large areas cultivated per household with long-cycle millet. The very large average area, of more than 22 ha per household, is the result of the abundance of cultivable land, large household size, and the use of ox-drawn plough teams. There is a wide range in holding size as indicated by the high coefficient of variability, equal to 65 per cent in both years. The great range in size of bush field is further demonstrated in Table 4.4, this

TABLE 4.4. *Distribution of bush fields by size, 1981*

Hectares	No. of households (n = 29)
0–10	7
11–20	12
21–30	1
31–40	4
41–50	3
51–60	—
61–70	1

varying in 1981 from a low 6.1 ha for a small household containing only two adult workers to 67.2 ha for the largest household in the village which has more than 20 workers in the family. Total bush-field size is strongly related to the size of the household's work-force, field size being expanded when the household acquires new working members. When the relationship between household and bush-field size was examined, the correlation equations produced highly significant R^2 values of 82.7 per cent and 89.1 per cent for 1980 and 1981 respectively.

The second row in Table 4.3 shows the average bush-field area farmed per working household member. These figures of around 3 ha per worker contrast greatly with data from most other West African studies in which the area cultivated per worker usually lies between 0.5 and 1.0 ha. The high figure for Kala is due to the abundance of cultivable land and wide-spread ox-plough ownership. Given the strong correlation between household and bush-field size, it is not surprising that the coefficient of variation for area cultivated per worker is much lower than that for total bush-field area, at between 20 and 30 per cent. Several correlations were run in order to account for this variation in bush-field area farmed per worker. It was found that households with a larger area per worker tended to have access to non-household sources of labour and higher ratios of oxen per worker. There was, however, no evidence of scale economies leading to larger households having greater areas cultivated per worker, nor of an inverse relationship between bush-field and village-field holding size per worker. The lack of the latter is partly due to the method and timing of bush-field sowing, which means that large areas can be rapidly sown with the first rains of the season (see the calendar in Fig. 4.1). The village fields are usually ploughed and sown considerably later when the rains have set in properly. Thus, there is minimal competition for the allocation of resources at sowing time between the two millet crops.

Age-profile of the bush field

A household's bush field is made up of several strips of land cleared in
different years and abandoned after four to five years of cultivation. A
household that decides to add a large proportion of new land to the bush
field faces a number of disadvantages. First, more time must be spent
during the dry season in chopping down trees and clearing the land ready
for the farming season although the common use of *ton* labour for clearing new land reduces the demands on the household's own work-force.
Secondly since new land must be ridged before it can be sown, millet on
this land will have a later sowing date, a factor of great importance within
the context of short and unreliable rainy seasons. A household with a
very high proportion of new land is thus taking a bigger risk than a
household whose field has a more balanced age-profile. Before ox teams
were widely available, households clearing a completely new field would
commonly continue to sow part of their old bush field at the start of the
rains before tackling the new field, hoping by this means to spread their
risks. With the widespread adoption of ploughs, this two-field policy is no
longer followed as new land can be ridged more rapidly than was possible
with the hoe alone.

The mean proportion of new land to total bush-field size for 1980 and
1981 is presented in Table 4.5. The high figure for 1980 is due to the
influence of five households with completely new fields cleared in that
year. In 1981, there were no newly cleared fields but in the dry season of
1982, two households started clearing new bush-field sites for the following season. The reasons for moving to a new bush-field site include the
nature of soils (the two households noted above moved in 1982 to sandier
sites) and the risk of crop damage where bush fields lie close to rain-filled
ponds at which village and transhumant cattle are watered.

Labour input into the bush field

The timing of farm operations during the short rainy season is presented
in Fig. 4.1. With a cultivation season which may be as short as 7 or 8
weeks, from sowing to the end of weeding, farmers in Kala must carry
out the different operations at great speed in order to maximize the
usefulness of any rain which falls.

Early sowing of the crop is essential for the 120 day bush-field millet if
it is to have long enough to flower and fill out its grains before the rains
draw to an end in early to mid-September. To sow as much seed as
possible with the first rains, farmers practise a very rapid sowing of grain
on unridged land. Pockets are made on the unprepared bush-field surface
with a long-handled hoe, while someone follows them dropping a few
grains into the pocket and using a foot to press the seed firmly into the

TABLE 4.5. *Percentage of bush fields made up of newly cleared land*

	1980 (n = 29)	1981 (n = 28)
Percentage of new land	41.6 (32.6)	20.2 (23.8)

Note: Figures in brackets refer to the standard deviation.

pocket. This method of sowing is termed *paki* and it permits the farmer to take advantage of the first rains of the season, which may not be heavy enough to prepare land with a plough. Before the advent of the weeding plough in the 1950s and 1960s, it is said that a farmer would only cultivate a field that took three days or less to sow *paki*, knowing that an area larger than this would prove impossible for him to weed by hand. Now households cultivate bush fields which may take at least six days to sow *paki*, because the weeding plough enables them to weed a much larger area than could be managed by hand.

Bush-field millet is also sown on ridged land in some circumstances. All newly cleared land is ridged before sowing to provide a raised seed-bed for the young plant. As noted earlier, the bush field will also be ridged in years when an early rainfall has caused many weeds to germinate before the first millet is sown, as in 1981. Ridging of land also may be done in areas such as clay depressions where weed growth is likely to be a particular problem. Sowing millet on unridged land is a much faster operation than where land must be ridged before sowing and it also demands only simple equipment, thus making no demands on the oxen plough team at a time of year when the animals are in poor condition following the deprivations of the long dry season. Farmers said they would try to combine different methods of sowing in the bush, not knowing beforehand which would prove the best strategy, given the rains of the coming weeks. They would always try to get some millet sown on ridged land, since the latter does not need to be weeded as promptly as *paki* millet, giving the work-force a little extra time for other tasks.

Millet must be weeded soon after it has been sown if it is not to face strong competition for water and nutrients. This is a less stringent requirement for millet that has been sown on ridged land as much of the weed growth will have been retarded by the passage of the plough before sowing. Unridged land must be weeded as soon as possible, this being done by an ox-drawn weeding plough followed by a team of hoers who clear away the remaining weeds. The speed at which this task can be done will affect the success of the millet harvest, those parts of the field that have received little and late weeding exhibiting spindly, yellow millet plants with few and only partially filled spears of grain.

The speed of weeding will depend on the size of field that the farmer has decided to cultivate, on the possibility of supplementing the household work-force by hiring labour from outside and by help from friends and neighbours, and on the availability of oxen plough teams, which allow a rapid weeding of the field with animal-drawn equipment, reducing the subsequent work that must be done with the hoe. Households differ in the speed with which weeding is accomplished; for example in 1981, the date on which weeding of the bush field was finished varied from 15 August to 6 September. Several households also went back and did a second rapid weeding of the fields in late September, following light rainfall.

Table 4.6 presents the labour input to bush fields in 1980 and 1981. There is little variation between households in man-days per hectare, with a coefficient of variation of around 20 per cent in both years. The amount of work done in 1981 was considerably below that of the previous year, due to the late arrival of the sowing rains which left less time available for the different operations. This meant that many farmers only carried out a single weeding of their bush fields in 1981, in comparison with the double weeding of the same fields in 1980. As may be seen, hand-weeding labour makes up the major part of the total labour input to the bush field, representing 60 per cent of all work done in both years. The other operations, making up the remaining 40 per cent, consist of sowing work and the labour involved in managing the oxen plough team.

Accounting for variation in labour input per hectare

There are two important dimensions to work done per hectare: the amount of time spent on any operation and its timing. Area cultivated per worker is a major determinant of the first variable, the number of days work per hectare declining with rising area cultivated per worker, as there is little effective access to non-household labour with which households can supplement their own work-force.

So far as timing of the different operations is concerned, neither the proportion of early-sowing labour nor of early-weeding labour done was significantly correlated to area farmed per worker. In the case of sowing labour, this is because, with much of the bush field sown very rapidly on unprepared land, differences in area cultivated per worker made little difference to sowing dates, the entire operation taking only five or six days to complete. The only important determinant of the speed at which sowing is accomplished is the proportion of new land within the bush field. A significant inverse relationship was found between the proportion of new land in the bush field and the proportion of sowing labour com-

TABLE 4.6. *Man-days of work spent per annum in the bush fields* (includes all labour spent in sowing, ploughing, and weeding)

Mean man-days	1980	1981
per household	406.5	269.1
	(285.1)	(167.9)
per hectare	19.4	12.6
	(4.4)	(2.4)
of which:		
hand weeding /ha	11.7	7.5
	(3.2)	(1.6)
% of total input to the bush fields	60	60

Note: Figures in brackets refer to the standard deviation.

TABLE 4.7. *Ratio of work-force and bush-field area to oxen*

	1980	1981
Workers/ox	2.09	1.86
	(0.70)	(0.71)
Hectares/ox	5.90	5.39
	(2.35)	(1.60)
No. of households	25	27

Notes: The table above excludes those without permanent access to an oxen plough team in that year and those who did not cultivate a bush field.

Figures in brackets refer to the standard deviation.

pleted in the first few weeks of the farming season, confirming that those households with most new land complete their sowing more slowly than those with less. As far as weeding is concerned, days of work per hectare decline with rising area per worker, indicating a more rapid and cursory weeding of the land.

Plough-team inputs into bush-field millet

Ox teams make an important contribution to bush-field millet production, both by preparing some land before sowing and by weeding the crop. Almost all households had permanent access to a plough team in 1980 and 1981, although some of these animals were on loan from another household as described in more detail in Chapter 9. Table 4.7 presents data on the different ratios of oxen per worker and per hectare of bush-

TABLE 4.8. *Use of oxen plough teams in the bush fields*

	1980 (n = 25)		1981 (n = 27)	
	No.	%	No.	%
Total days spent per plough team	28.3		19.2	
	(7.4)		(6.2)	
of which:				
ridging days	7.6	27	5.8	30
	(5.8)		(3.4)	
weeding days	20.7	73	13.4	70
	(8.3)		(6.2)	
Total plough-team days/ha	2.06		1.52	

Notes: This table excludes those households which did not have permanent access to a plough team during the farming season concerned.

Figures in brackets refer to the standard deviation.

field land. Oxen numbers are taken rather than plough-team numbers, since households differ in the number of oxen used per plough team. Several households had more than two oxen per plough, partly to allow a longer working day by resting each ox in turn and partly to 'break-in' a newly trained animal to the work of ploughing.

Between 1980 and 1981 there was an increase in the number of oxen used for ploughing in the village from 109 to 120, which accounts for the fall in the two ratios shown in Table 4.7 from one year to the next. With an average of 2.4 oxen per plough team, this gives an average bush-field area per plough team of 12.9 ha. This figure is high in comparison with the estimated area which can be managed by a single oxen plough team in other parts of West Africa. For example, Coulomb *et al.* (1980) note an average area of around 5 ha per plough team from surveys in Mali and Senegal. The high figure in the case of Kala is only possible because much of the land is not actually ridged before sowing.

Table 4.8 shows the total number of plough-team days spent in the bush field in both years. The lower input in 1981 was the result of the shorter farming season in this year, caused by the late arrival of sowing rains and the consequent concentration of different operations in the two fields within tight time limits. Ridging work made up 30 per cent or less of time spent by the plough, confirming the importance now attached by farmers to the use of the plough team for weeding. The low mean value for ridging work per hectare (between 0.45 and 0.60 days of work) is due to the practice of sowing much bush-field millet on unridged land, with the plough team being used only to ridge newly cleared land and to weed

TABLE 4.9. *Mean bush-field millet yields per household, per hectare, and per worker* (in kilograms of threshed grain)

Mean yield	1980 (n = 27)	1980 (n = 28)
per household	4,988 (3,656)	5,179 (4,116)
per hectare	210 (81.0)	215 (68.6)
per worker	602 (208.4)	659 (250.2)

Note: Figures in brackets refer to the standard deviation.

the bush field. Those households which ridged much of their bush-field land subsequently spent less time weeding with the plough, this being carried out manually on the ridged areas.

Bush-field millet yields

Table 4.9 presents data on yields of bush-field millet. Variation among households in the size of the harvest is high with a coefficient of variation greater than 70 per cent in both years. However, the range in output of this crop is largely accounted for by size of field, a strong positive relationship existing between bush-field size and total harvest (R^2 = 74 per cent and 86 per cent for 1980 and 1981 respectively).

The mean yield per hectare for this millet is very similar for the two years, at slightly over 200 kg per ha, although this hides some variability, as may be seen in Table 4.10. There was no consistent ranking of households in terms of bush-field yield per hectare between the two years, many households getting significantly better, or worse, yields from one year to the next. The lowest yields lie below 100 kg per ha for those households with newly cleared fields or for those without their own plough team, while the highest yields approach 400 kg per ha. The average yield per hectare for bush-field millet compares very unfavourably with that for the village-field millet where manuring brought average yields of around 1,000 kg per ha in both years studied. However, villagers commented that both 1980 and 1981 produced below-average bush- and above-average village-field harvests. In most years they would expect less of a disparity between yields of the two crops.

Yields of millet per worker were somewhat higher in 1981 than in 1980, due to the slightly higher yield per hectare and the slight increase in area

TABLE 4.10. *Distribution of bush-field millet yields* (in kilograms of threshed grain)

Yield per hectare	No. of households	
	1980 (n = 27)	1981 (n = 28)
<100	1	1
100–150	3	4
150–200	11	9
200–250	5	6
250–300	2	5
300–350	3	2
>350	2	1

cultivated per worker in 1981. The high overall yield of bush-field millet per worker in Kala is the result of very extensive farming practices, low yields per hectare being offset by the large land area farmed per worker.

Thus this variety of millet provides a roughly equivalent harvest per household worker as does the much higher yielding village-field millet, given the small area farmed per worker with the latter crop.

THE VILLAGE FIELD

Village fields are permanently cultivated plots surrounding the settlement, manured by the droppings of animals and household refuse and sown with a short-cycle millet variety, *souna*, which takes from 60 to 80 days to mature. Households own several plots scattered around the village lands, each having been cleared at a different date in the past. Clearing of land is done in the dry season and involves very little work, the land surrounding the settlement being covered in light scrub as a result of having been used in the recent past for shifting plots of groundnuts and fonio. The different plots making up the household's holding will have received varying amounts of manure; households generally follow a policy of manuring land every three to five years, depending on their access to this resource. When a household digs a new well, this is translated into increased village-field millet production, by raising yields on existing plots and by allowing the household to manure a larger area.

In recent years, many households have rapidly expanded the area cultivated with short-cycle millet as a result of their gaining access to increased supplies of dung, both from their own livestock and from the herds of dry-season visiting pastoralists. In 1981, 21 households added

TABLE 4.11. *Mean village-field area cultivated per household and per worker* (in hectares)

	1980 (n = 29)	1981 (n = 29)
Area cultivated per household	4.3	5.7
	(3.2)	(3.6)
Area cultivated per worker	0.62	0.89
	(0.39)	(0.53)
Average no. of plots	2.9	3.7

Note: Figures in brackets refer to the standard deviation.

some new land to their village fields, many of these having dug a new well in the previous two dry seasons, leading to a total increase in village-field area of 33 per cent.

Village fields are ridged before sowing if the farmer has access to a plough team, the ridging plough mixing in the dung and refuse deposited on the soil as well as removing the first crop of weeds. The ridges and distance between the millet plants are kept close to make the most of the manured soils. Weeding of the crop is done some 15 to 20 days after sowing. The timing of this operation is considered very important as weeds on the permanently cultivated manured soils are particularly dense and tenacious.

Area cultivated

Table 4.11 shows the mean village-field holding size per household and per worker. It may be seen from this that the average area cultivated with this crop is much smaller than that for bush-field millet, the village and bush fields occupying on average 5.7 ha and 22.9 ha respectively in 1981. The number of plots has increased from 1980 to 1981 with the addition of new land to village-field holdings as many farmers want to grow more of the short-cycle millet variety. As will be seen later in this chapter, the marginal returns to farm inputs are much higher in village- than bush-field millet, despite the average product per worker being very similar. However, village-field holdings have developed very unevenly between households, as may be seen by the high coefficient of variation in area cultivated per worker, at more than 60 per cent, in comparison with the lower figure for bush-field area per worker of from 20 to 27 per cent.

Variation in the scale and productivity of village-field millet for different households is related to a number of factors which include household size, the amount of manure available, and the household's access to labour and plough-team inputs. Household size plays an important role in determining the area cultivated with this crop, producing a correlation coefficient of 53 per cent in 1980 and 49 per cent in 1981 when village-field size is regressed on the size of the household's work-force. However, household size is of less importance for this millet variety than for bush-field millet (for which the correlation coefficients already quoted were found to be 83 per cent and 89 per cent for 1980 and 1981 respectively). This suggests that other factors, such as access to manure, may play an equal role in determining the size of village-field holding.

Manure availability

The amount of manure available to the household is a major determinant of the area which it can cultivate with village-field millet. This millet variety performs poorly on unfertilized soils, so it is only by having a regular supply of dung that households can ensure themselves a good harvest. Dung comes from two sources: a household's own livestock holdings and the amount of dung which a household can get through manure–water contracts with visiting pastoralists during the dry season. This dung is deposited on the fields, either by kraaling the animals overnight on the household's plots or by carting manure from the rainy season cattle pen to the field. Kraaling of animals is especially advantageous as it minimizes the amount of labour which must be expended on transport and spreading, the herd being moved about the field to ensure an even distribution of the dung. Farmers in Kala value dung very highly because in a year with good rainfall a well-manured field can produce a yield of up to 2,000 kg per ha.

The manuring index In order to quantify and compare the availability of manure to different households in Kala, a 'manuring index' was constructed composed of the following three elements:

(i) Each animal in the household's cattle holding was counted as 1.0 on the index, with horses and donkeys valued at 0.5, given that much of the dung from the latter stock is taken out by women to their private plots rather than being used for manuring the household's millet fields.

(ii) The wells owned by a household were valued in terms of their cattle equivalents. An average well waters around 60 head of cattle over a three-month period during the dry season and is therefore taken as equivalent to having year-round access to 15 cattle. Since the fertility produced by manure lasts over several seasons, the value of a well in its first year of life was taken as worth only 5.0 head, in its second year as worth 10.0 head, reaching a long term value of 15.0 head in its third year and all subsequent years.

(iii) Circumstances particular to the household concerned may add extra units to its manure index if it has access to dung in excess of the above two sources. In one case, the four households making up the chiefly lineage take it in turns to receive on their land the tents and flocks belonging to a group of Maure herders. These herders have been coming for more than 40 years and water their animals in the evening at the communal village well. In another case, one well owner has an exceptionally productive well, due to it having been dug more deeply than others and to its favourable position which means it can water more than 200 stock a day in contrast to an average well's capacity of 60 head. Another household has no private well and only a pair of oxen, yet has dung far in excess of many other well-less households, because its fields lie close to the communal village well and stock wait to be watered in the shelter of the *balansan* tree (*Acacia albida*) which stands on this household's land.

A strong correlation was found to exist between access to manure and household size (R^2 = 71 per cent in both years), the larger households having access both to greater absolute quantities of manure and to more manure per household member. This is a result of the greater livestock wealth of larger households and their greater ease in getting a private well dug (examined in Chapters 8, 9, and 10), as they have a larger domestic labour-force available for this task.

Total village-field holding is also strongly correlated with access to dung, shown by R^2 values of 69 per cent for 1980 and 1981, when the size of a household's field is regressed on the manuring index. This strong correlation confirms that households tend to increase the area cultivated with village-field millet when they gain access to more manure. The size of the manuring index, village-field area, and household size are all strongly interrelated, the correlation between any two being complicated by their interdependence with the third. To eliminate the effect of scale interfering with village-field area and manure availability, the relationship between village-field area per worker and manure availability per worker was examined. Simple regression analysis showed a significant positive relationship between the two variables, confirming that manure availability is a major determinant of the area that can be cultivated with this crop.

Table 4.12 presents data on the average availability of manure per household, per hectare, and per worker. The average household has access to the manure from one well and 15 or more cattle. There is, however, great variability in access from one household to another, as can be seen from the size of the coefficient of variation, which exceeds 100 per cent in both years. Average manure use per hectare lies around 5 to 6 units, so that a well (equal to 15 units on the scale) can effectively manure 3 ha of land. Manure use per hectare fell between the two years

TABLE 4.12. *Level of manure index per household, per hectare, and per worker*

Mean manure index	1980	1981
per household	31.8	33.9
	(36.3)	(36.4)
per hectare	6.1	5.1
	(4.7)	(3.9)
per worker	3.5	3.9
	(3.1)	(3.7)

Note: Figures in brackets refer to the standard deviation.

due to the large growth in area cultivated with this crop. There is fairly high variation in levels of manure use per hectare, with a coefficient of variation greater than 75 per cent. Some households have a small well-fertilized plot whereas others have an extensive land-manuring policy, taking in large additions to village-field holdings requiring several years to manure sufficiently to get a good yield. As will be seen in the following chapter, the marginal returns from an extra unit of manure vary very greatly, depending on the existing level of manure use. Households with a light manuring policy gain much higher marginal returns to manure than those with a heavily fertilized plot of land. A low level of manuring is adopted by farmers where they fear the effect of drought on their crops. When rainfall is low and badly distributed, a heavy dose of manure can burn the crop, producing a very much lower yield than land which has been more lightly manured. The relationship between levels of manuring and yields is looked at in more detail later in this chapter.

The level of manure available per worker also shows a high degree of variability, indicating the unevenness of access to this input between households.

Labour input into village fields

Table 4.13 presents data on the labour input into a household's village fields. The average number of days worked by the household on this crop compares with a total of 430 and 288 man-days for bush-field millet in 1980 and 1981 respectively. The proportion of total time spent in the farming season on the village-field crop grew from 14 per cent in 1980 to 21 per cent in 1981 due to the expansion in village-field area that took place in 1981 and to the very short rainy season in that year which meant that the time available for bush-field work was limited. Total time spent per hectare on the village-field crop was roughly similar in the two years,

TABLE 4.13. *Labour input into the village fields*

Total man-days	1980	1981
per household	68.0	76.7
	(51.6)	(48.3)
per hectare	16.5	14.4
	(4.8)	(4.7)
of which:		
hand weeding/ha	7.8	6.3
	(3.0)	(2.9)

Note: Figures in brackets refer to the standard deviation.

unlike for bush-field millet, where only 12.6 man-days per ha were spent in 1981 in comparison with 19.4 man-days in 1980.

For sowing, weeding, and harvesting households co-ordinate their activities in the village fields, undertaking these tasks together. This is to minimize losses of seed and grain to birds at sowing and harvest time. However, the villagers also place a moral value on being seen to be acting together.

Households turn to sow their village fields with the first major rainfall after the bush fields have been sown and once the ground is moist enough for the plough to ridge the soil. Sowing dates for this millet variety are tightly spaced; in 1980 and 1981, all land was sown within a two-week period, in contrast to sowing of bush-field millet where six or more weeks may separate the first sowing from the last. The compactness of sowing dates for short-cycle millet is to ensure that it completes its cycle within the short central period of the rainy season when showers are more likely to fall, as this millet variety is less able to resist a long period of drought than the longer-cycle bush-field variety.

Plough-team inputs into village-field millet

Oxen plough teams play a relatively greater role in village than in bush-field millet production. This is because all village land is ridged before millet is sown in contrast to fields in the bush where much millet is sown on unridged land.

Table 4.14 presents data on the use of oxen plough teams in village-field millet production over the two years studied and may be compared with Table 4.8, where equivalent data for bush field-millet production was presented.

Plough teams are used more intensively on village as opposed to bush fields and the composition of this input also differs between the two

Farm Production

TABLE 4.14. *Use of oxen plough teams in the village fields*

	1980 (n = 26)		1981 (n = 27)	
	No.	%	No.	%
Total days spent	9.35		8.51	
per plough team	(4.20)		(4.03)	
of which:				
ridging days	3.55	38	4.00	47
	(1.26)		(1.34)	
weeding days	5.80	62	4.51	53
	(2.69)		(2.72)	
Total plough-team	3.38		2.48	
days per hectare	(1.17)		(0.45)	

Note: Figures in brackets refer to the standard deviation.

fields, with a much higher proportion of this work being devoted to ridging land in the case of village-field millet. In 1981, almost half of the plough-team days worked were spent on this operation, as opposed to from 20 to 27 per cent in the case of the bush field.

Village-field millet yields

Table 4.15 presents data on the size of village-field millet harvests which may be compared with those from the bush field in Table 4.9.

Out of a total millet harvest from both varieties of 9,050 and 10,890 kg in 1980 and 1981 respectively, the proportion gained from the village fields grew from 45 per cent to 52 per cent, due to the expansion in their area. Yields of village-field millet were roughly similar in both years, at around 1,000 kg per ha, although as can be seen from Table 4.16, there was wide variation in yields for different producers. Households with the lowest yields of less than 500 kg per ha were either those with little or no manure, or those which had rapidly expanded the area they cultivated with this millet variety, following the sinking of a well, leaving much of the new land barely fertilized. Households with the highest yields of over 1,500 kg per ha were those with small, well-manured plots on sandy soils.

The average yield of village-field millet per worker grew by 46 per cent between 1980 and 1981 as a result both of the increase in area cultivated per worker and of the slightly higher yields per hectare in the latter year. The coefficient of variation for yield per worker is greater for village- as opposed to bush-field millet, at 58 per cent and 40 per cent respectively, in 1981. This is attributable to the wide differences in the availability of

TABLE 4.15. *Mean village-field millet yields per household, per hectare, and per worker* (in kilograms of threshed grain)

Mean yield	1980 (n = 29)	1981 (n = 29)
per household	4,058 (3,007)	5,707 (4,063)
per hectare	993 (411)	1,011 (396)
per worker	553 (343)	808 (474)

Note: Figures in brackets refer to the standard deviation.

TABLE 4.16. *Distribution of village-field millet yields* (in kilograms of threshed grain)

Yield per hectare	No. of households	
	1980 (n = 29)	1981 (n = 29)
<250	1	0
250–750	5	8
750–1,250	15	15
1,250–1,750	6	5
>1,750	2	1

dung between households, since this is an input with major influence on area cultivated and yield per hectare for the short-cycle variety.

PRODUCTION OF THE TWO MILLET VARIETIES

This chapter has described production of the two millet varieties, their methods of cultivation, the main factors affecting their performance, and the yields obtained from each crop. Table 4.17 summarizes this data for the farming seasons of 1980 and 1981.

Bush-field millet is grown in a very extensive manner, with low yields per hectare but a high average area per worker. By contrast, the village fields produce a much higher yield per hectare but on a much smaller area. Farmers noted that in both years the bush fields had done less well than expected, whereas the village fields had produced a better than

TABLE 4.17. *Production of bush- and village-field millet, 1980 and 1981*

	Bush-field millet	Village-field millet
1980		
Mean area/household (ha)	22.2 (n = 28) (14.5)	4.3 (n =29) (3.2)
Mean area/worker (ha)	2.91 (n = 28) (0.80)	0.62 (n = 29) (0.39)
Mean yield/ha (kg of threshed millet)	210 (n = 27) (81.0)	993 (n = 29) (411)
Mean yield/worker (kg of threshed millet)	602 (n = 27) (208.4)	553 (n = 29, (343)
1981		
Mean area/household (ha)	22.9 (n = 28) (15.0)	5.7 (n =29) (3.6)
Mean area/worker (ha)	3.05 (n = 28) (0.63)	0.89 (n = 29) (0.53)
Mean yield/ha (kg of threshed millet)	215 (n = 28) (68.6)	1,010 (n = 29) (395.9)
Mean yield/worker (kg of threshed millet)	659 (n = 28) (250)	808 (n = 29) (474)

Note: Figures in brackets refer to the standard deviation.

average yield. This they attributed to the pattern of rainfall and, in particular, to the absence of heavy rain at the end of the growing season in mid- to late September in both years, when the longer-cycle crop should be filling out its grains.

Daily rainfall distribution in 1980 and 1981 was presented in Fig. 4.1 in relation to the main farming operations and, in particular, to dates of sowing. While total rainfall and total useful rainfall were lower in 1981 than in 1980, they were better distributed in 1981 in relation to village-field millet, leading to higher yields of this crop. As noted earlier, the crucial moments in the millet's growth-cycle are at sowing and when the grains are filling out. A heavy rainfall is needed at sowing in order that the seed can germinate fully and establish itself. Occasional rain is needed during the growth of the plant but it can survive relatively long periods without rain once its root system has developed. The plant needs heavy rain after flowering, when its grains are forming, some two months or so after sowing.

In 1980, while reasonable quantities of rain fell during late July and August, when the village-field crop was in mid-cycle, there was no useful

rain after the first week of September. Given the relatively late sowing date for village-field millet in this year, this meant that there was
insufficient moisture for the grains to fill out properly. By contrast, in
1981, the village crop was sown much earlier and, despite fairly poor
rainfall during its mid-cycle in July and August, a very heavy rainfall in
the first week of September allowed the grains to fill out well.

Competition for labour between the two crops is limited and varies
from year to year, depending on the volume and pattern of rainfall.
Competition is usually greater in mid-season than at the start of the rains.
In many years, the bush fields will be sown and partially weeded before
sufficient rain has fallen to allow the ridging and sowing of the village
fields. This was the case in 1980, when most households had sown their
bush fields in early June and had completed a first hand-weeding of the
crop by mid-July. Work on the village fields did not start until 19 July,
after a fall of more than 50 mm of rain. In 1981 by contrast, sowing of the
bush field did not start until mid- to late June, by which time enough rain
had fallen to start ridging the village fields. Consequently, cultivation of
the two crops was more competitive in the latter year and several households had to abandon their plans to sow new bush-field land because of
the constraints on their time.

The greatest competition between the two millet varieties occurs in the
peak weeding season in late July to mid-August, during which the household must perform a careful weeding of its village fields while also keeping weed growth in the bush fields under control. The village fields
receive priority at this time and those households with large new village-
field plots experienced relatively low yields of bush-field millet because of
having spent much time away from the latter field in the peak weeding
season.

Harvesting of the two crops takes place sequentially. The village fields
are harvested in October, the millet threshed, winnowed, and stored
before the work-force starts to cut the bush-field crop in early December.
The latter crop has a much stronger stem which resists wind damage
better than the brittle short-cycle millet of the village fields. In addition,
especially in years when rain has fallen in late September or October,
the longer-cycle bush-field millet will still be green in mid-November
and the grain not yet dry enough for harvesting. By the end of January,
the village will have safely stored the bush-field crop.

5

MILLET-PRODUCTION ANALYSIS

A production analysis of the two millet varieties in the two farming seasons of 1980 and 1981 will throw light on a number of issues which relate not only to the productivity of resources in different uses in any one year, but also to longer-term questions associated with the choice of patterns of investment and the means by which farmers acquire access to productive assets. Thus, the analysis in this chapter provides the basis for assessing the size and variability of returns to different farm inputs and in particular to the key investments in an oxen plough team, in acquiring access to more dung through the digging of wells, and in getting control of more labour. The results of the regression analysis including the marginal returns to factors between uses, from one year to the next and between farmers are presented in the following chapters.

EXPECTATIONS, CROP OUTPUT, AND INVESTMENT

The decision by a household head to allocate resources to a particular investment will depend on its expected return relative to those of other assets. Returns will vary between different activities and from year to year, given the interactions between rainfall variation and yields in each sector. Returns will also vary from one producer to another, depending on the mix of resources available to each farmer, the opportunity cost of these resources, and the extent to which different farmers can bear risks.

Rainfall in the Sahel is highly variable from year to year, both in its distribution within the rainy season and in its distribution from place to place. This high variability is the backcloth against which producers must assess expected returns from different assets and activities. Farmers in Kala base their expectations on their own past experience, those of other people, and on the views they hold about future trends. In the construction of current expectations, farmers are likely to place more weight on recent results and less weight on those which occurred in the more distant past. Each year which passes provides the farmer with further information which either confirms his beliefs or casts doubt upon them. As far as past experience is concerned, a good village-field millet harvest, such as happened in 1980 and 1981, tends to shift farmers' beliefs towards higher expected returns from this millet variety and will lead to a reallocation of resources at the margin towards this crop. Conversely, after a disastrous village-field harvest in 1984, some farmers said that they would be devoting fewer resources to this crop in future. In general, however, farmers are cautious about changing their production strategies; a couple of years' experience will not be sufficient to make them completely revise their expectations, as they know too well that each year will provide a slightly different pattern of rainfall to which they must adapt their farming practices. Farmers also observe the experience of others in their own and in neighbouring communities. The adoption of plough teams and the spread of well-digging in Kala owes much to the ease with which farmers can observe and discuss the results and advantages of changes in technology within the village. The close similarity in environmental conditions within the village means that knowledge obtained here is more immediately applicable than that acquired elsewhere. Much travel takes place between settlements leading to the exchange of information and ideas. Knowledge of ploughs was first acquired by people who had seen them at work in the irrigated areas of the Office du Niger and in villages close to Ségou town. However, it is difficult for farmers to build up an accurate picture of the likely returns to be gained from a new technology until they have tried it out under their own local conditions. Hence, new methods of production and new seed varieties are tried out by farmers in Kala and other villages on a small scale before widespread investment takes place.

As far as future trends are concerned, farmers in Kala and elsewhere try to predict what will happen in the year to come and in the longer term, either on the basis of some general rule, such as 'seven years of plenty, seven years of want', or by using fortune-telling techniques, of which several elderly men in Kala are reputed masters. Alternatively, the aspect of the stars is thought to provide interpretable evidence as regards the next rainy season. However, villagers admit that these techniques are often not very satisfactory and do not give them clear guidance as to future events.

Farmers also recognize that there may be major shifts in climate which demand a reassessment of the relative returns to be expected from different activities and they give the example of the last 15 years as evidence for such a shift. The substantial fall in mean rainfall since the end of the 1960s has led to a progressive revision of expectations during the 1970s, by the end of which period most farmers had reallocated resources away from groundnuts and towards increased production of manure-based short-cycle crops, like village-field millet. There has been relatively little movement out of the longer-cycle bush-field millet and farmers stress the need to spread their risks between the two varieties of millet. One or two farmers expressed the fear that the experience of a year like 1984 (with only 230 mm of rainfall, compared with around 400 mm in 1980 and 1981) might presage the start of a new and yet more arid period with rainfall levels below even those of the last 15 years. This was a prospect which naturally filled them with much dread, as adaptation to a mean rainfall of 200 to 300 mm would demand an even greater revision of crop and investment strategies than the shift from 600 to 400 mm experienced at the end of the 1960s. Continued decline in rainfall would probably have led to migration from the region by households or individuals in search of land or employment in a more favoured area. The heavy rainfall received in 1988 confirmed their view that change and variability are inevitable features of their life as farmers in Kala and many farmers expressed the hope, as they happily surveyed the 1988 crops, that perhaps better rainfall had now returned.

A comparison of marginal returns

In order to assess the size and variability of returns to different invest-ments, a production function will be used to provide for an analysis of the following:

The relative returns to factors in production of each millet variety   The data will show the high returns to farmers from expanding village-field millet production, the profitability of which may also be seen both in the priority given to work on these fields during the central part of the rainy season and in the rapid growth of well-digging as a way of acquiring dung, since dung is only used for the short-cycle village-field crop. The shift in resources to the short-cycle millet has become increasingly necessary for households if they are to assure themselves a sufficient grain harvest, because of the current prolonged period of low and uncertain rainfall. However, farmers have not abandoned their bush fields, despite the low returns apparent in 1980 and 1981. This is because harvests of each millet variety are subject to considerable uncertainty from year to year, depend-ing on the pattern of rainfall. The almost total failure of the village-field harvest in 1984 illustrates the dangers of relying exclusively on one crop. In addition, as noted in the previous chapter, the two millet varieties are only partially competitive in the use of resources.

The difference in returns to factors in the same use from one year to the next   This difference is due in large part to the volume and timing of rainfall during the farming season. It had been hoped that the two rainy seasons studied would exhibit marked variations in yield of the two millet varieties. These data would then contribute towards the discussion in the following chapters of the variability in returns to investment experienced by farmers as a result of climatic factors, allowing the appraisal of dif-ferent assets not only in terms of their expected return but also in terms of the variability in this return from year to year. Despite the similarity between mean yields per hectare across the two years, considerable differences do emerge in the marginal productivity of different factors in the same use from one year to the next, as a result of differing levels of input use and their interaction with the pattern of rainfall in that year. Farmers said that in both years village-field harvests had been above average while those from the bush field had been disappointing. Over a longer period of years, one would expect yields of both varieties to show more variation in yield per hectare than that exhibited in 1980 and 1981 and this would lead one to expect even greater variation in the marginal returns to different factors than was found for the two years studied.

The divergence between each factor's marginal product and the price at which it is occasionally available This divergence is consistent with the very limited development or total absence of markets for the main resources used in farming. In the later analysis of investment by farmers, it will be shown that digging a well or buying a plough team may be the only way in which households can ensure themselves certain access to the services which these assets provide. Choice among alternative investments must therefore take into account not only the distribution of expected returns from each asset but also the consequence for a household's farming strategy of not owning a particular asset, given the very limited opportunities for buying inputs on the market.

The widely differing returns to factors from one farmer to another Farmers in Kala exhibit a wide variation in the marginal returns gained from different assets as a result of their differential access to labour and other factors of production. The poor development of markets in different services compounds and partly explains the differences in marginal returns as farmers are unable to exchange the services of costly and indivisible assets.

Problems with production function analysis

There are various drawbacks to the use of production functions, some of which are due to problems with the definition of variables to be used in the analysis and with the accurate measurement of these variables, some with the specification of the production function and others with the interpretation of the results and formulation of policy. Each of these will be discussed below, looking in particular at how such problems can be met in the case-study of Kala.

Problems with data

Studies vary in the units used to measure the different elements in the production function, some relying on physical quantities while others convert all the variables to monetary values. In the case of Kala, the analysis is conducted using physical quantities of the different inputs and outputs; millet is measured in kilograms of threshed grain, labour and capital inputs in days of work per hectare, and manure by an index in which each household's access to this commodity is measured in terms of cattle owned and the household's ability to establish manuring contracts through well ownership. The prices of inputs and output are only introduced later when the marginal value productivities of factors are compared with the value at which they are available on the market.

Homogeneity of output was easily satisfied in the case of Kala, kilograms of millet being by far the most important output from the two millet fields. Other outputs consist of millet stalk, which is eaten as fodder by livestock and used for thatching, and cowpea grain and hay, which provides food for people and stock respectively. Cowpea production was of negligible value in both years studied.

A decision had to be made how far to break down labour and oxen inputs by type of work done and its timing and how to aggregate inputs of different quality, such as child and adult labour. Oxen also present a problem, since they vary in quality and consequently their services are of differing value. Some studies take the number and value of oxen owned as a proxy for their services, but in the case of Kala, oxen plough-team days are taken as the measure of capital services flowing from this asset. This does not, however, take into account the evident differences in productivity between oxen pairs and the amount of work that can be achieved in one day, as noted earlier. Labour inputs have been broken down into their major components, sowing and weeding labour, land preparation being done almost entirely by oxen and therefore included in oxen plough-day inputs. Measurement of the labour input variable presented considerable problems which were not satisfactorily resolved. Issues relating to the collection of the labour data and to the weighting of different age and sex classes were discussed in Chapters 1 and 4 respectively. As a result of measurement problems, this variable did not perform well in the production analysis.

The manuring variable presents other problems due to the difficulty with which this input can be measured. Production analyses using a fertilizer variable usually measure this input in terms of a given weight applied per hectare. In the case of Kala, however, this approach would have been very difficult, given the method by which most manuring is achieved—the kraaling of cattle on the village fields overnight—and the very extensive areas involved. An index measuring the household's access to manure was described in the previous chapter which aims to capture the variability in control over this factor from one household to another.

Manure also presents a problem of measurement because of the residual effects of manuring on soil fertility. The actual fertility in the soil depends not only on manuring received this year but also on past applications, nor will the value of manure applied in this year be totally used up during the production process. Where a farmer is using roughly similar quantities from year to year with constant land area, it can be assumed that last year's residual fertility is balanced by the incomplete use of this year's application. But where farmers are in the process of rapidly expanding the area of manured land through access to increased supplies of dung, this balancing-out is unlikely to occur, a point which must be kept in mind when interpreting the production elasticities of the manuring index. However, the manuring index takes some account of residual fertility effects by attributing a lower value to wells in their first two years of operation, during which the household is gradually building up the fertility of its village lands.

In aggregating cross-sectional data into a single production function, two assumptions must be made. The first is that farmers are producing with roughly similar technologies so that the aggregation of their production data is valid. This would seem to be a reasonable assumption to make in the case of Kala because of the common methods and technologies used in the cultivation of each millet variety. The second assumption is that the production of each crop is independent of the output of other crops and activities, also largely the case in Kala, given the limited competition between cultivation of the two millet varieties.

A way must be found of dealing with zero inputs—that is inputs that can take a value of zero without total output also being zero. An example of this is the input of oxen plough-team weeding; a zero value for this will not mean that output will be zero, unlike for example, a zero value for sowing labour. In the case of Kala, two inputs can take a potential value of zero, although for these variables in either year there were in fact no zero observations made. Both manure use in the village fields and plough-team use in either field can take zero values without yield per hectare also falling to zero. Account is taken of this possibility in the formulation of the manuring variable used in the production function in the way suggested by Burt (1971), by the addition of a small constant to the independent variable in the regression analysis. The size of this constant represents the residual fertility in the soil in the absence of any manure applied, as discussed later.

CHOICE OF VARIABLES FOR THE ANALYSIS OF MILLET PRODUCTION

The analysis is based on data collected at the household level rather than concentrating on input–output data from specific plots of land. As a result, the estimates from the regression analysis represent average returns to factor use at the household level rather than a more precise technical relationship at the per hectare level. The advantages of the approach adopted here lie in the estimated returns being more typical of the household's general production pattern than would be the case were a single plot of land to have been taken, and in the lower cost of data collection than is the case where per hectare inputs must be closely monitored and measured. The disadvantages stem from the lower over-all level of statistical significance that can be attributed to the results because of errors in measurement and the aggregation of material over a larger area of land.

Choice of variables was limited to those thought likely to be of import-ance and for which data could be sought. The method and problems of data collection and aggregation have been discussed in earlier chapters. Their implications for the production analysis and its interpretation will be commented on in the following chapter. For both varieties, it was decided to use output per hectare as the dependent variable, rather than total harvest size. Initially, the data were regressed in their absolute quantities, total output being taken as a function of total labour input, total plough-team input, and so on. While the correlation coefficient obtained was high, with R^2 greater than 80 per cent, there was obviously very great multi-collinearity between the independent variables, which meant one could have little confidence in the estimated coefficients on each variable. Using output per hectare is justified here since there is no evidence of any relationship between yield per hectare and total area cultivated. Taking input use per hectare greatly diminishes the incidence of multi-collinearity, but there nevertheless remains a degree of correla-tion between some of the independent variables. The significance of these relationships and their interpretation are examined later, in discussion of the partial correlation matrix.

Village-field millet

For this crop, the major inputs are labour, plough-team inputs, and dung, although other factors may also be of significance in affecting the yields of particular plots, such as soil characteristics and the plot's slope and position.

Labour　Only labour input during the short cultivation season is relevant here. There are a number of possible labour variables which may be taken, depending on which operations are included and on whether any account is taken of the timing of these operations. The two main opera-tions carried out by hand on the village fields during the rainy season are sowing and weeding, work done by the plough team in ridging and weeding being put into a separate variable. There was felt to be no justification for including sowing labour per hectare as a variable, as sowing practices do not vary across households, a high input of man-days per hectare spent sowing resulting as much from slower work as from differences in technique likely to produce different yields. Only hand-weeding labour per hectare was included in the labour variable for the village-field regressions. This was measured in half-days of work and weighted for different age and sex groups. The tight spacing of all operations on these fields meant that no effective differences in timing were observable between farmers, the entire village co-ordinating the start of sowing and of weeding operations. Thus, no account was taken of the timing of inputs in the case of this millet variety. As will be seen later, the labour variable performed particularly poorly in the analysis of village-field millet production. Possible causes of this performance will be discussed later.

Plough team work Plough teams were used by almost all households both to ridge the village fields before sowing and to weed the crop fifteen days or so after sowing. Passage of the plough team serves largely to keep weeds under control, allowing the millet plant to make best use of the moisture and nutrients available from the manured land. The work of both ridging and weeding the village fields was included in a single variable. Measuring the number of days spent in all plough-team operations also avoided the problem posed by a zero input for either plough-team operation. While all households used a plough team for some work on their village fields, several households weeded their village fields entirely by hand, either because they owned no plough team of their own, having only managed to borrow a team for the ridging work or because, with a very small work-force, the household found it difficult to manage the oxen and have a hoe team clearing away the weeds after the passage of the plough.

Manure A household's access to manure is measured by the manuring index per hectare of village-field land. Construction of the manuring index, described in the previous chapter, combines the dung a household gets from its own livestock holdings with access to dung acquired through its ownership of a private well, the water from which is exchanged for the manure from visiting herds in the dry season. Earlier, there was a discussion of the problem posed by variables which can take a zero value without output also becoming zero. One way around this problem was shown to be the addition of a constant to the variable in question. This approach is adopted for the manuring variable in this case. Massel and Johnson (1968) note that this constant should represent the soil's natural fertility. However, it may be difficult to estimate this in practice. Instead, they take several arbitrary constants, choosing that figure which seemed best to explain output when no manure was used. In the case of Kala also, a constant was sought which could reasonably represent the residual fertility of the soil which allowed some harvest to be gained without any additional manure being applied. Several values were tried for this constant, taking it equal to 0.1, 0.3, and 0.5 manuring units per ha, before opting for the intermediate value in the main regressions on the basis of its plausibility and the goodness of fit achieved.

Soils   The soils surrounding the village are mainly light sands, but some differences do exist in the nature of soils from one plot of village land to another. In particular, fields to the south and west tend to be on harder gravels and it is for this reason that most recent village-field expansion has taken place towards the north and east. However, households have a number of plots of varying quality and in different positions; hence, it is not possible to attribute a single soil dummy variable to each household.

Slope   The village of Kala is situated in a saucer-like depression, the land rising slightly on all sides before sloping away again into the bush. Fields immediately surrounding the settlement are at the base of a gentle slope, which is nevertheless probably steep enough to generate a significant run-off of moisture and nutrients from higher to lower areas. Conversely, farmers recognize that millet sown on the top of a slope will not do so well because there is less moisture available. These differences in position are of especial importance in accounting for variation in yield per hectare during years of low rainfall, when millet on a well-manured but dry soil will suffer from 'burning', producing a brittle plant with few grains. As with soils, households tend to have a variety of plots, each with a different position and slope; some plots are so large that there are high and low-lying areas within them. No household has village land which is universally high or low-lying and so no account is taken of this variable in the analysis.

Plot fragmentation   A household's village fields have been added to over the years, especially in the last decade with the growth of private wells dug. Households typically farm several plots, varying from 1 to 10, with a mean of 3.7 in 1981, when the average plot size was 1.5 ha. Fragmentation of plot size is likely to be detrimental to yields where plots are so small that it is cumbersome to use plough teams and where much time must be spent walking from one plot to another. In the case of Kala, fragmentation is not likely to affect yields, because of the large mean size of plot, which means that none are so small that oxen cannot be used. In addition, the household's different plots are never more than 1 km or so apart and the household's work-force will have to move, at most, once during the day from where they are working. Data from both years confirmed that there was no significant relationship between yields and fragmentation, so this variable was not included in the regression equation.

Form of the village-field millet regression equation

The following regression equation was estimated for the village-field millet data:

$$Q/ha = A(HWL/ha)^a(PTD/ha)^b(k + MN/ha)^c$$

where:

Q/ha is output of millet per hectare of village field, measured in kilograms of threshed grain.

HWL/ha is hand-weeding labour spent per hectare, weighted to account for sex and age and measured in man-day equivalents.

PTD/ha is plough-team days spent per hectare, both ridging and weeding the village field.

$(k + MN/ha)$ is the manuring variable, k taking a value of 0.3 manuring units per hectare, to account for residual fertility in the soil.

A is a constant and ^{a}, ^{b} and ^{c} are partial elasticities of production for each variable input.

Regression of the above function was carried out using the log-linear form, inputs and output being put into natural logarithms:

$$Log(Q/ha) = LogA + aLog(HWL/ha) + bLog(PTD/ha) + cLog(k + MN/ha)$$

The results from this analysis are discussed later in this chapter.

Bush-field millet

A number of different variables were taken for this crop to assess their role in determining output per hectare. As with the village-field millet, both labour and plough-team work were included. No measure was taken for dung since dung is not used in bush fields. Other variables include the proportion of new land in the field, a sowing-date dummy, and a dummy variable to incorporate differences in soils and rainfall received between fields.

Labour In the choice of an appropriate labour variable one has to consider several issues: firstly, which operations to include; second, whether to keep the operations separate, and third, how far to take account of the timing of each operation. It was decided to treat sowing labour by use of a dummy to take account of the timing of this operation. With plough-team work taken as a separate variable, this left only hand-weeding labour to be dealt with here. All labour inputs were weighted for the age and sex composition of the work-force. It was also felt necessary to give some time-weighting to hand-weeding labour, given the spread of two to three months over which this work takes place. There are two ways in which the timing of inputs can be taken into account. The first is to take labour done in different periods as a different variable; for example, weeding labour carried out in June, July, and August could appear in the production function as L_1, L_2, and L_3 respectively. Given the small number of observations in the farm data from Kala, this option was not taken up, as increasing the number of variables would progressively reduce the degrees of freedom of the analysis. The second option is to aggregate the work done in different weeks into a single variable, using a system of weights to take account of the relative value of work done at different times. This was the option adopted here. As with all aggregation procedures, it suffers from the inevitably rather random weights attached to labour inputs in different periods.

Both farmers and agronomists are in agreement over the need to weed millet early to get good results. Several weighting systems were tried to see which gave the best correlation with yield in both simple and multiple regression analysis. For example, in one case all labour up to the end of week 10 (11 August) was weighted by 1.0, that done between week 11 and week 13 weighted by 0.5, while all further work was valued at 0. In another case, all work done before the end of week 12 (25 August) was weighted by 1.0 while all subsequent work was valued at 0. The latter system was chosen in the end for bush-field production in 1980 because this variable performed best in regression on yield per hectare. The zero-weighting for all work done from the last week of August onwards may be justified by the fact that several of the fastest weeding households had already finished work on their bush fields by this date and, with a long dry period during much of August, soils were hard and difficult to work. A few households abandoned parts of their fields in this year because the additional work was not thought worthwhile. Nevertheless, some households continue to weed their fields at this late date because, in the event of late rainfall, such a weeding would improve the chances of a good harvest.

In the case of 1981, it proved more difficult to obtain a labour variable of any significance in regression against output per hectare. The farming season of 1981 was very much shorter than that of the previous year, due to the late arrival of the first sowing rains. The overall labour input per hectare was only 65 per cent of that in 1980, the result both of a more rapid pace of work and of only doing a single weeding of most of the field, instead of the more usual double weeding. Having tried out a number of time-weighted systems, the adopted one for 1981 takes all labour up until the end of week 10 (16 August) to be weighted by 1.0 after which it is valued at 0.

Neither the labour variable in 1980 nor that in 1981 proved to be very satisfactory, a problem which is examined later in the discussion of the results from the production function analysis.

Plough-team work There are several alternatives for treating plough-team inputs into the bush field: first, should the ridging and weeding inputs be treated separately or together and, second, should timing of these inputs be taken into account? On the first question, examination of the data showed that there was a slight inverse correlation between plough-team weeding and ridging work per hectare, supporting the observation that households ridging much of their bush field subsequently used the plough team very little for weeding. Several households with completely new bush fields in 1980 gave up all work with the plough team after the land had been ridged, leaving all weeding work to be done by hand. This was because, with ridges already made, one of the main functions of weeding had already been carried out. Thus, it was decided to combine ridging and weeding work per hectare into a single plough-team variable.

As far as timing is concerned, work by plough teams occupies the central part of the rainy season. Almost the entire first weeding of the bush field in 1980 was performed by hand, because the land was dry and the oxen in poor condition. Plough teams were not used on any scale until week 7, in mid-July, to ridge the village fields, although the first sowing of the bush fields had been as early as 4 June. In 1981, plough teams started work by the fourth week in June to help ridge bush-field land and clear it of weeds. This crop of weeds and the relatively good condition of the work-oxen were both due to the very heavy rainfall received at the start of May, giving animals six or seven weeks of new pasture growth before being put to work. In both years, the plough team finished work long before the bush-field weeding had been completed, teams working an average of 28 days in 1980 and only 19 days in 1981. Once the weeding plough has passed over the bush field, the oxen are abandoned and the rest of the work is done by hand-held hoe. Because of the concentration of plough-team work in the central part of the rainy season, it was decided not to weight plough-team input by the timing of this work.

The proportion of new land in the bush field This variable represents the share of the bush field made up of land newly cleared in that farming season. As noted in Chapter 4, a completely new bush field presents certain risks to the farmer, as all of the land must be ridged before sowing. This means waiting for heavier rains which will enable the plough to pass. In addition, ridging the land is a slow operation, the plough team completing slightly under one hectare per day, given good working conditions. Consequently, sowing dates for newly cleared land are later than those for land that has already been farmed for one season or more, since millet can be sown in this latter case on the old ridges from the previous farming season. Later sowing dates lead to reduced yields of this millet variety since it must rely on rainfall received towards the end of the wet season to fill out its grains. However, rainfall in September is highly variable and often very localized in its incidence. Thus, this variable is likely to have a negative effect on yield per hectare, lower yields being associated with a higher proportion of the bush field made up of newly cleared land.

Soil dummy　This is a dummy variable which tries to take account of major differences in the soils found in bush fields. In general, bush fields cover very large surfaces of land (mean size for the village is over 22 ha), within which there is considerable variation in relief, soil type, number of large trees, and so on. While most bush fields were predominantly sandy with a few clay depressions or lateritic mounds, several households had noticeably less favourable soils. Households 13 and 20 had fields on heavier clays which were abandoned after the 1981 harvest for this reason. Households 3, 16a, and 21 cleared new fields in 1980, attaching themselves to the western end of the line of bush fields cleared by other households some years before, but found these sites to be lateritic, giving poor yields in both years. The five fields mentioned above were attributed a value of 0 on the soil dummy, the other 24 taking a value of 1.0. The land around Kala is fairly flat with very limited run off to small local depressions; thus, slope of bush field was not considered a significant variable.

Sowing dummy　Several sowing dummies were tested against bush-field yield per hectare to find one which could account for some of the variation in output per hectare. Only in the case of 1980 was a dummy found of any significance, which is no doubt due to the very extended period over which sowing was done in this year in contrast to the tighter schedule of 1981. Thus, this variable was only used for regression of 1980 bush-field data. The sowing dummy was constructed on the following basis: all households with bush fields entirely sown by the end of week 5 (the first week in July) took a value of 1.0, all other households taking a value of 0.

Rainfall　Rainfall figures for 1980–4 were presented in Chapter 3 where it was also seen that the amount of rain at the start and at the end of the wet season is much more variable than that in mid-season, that is in July and August. A late shower may touch a number of bush fields and leave adjacent fields dry. The longer-cycle millet grown in the bush is more dependent on rainfall received at the end of the rainy season to fill out its grains, than is the short-cycle village-field millet. This means that considerable variation in yield of the bush-field millet may be accounted for by the chance occurrence of a shower received by the field in late September. In 1981, three households with fields to the south-east of the village gained a late shower which probably added significantly to their yields in contrast to those of fields to the north which had no rain after August. However, since the rain-gauges were not established in each field, it was impossible to estimate more precisely the importance of variations in rainfall when accounting for differences in millet yields. In order to take account of the late September rainfall in 1981, a rainfall dummy was constructed for this year, taking a value of 1.0 for the three households with bush fields in the south-east, all other households taking a value of 0.

Form of the bush-field regression equation

The following regression equation was estimated for the bush-field millet data:

$$Q/ha = B(CTW/ha)^d (PTD/ha)^e PNB^f SOIL^g SWI^h RAIN^j$$

where:

Q/ha is output of millet in kg per ha of bush field.
CTW/ha is hand-weeding labour per ha, weighted by sex and age. In 1980, the time-weights take all work after 25 August as equal to 0, while for 1981, all work done after 16 August is taken as 0.
PTD/ha is plough team days spent per hectare on ridging and weeding work.
PNB is the proportion of newly cleared land in the bush field.
$SOIL$ is a dummy variable taking a value of 0 for five households with particularly hard soils (all other households taking a value of 1.0).
SWI is a dummy variable used in the regression of 1980 data, taking a value of 1.0 for those households which completed sowing of their bush fields by the end of week 5 (7 July), otherwise taking a value of 0.
$RAIN$ is a dummy variable used for regression of the 1981 data taking a value of 1.0 for three households whose fields received a shower in late September, all other fields taking a value of 0.
B is a constant and $d, e, f, g, h,$ and j are partial elasticities of production for each variable input.

RESULTS OF THE REGRESSION ANALYSIS

Data from village- and bush-field millet production were used in the regression equations outlined above. The equations were estimated in their log-linear form; labour, plough-team, and manuring variables were

TABLE 5.1. *Partial correlation coefficients: Village-field millet, 1980, 1981, and pooled data*

	Mean	Standard deviation	VFM/ha	MN/ha	PTD/ha	HWL/ha	YRDUM
1980:							
VFM/ha	6.804	0.483	1.000	0.527[a]	0.539[a]	0.152	
MN/ha	1.515	0.939		1.000	0.134	0.000	
PTD/ha	1.166	0.316			1.000	0.000	
HWL/ha	1.978	0.389				1.000	
1981:							
VFM/ha	6.333	0.444	1.000	0.554[a]	0.404[b]	0.000	
MN/ha	1.353	0.931		1.000	0.283	0.000	
PTD/ha	0.853	0.343			1.000	0.000	
HWL/ha	1.748	0.422				1.000	
Pooled data:							
VFM/ha	6.819	0.460	1.000	0.546[a]	0.440[a]	0.134	0.000
MN/ha	1.434	0.930		1.000	0.288[c]	0.000	0.000
PTD/ha	1.004	0.364			1.000	0.319[a]	−0.417[a]
HWL/ha	1.863	0.419				1.000	−0.247[b]
YRDUM	0.500	0.504					1.000

[a] Statistically significant at the 99% confidence level.
[b] Significant at the 95% level.
[c] Significant at the 90% level.

Note: All variables are in their logged form, except for the year dummy (YRDUM) in the pooled data matrix.

taken in their natural logarithms while the dummy variables remained unlogged. In addition to performing the regression analysis for each crop year taken separately, a joint-production function was also estimated by pooling data from the two years for each crop and using a dummy variable (1980 = 0, 1981 = 1) to take account of the year from which the observation was derived.

The results of the regression analysis are shown in Tables 5.4 and 5.5 and are discussed below these tables. Before looking at the estimated coefficients on each input, the partial correlation matrices will be presented and discussed in order to clarify the relationships existing between the different variables.

The partial correlation matrix

Tables 5.1, 5.2, and 5.3 present the partial correlation matrices for inputs into the two crops in 1980 and 1981 and for the estimated joint production function which pools the data for each crop over the two farm-ing seasons. These tables show the significance of each variable when regressed singly on output per hectare and of the degree of association between variables. Each millet variety will be discussed in turn.

Village-field millet In the separate year production analyses, the only relations of high significance between yield per hectare and the indepen-dent variables involve the level of manuring and the plough-team vari-able. Hand-weeding labour per hectare was not significantly correlated with yield in 1980 and no relationship was found at all between these two variables in 1981. The reasons for the absence of a significant relationship between labour and yields are investigated later. As far as factor–factor relations are concerned, there was a low positive correlation between plough-team and manure use per hectare, especially in 1981, when the partial correlation coefficient, r, was equal to 0.283, which indicated an association between the two variables of significance at the 90 per cent level of confidence. The impact of this low but positive correlation will be seen in the relative size and significance of the estimated coefficients on manure and plough-team inputs in the main regression equations. In addition, this association must be kept in mind when considering the variations in marginal returns to different factors between farmers, since the positive value for r suggests a relationship of complementarity be-tween manure and plough-team inputs. Complementarity between inputs will also be looked at in the chapter on investment, since it is likely that the returns to digging a well, for example, will be partly determined by the household's access to plough-team inputs. Overall, however, there was very little correlation between the independent variables thus reduc-ing bias in the estimated coefficients.

For the pooled-data regression, the partial correlation coefficients showed a similar pattern to those for the separate years. The figures confirmed the importance of manure and plough-team inputs in determin-ing yields per hectare and the insignificance of the hand-weeding labour variable. A positive and significant association emerged between the hand-weeding labour variable and plough-team work ($r = 0.319$), which was probably due to the tendency for those households with more ex-tensive village-field holdings to use lesser amounts of both labour and plough-work. The negative association between the year dummy and both labour and plough-team use was the result of the much faster pace of work in 1981, shown up in lower levels of input use not only in the village but also in the bush fields.

Bush-field millet For the separate year analysis in 1980, yield per hectare had a strong positive correlation with weeding labour per hectare and a strong negative correlation with the proportion of new land in the bush

TABLE 5.2. *Partial correlation coefficients: Bush-field millet, 1980 and 1981*

	Mean	Standard deviation	BFM/ha	CTW/ha	PTD/ha	PNB	Soil	SWI	Rain
1980:									
Logged variables									
BFM/ha	5.272	0.397	1.000	0.537[a]	0.000	−0.629[a]	0.321[c]	0.279[c]	
CTW/ha	1.879	0.381		1.000	0.000	−0.643[a]	0.345[b]	0.000	
PTD/ha	0.579	0.491			1.000	−0.063	0.000	0.000	
Unlogged variables									
PNB	0.452	0.326				1.000	−0.563[a]	0.167	
Soil	0.828	0.384					1.000	0.063	
SWI	0.296	0.465						1.000	
1981:									
Logged variables									
BFM/ha	5.320	0.326	1.000	0.276[c]	0.295[c]	−0.063	0.361[b]		0.205
CTW/ha	1.645	0.342		1.000	0.467[a]	−0.114	0.000		0.000
PTD/ha	0.333	0.376			1.000	0.000	−0.263[c]		0.000
Unlogged variables									
PNB	0.202	0.238				1.000	0.000		0.190
Soil	0.828	0.384					1.000		0.000
Rain	0.107	0.315							1.000

[a] Statistically significant at the 99% confidence level.
[b] Significant at the 95% level.
[c] Significant at the 90% level.

field. As noted earlier, this latter association was caused by the existence in 1980 of five completely new bush fields which suffered lower yields because of their later sowing dates and which had poorer laterite soils than the other bush fields. There was also a low correlation between yield and both the soil variable and the sowing dummy. In terms of factor–factor relationships, the proportion of newly cleared land in the bush field showed a strong negative correlation with both the weeding variable and the soil dummy. The first of these correlations results from the practice of those with new bush-field land of ridging this before sowing; this land then only needs a single weeding (unlike unridged bush-field land which usually gets a second weeding), so that the hand-weeding labour variable will be negatively associated with the PNB variable. The correlation between PNB80 and the soil dummy can be explained by the following: of the five fields given a dummy variable of 0, due to poorer soils, three had cut completely new bush fields in 1980, hence the significant inverse correlation between these two variables in 1980, which was lost the following year. The positive correlation between the hand-weeding labour variable and the soil dummy may be accounted for by the same explanation as that given above; namely, three out of the five newly cleared bush fields took a 0 value for the soil dummy, these being fields where the land was entirely ridged before sowing so that only one weeding was subsequently performed.

For 1981, only the soil variable was found to be significant at the 95 per cent confidence level when regressed singly on yield per hectare. Between the variables, only the hand-weeding and plough-team inputs were significantly correlated, due to a tendency for the use of both inputs to be inversely related to the area cultivated per worker. A low negative correlation was found between the plough-team variable and the soil dummy, indicating a greater use of the plough team on those fields taking a 0 value for the soil dummy. Of those five households with a 0 value, two used a particularly high plough-team input per hectare because of the heaviness of their clay soils.

The partial correlation coefficients for the pooled data are shown in Table 5.3. The results are in line with those expected, the value of coefficients lying between those obtained when each year was taken separately. However, the larger sample size does allow a greater degree of confidence to be attached to the coefficients than when each year was taken separately. In addition, inspection of the *r* values for the year dummy showed that while overall yield per hectare was not significantly different in the two years, there were significantly lower levels of labour and plough team use per hectare in 1981, in comparison with 1980, a fact already noted and put down to the later start of the cultivation season in 1981 and the consequent concentration of operations within a short space of time. The *PNB* variable was also negatively correlated with the year

TABLE 5.3. *Partial correlation coefficients: Bush-field millet, pooled data*

	Mean	Standard deviation	BFM/ha	CTW/ha	PTD/ha	PNB	Soil	Rain	SWI	YRDUM
Logged variables										
BFM/ha	5.297	0.360	1.000	0.401[a]	0.300[b]	−0.440[a]	0.362[a]	0.000	0.202[c]	0.000
CTW/ha	1.762	0.378		1.000	0.230[c]	−0.276[b]	0.100	0.000	0.000	−0.285[b]
PTD/ha	0.453	0.450			1.000	0.000	0.187[c]	0.130	0.000	−0.243[c]
Unlogged variables										
PNB	0.327	0.313				1.000	−0.297[b]	0.000	0.245[c]	−0.382[a]
Soil	0.826	0.381					1.000	0.000	0.187[c]	0.000
Rain	0.052	0.223						1.000	0.000	−0.195
SWI	0.448	0.502							1.000	0.000
YRDUM	0.500	0.504								1.000

[a] Statistically significant at the 99% confidence level.
[b] Significant at the 95% level.
[c] Significant at the 90% level.

dummy, which may be explained by the higher proportion of newly cleared land in bush fields in 1980 when compared with 1981.

The regression coefficients

Six regression equations were estimated for each millet variety, the coefficients from which are shown in Tables 5.4 and 5.5.

Village-field millet In the separate year analyses, the two main variables—manure and plough-team inputs per hectare—were both significant at the 95 per cent confidence level when these two variables alone were used in the regression equation. The coefficient on the plough-team variable was of greater absolute value in both years, but became of lesser significance in 1981 when the level of manure use grew more important in accounting for variation in yield per hectare. Inclusion of the hand-weeding labour variable did nothing to improve the goodness of fit between the variables and output per hectare, nor was the coefficient on the labour variable high either in value or in significance in either year. The pooled-data regressions provided coefficients whose value lay between those for the separate years. Their significance, however, was considerably greater, with *t*-values statistically significant at the 99 per cent confidence level.

Bush-field millet Several regressions were tried for the bush-field data, including or omitting different variables to assess their relative impact on the coefficients and degree of correlation found. In general, the coefficients were relatively stable with the addition or exclusion of different variables, although when the proportion of newly cleared bush-field land (*PNB*) was included, there was some shift in the value of other coefficients, especially that on the weeding-labour variable. As noted earlier, this was due in 1980 to there being a strong negative correlation between these two variables. In 1981, the *PNB* variable was of much lesser importance and was omitted from the final regressions run. In 1980, two variables were found to be of greatest significance, that for hand-weeding and that for plough-team work per hectare. The coefficients on these two variables were both significantly different from 0 at the 95 per cent level of confidence. The sowing dummy lacked significance at the 95 per cent level but was significant at the 90% per cent level in 1980. In 1981, while many different labour variables were tried out in the regression, none produced a relationship of any significance. However, both plough-team use and the soil dummy were strongly significant in this year. The rainfall dummy did not prove useful in capturing the effects of a late shower felt by three bush fields at the end of the rainy season.

The regression analysis using the pooled data for both farming seasons provided coefficients intermediate in value to those obtained when each

TABLE 5.4. *Regression equations: Village-field millet, 1980, 1981, and pooled data*

Variable	1980 Coefficient	1980 Coefficient	1981 Coefficient	1981 Coefficient	Pooled Coefficient	Pooled Coefficient
Constant	5.93 (24.13)	5.68 (15.88)	6.22 (33.59)	6.12 (19.64)	6.01 (33.83)	5.84 (22.80)
MN/ha	0.130[b] (1.79)	0.131[b] (1.80)	0.230[a] (3.00)	0.231[a] (2.95)	0.182[a] (3.44)	0.183[a] (3.45)
PTD/ha	0.617[a] (3.03)	0.567[a] (2.70)	0.358[b] (1.72)	0.336[c] (1.53)	0.482[a] (3.32)	0.447[a] (2.97)
HWL/ha	—	0.155 (0.96)	—	0.065 (0.38)	—	0.105 (0.91)
YRDUM					0.168[b] (1.68)	0.181[b] (1.79)
R^2	34.8%	34.5%	35.4%	33.2%	34.8%	34.6%
n	27	27	29	29	52	51

[a] Statistically significant at the 99% confidence level.
[b] Significant at the 95% level.
[c] Significant at the 90% level.

Note: Figures in brackets refer to the t-statistic for that coefficient.

TABLE 5.5. *Regression equations: Bush-field millet, 1980, 1981, and pooled data*

1980

Variable	Coefficient	Coefficient
Constant	3.97 (12.71)	4.37 (6.99)
CTW/ha	0.604[a] (3.77)	0.388[b] (1.82)
PTD/ha	0.305[a] (2.51)	0.252[b] (1.84)
Soil	—	0.100 (0.47)
PNB80	—	−0.274 (−0.82)
SWI80	—	0.185[c] (1.53)
Rain	—	—
R^2	41.2%	48.0%
n	27	26

1981

Variable	Coefficient	Coefficient
Constant	4.92 (15.75)	4.59 (16.53)
CTW/ha	0.201 (0.99)	0.133 (0.78)
PTD/ha	0.211 (1.15)	0.382[b] (2.34)
Soil	—	0.439[a] (3.17)
PNB81	—	—
Rain	—	0.177 (1.10)
R^2	8.7%	36.5%
n	28	28

Pooled data

Variable	Coefficient	Coefficient
Constant	4.38 (18.90)	4.38 (14.13)
CTW/ha	0.410[a] (3.34)	0.259[b] (2.08)
PTD/ha	0.233[b] (2.32)	0.305[a] (3.08)
Soil	—	0.338[a] (2.91)
PNB	—	−0.147 (−0.84)
SWI	—	0.072 (0.88)
Rain	—	0.002 (0.01)
YRDUM	0.193[b] (2.14)	0.134[c] (1.31)
R^2	24.8%	39.2%
n	55	54

[a] Statistically significant at the 99% confidence level.
[b] Significant at the 95% level.
[c] Significant at the 90% level.

Note: Figures in brackets refer to the t-statistic for that coefficient.

year was taken separately. The inclusion of a larger number of variables reduced the size of the coefficient on the hand-weeding labour variable and its significance, as was also the case for the year dummy. Conversely, the plough-team coefficient grew in size and significance when the regression took account of other independent variables.

Overall significance of the results

The regression of input–output data both for the four crop-years and for the pooled data produced coefficients on several variables that were highly significant. This was particularly true of the variables measuring:

Manure use per hectare This was significant at the 95 per cent level in 1980, and at the 99 per cent level in 1981 and in the pooled regression.

Plough-team use per hectare For village-field millet this was significant at the 99 per cent level in 1980 and in the pooled data, and at the 90–95 per cent level in 1981, depending on the number of variables included in the regression equation. For bush-field millet this variable was of significance at the 90–95 per cent level in both years, again depending on the number of other independent variables included in the regression. These results are of particular importance for the discussion of returns to the key investments made by farmers in Kala, those of well-digging and of oxen plough-team purchases.

Dummy variables Soil emerged as a significant dummy variable for bush-field millet in 1981 and for the pooled data. This variable referred to five households with exceptionally hard soils in their bush fields, either due to high clay content or because they were lateritic. The *PNB* variable had important interrelations with other variables, such as levels of labour and plough-team use, but it was not significant overall in determining bush-field yields. The hand-weeding labour variable performed poorly in three out of the four cases analysed, the reasons for which are discussed in more detail below.

Correlation coefficients These are not as high as had been hoped for the regressions in both years and for the pooled data, but they are not untypical of the results obtained by other cross-section production studies of small farmers in developing countries. For example, Massell and Johnson's (1968) regression equations gained R^2 values lying between 30 per cent and 56 per cent for their sample of subsistence farmers in Zimbabwe (formerly Southern Rhodesia). However, Bliss and Stern (1982) obtained much higher values for R^2 in their analysis of yields in an Indian village. This is probably due to their having closely monitored inputs into a small plot of land rather than taking the entire area farmed by the household as done in the case of Kala.

Problems with the labour variable

In three out of the four cases analysed, the coefficient on the hand-weeding labour variable was low and statistically insignificant. This was surprising, given the importance attached by farmers to an early weeding of the millet and the researcher's expectation that labour input would be an important determinant of crop yield. There are two possible explanations for these poor results. First, the way in which the labour data was collected and aggregated may have been faulty. Collection methods were described in Chapter 1, where questions of accuracy were also discussed. It was noted that the methods followed represented a compromise between getting much more detailed information on hourly labour inputs and the much greater time this would take of both the research team and the village population, given the very large size of households, and the non-familiarity with western measures of time. The remarkable similarity in working hours between households and throughout the farming season prompted the researcher to measure labour in terms of half man-days of work in the field.

The method used for aggregating labour input from workers of different age and sex, described in Chapter 4, consisted of a system of weights. The relative weights used were chosen to reflect differences both in hours of work per day spent in the field and in the speed and intensity of work. The resulting figure for labour input may be a poor measure of actual work done in the field. However, it is not clear how the procedures followed could have been greatly improved without a much heavier and more intensive effort at labour-data collection involving, for example, monitoring the activity of each household's work-force with a stop-watch. Such a measurement exercise might well, in itself, have produced an inaccurate measure given the possible effect of close observation on work-force behaviour.

A second possible explanation for the poor correlation between labour input and grain yield lies in the fact that much of the weeding work is done by the plough. In such cases, hand-weeding is restricted to clearing away the few weeds not dealt with by the weeding plough. The production analysis only produced one case in which the labour variable was of significance, that for bush millet in 1980. In this year, the dearth of rain following the first sowing in early June lasted until mid-July, precluding much use of work-oxen as the ground was dry and the animals short of grass. Consequently a large amount of weeding work was done by hand. The second weeding was done by both plough and hoe, giving a total weeding-labour input per hectare of 11.7 man-days. By contrast, the bush field in 1981 and the village fields in both years were weeded for the first time by plough and hoe and subsequently received little or no attention. Thus, both the problems in measuring labour input and the lesser importance of hand-weeding labour in relation to plough weeding are probable reasons for the poor performance of this variable in the regression analyses.

The residual error term

This term usually picks up errors stemming from several sources: misspecification of the production function, inaccurate measurement of inputs and output, exclusion of significant variables and differences in the efficiency with which inputs are combined. Before looking at the relative significance of these components in the case of the Kala farm data, it is necessary first to investigate whether the estimated residual term is related to the predicted yield in a systematic way. Were a definite relationship to exist between these two variables (for example, suppose the residual term increased in size with rising yields), this would provide evidence either for the production function being wrongly specified, or for there being an important variable which had been omitted from the analysis. Where the estimated residual error is not correlated with predicted yield, this term is picking up errors resulting from inaccurate measurement of the various inputs and of differences in the efficiency with which the factors are combined. In the case of Kala, the estimated residual errors for each crop year were regressed on predicted yield for each observation but no relationship was found between these two variables ($R^2 = 0.0$ per cent) in either year.

Correlation of the residual with input levels also creates problems, especially where ordinary least-square regression analysis procedures are followed. Nowshirvani (1967) points out that coefficients on the input variables will be biased and inconsistent in such cases. Correlation between residuals and input levels is particularly likely where there are major differences in managerial efficiency between farmers, leading to higher input levels for 'good-practice' farmers. In the case of Kala, differences in managerial performance were not considered significant, given the marked similarity in work patterns, timing of farm operations, and the absence of purchased inputs, such as pesticides or fertilizer.

Tables 5.6 and 5.7 present data on those farmers for whom there was a large difference between predicted and actual crop yield, taking all observations in which the standard residual[1] was either less than −1.0 or greater than +1.0. Comments are provided to try to explain the poor accuracy of the predicted yield for each observation. However, given the

---

[1] The residual divided by the standard deviation of that residual.

TABLE 5.6. *The residual error: Village-field millet production*

Household	Name	Actual yield	Predicted yield	Standard residual	Comment
22 (81)	Tijani	263	602	−2.69	Large field, no plough team, no dung, only two household members.
18 (81)	Makono	523	1,178	−2.47	Large new field, no well, little dung.
3 (80)	BaSantigi	468	837	−1.78	3 years since any manure obtained.
7 (80)	Brahima	675	1,040	−1.31	Very uneven manuring, one plot never receives dung. Two wells but both draw little water.
13 (81)	Cesamon	465	693	−1.23	Very large new field cut for new well dug 1981.
3 (81)	BaSantigi	680	974	−1.09	Field doubled in size for new well dug 1981.
28 (80)	Kokenjini	360	502	−1.07	Very low and patchy manure use.
10 (81)	Sekou	595	829	−1.03	Large new field, several years since joint herd spent dry season on land.
29 (81)	Kumare	1,088	769	+1.06	Second year of new well, early arrival of herds at well, giving 6 months of manuring.
8 (80)	Cekoro	1,775	1,227	+1.13	Had large visiting herd for entire dry season.
11 (80)	Mable	1,177	814	+1.13	Above average well, Maure small stock and Fulani cattle herd watered for 5–6 months.
6 (81)	Samba	2,053	1,396	+1.21	Received joint herd for entire dry season.
11 (81)	Mable	1,284	837	+1.30	Above average well, many visitors.
8 (81)	Cekoro	1,444	880	+1.55	Small surface rapidly sown and weeded.
9 (81)	Niangoro	1,226	743	+1.63	Carted much village rubbish to fields, to compensate for very limited access to animal manure.
27 (80)	Cekura	1,645	706	+2.70	No well but received visiting herd in June in exchange for looking after herders' belongings in rainy season.

Farm Production

TABLE 5.7. *The residual error: Bush-field millet production*

Household	Name	Actual yield	Predicted yield	Standard residual	Comment
28 (80)	Kokenjini	101	145	−2.04	Large new bush field, late sowing and weeding.
13 (81)	Cesamon	128	208	−1.94	Large new village field, plus PNB81 of 80%.
29 (80)	Mamu	154	222	−1.58	Late re-sowing, small disheartened work-force.
12 (81)	Babani	199	281	−1.46	Field-sown *paki*, many weeds, short of food and one man out to work for others.
29 (80)	Kumare	73	93	−1.40	New field, sown *paki*, no oxen, late weeding.
4 (80)	Sirke	155	224	−1.38	Very large field, late weeding.
21 (81)	Njeba	137	180	−1.18	Field-sown *paki*, weeded late, large village field took up family's time.
2 (81)	Dansine	178	238	−1.17	Large village field given most attention.
19 (81)	Sirima	174	233	−1.16	Large new village field, late weeding work.
29 (81)	Kumare	97	117	−1.08	Field-sown *paki*, large new village field, no plough team.
12 (80)	Babani	159	208	−1.07	Large, late-weeded partly abandoned field.
14 (80)	Kako	260	198	+1.01	Average area per worker, early-weeded field.
15 (80)	Bensurun	287	222	+1.01	Young and hard-working members, women arrive very early in morning at field with food.
1 (81)	Dafe	265	205	+1.02	Most of field ploughed before sowing, weeds kept down, 5 ploughs working at peak.
27 (80)	Cekura	174	138	+1.12	No evident reason.

Household	Name	Actual yield	Predicted yield	Standard residual	Comment
18 (81)	Makono	208	155	+1.26	Large part field ploughed before sowing.
16 (80)	Ganiba	389	269	+1.35	Same as for 14 (80), 15 (80).
5 (81)	Toto	330	233	+1.40 ⎫	Large young male
10 (80)	Sekou	335	227	+1.46 ⎬	work-force, enthusiatic
19 (81)	Sekou	300	200	+1.70 ⎭	and hard working. Much of field ploughed before sowing in 1981. Spare oxen and hired labour.
16 (81)	Ganiba	368	240	+1.71	Note comment above, 16 (80). Very articulate.
5 (80)	Toto	367	206	+2.16	Note for 5 (81) above.

low overall explanatory power of the regression models estimated in this chapter, one would expect a significant number of farmers to have inexplicably high or low yields in comparison with those predicted. In addition, high residual errors are attributed to three other factors:

Problems in accurately measuring the different inputs and taking account of variation in their quality   For example, a standard weighting system was applied to aggregate labour according to different age and sex classes across households. While it was recognized that the labour-force in some households was either particularly hard working or rather slack, it was felt that these judgements provided an insubstantial basis on which to weight the work-force differentially between households.

The question of variation also arises for work-oxen inputs, since the effectiveness of one plough-team day of work will depend not only on the age and strength of the oxen but also on the number of teams working together; two or more teams working together are said to work faster because the oxen compete with each other. Further errors are likely in the measurement of a household's access to manure. Wells were valued in terms of their manuring value, an average well being able to water 60 cattle over three months. Some households had wells that performed somewhat better than this whereas others drew less water than average. In addition, some well owners were better able than others to maintain a visiting herd on their land for a longer period, due to existing ties of friendship or by providing the herder with food or extra labour to help with water-drawing. Thus, two households with the same figure on the manuring index may have actually had somewhat different levels of manure on their village fields.

Insufficient detail over the timing of different inputs may also explain high residual errors. Choices must be made, on the one hand, as to the degree of detail to consider in breaking inputs down into their components and, on the other hand, the degree to which aggregation is possible. One man-day of weeding work in late July will be more valuable than the same amount of work done in early September. For both years, account was taken of the timing of hand-weeding labour into the bush field by valuing all work done after late August as worth nothing. Nevertheless, variation in the timing of inputs, not only for the labour variable but also for sowing and plough-team work, has probably been inadequately captured and part of the residual error can be attributed to this cause. A greater degree of detail for the timing of inputs was considered, but balanced against this was first the loss of freedom in the regression analyses from including a larger number of variables and, secondly, the inevitably rather random values given to time-weighting systems.

Farmers are bound to differ among themselves in terms of their knowledge, aptitude, and judgement It is common for differences in 'managerial efficiency' to be used to explain large residual errors in production analysis. Thus, Bliss and Stern (1982: 281) note that 'apart from random factors, it is the care with which those inputs are used which one should look for in explaining the residuals'. However, the practice of attributing a high residual to differences in managerial efficiency seems both too loose and too convenient a procedure. It would obviously be preferable to measure managerial input and include this as an independent variable in the production analysis. Massell and Johnson (1968) adopt this method in their study of small farmers in Southern Africa, taking the classification of farmers by government extension agents into three groups, 'skilled', 'semi-skilled', and 'unskilled'. In the case of Kala, there was no obvious way to classify the farm households according to managerial efficiency. The village practice of co-ordinating the start of certain operations, such as the sowing and weeding of the village fields, reduces the scope for large differences in timing from one farmer to another. Nevertheless, there is bound to be variation in the efficiency and care with which inputs are used by different farmers. The regular visits made to the fields during the cultivation season allowed some judgement to be made about the relative conscientiousness of each farm household. Frequent conversations about farming methods gave an impression of greater awareness of alternative methods among certain producers. However, these judgements are not necessarily always accurate. For example, a farmer who is very articulate may not actually be more efficient than a less voluble farmer, although in the former case one does get the impression that the farmer has observed and considered many aspects of crop production and is therefore more likely to be aware of the possible areas for improving crop performance.

During visits to the fields, it was also noted that the work-force in some households appeared to be in better humour and to work harder than the work-force elsewhere. This was especially the case where there was a group of men in their late teens and early twenties who set the pace and drew the rest of the household along by their energy and enthusiasm. This difference in the efficiency of labour use across households was discussed earlier, where it was acknowledged that there were significant but unmeasured variations in the value of one man-day of work from one household to another.

Error in estimating the relationship between inputs and outputs This is also attributable to the per hectare form in which the data were analysed. It was noted earlier that severe problems with multi-collinearity prevented absolute values for inputs and outputs from being used in the production function. As a result, the per hectare formulation was adopted, greatly reducing partial correlation among the independent variables. However, the figure for input use per hectare hides considerable variation between different parts of the same field. Bush fields, in particular, are extremely large areas averaging more than 20 ha in size and within each field certain parts will have received a larger amount of weeding input at a more timely date than others. One farmer was quick to point out during a tour of his bush field the range of cultivation practices which he carried out: part of the field hand been sown *paki*, some sown on ridged land, some weeded by hand and some weeded by both plough and hoe and each of these mixtures had been carried out at different dates. Similarly, within a household's village-field holdings, there are uneven levels of manuring, although farmers try to keep their different plots at roughly equal levels of fertilization over a period of years. The estimated production functions therefore have to capture the response of output to variation in input use at a rather aggregate level. A high residual error may thus be partly accounted for by the variation in actual input use per hectare over the field concerned.

6

RETURNS TO FARMING

This chapter compares the returns in production of bush- and village-field millet during the two cropping seasons studied and discusses reasons for the wide divergence in returns between crops and from one year to the next. This is followed by a comparison of returns to different factors of production with the prices at which these are occasionally available, before turning to an analysis of the broad spread in returns for those farmers who demonstrated behaviour markedly different from the average of all observations. First, however, there will be a discussion of the problems associated with the analysis of marginal returns using a Cobb–Douglas production function.

Problems associated with the marginal returns analysis

The form taken by the Cobb–Douglas production function, used in the previous chapter to analyse millet production, imposes a certain kind of relationship between the level of factor use and marginal returns. This relationship is one of continuously declining returns to any one factor as its use is increased while other factors are held constant. This is a reasonable assumption at levels of input use which are not far from the mean, but less confidence may be placed on the predictive value of estimated coefficients where input levels take extremely low or high values. Looking at the range of per hectare input levels for the two millet varieties, it can be seen that labour use in the bush field and plough-team use in the village field both exhibited relatively low coefficients of variation, at 20 per cent and 30–40 per cent respectively. In contrast, manure use per hectare in the village fields had a coefficient of variation as high as 80 per cent in 1980, and plough-team use per hectare of bush field had a coefficient of variation of over 100 per cent in 1981. The marginal returns for these latter two inputs should therefore be used with more caution.

Manure use per hectare illustrates one of the difficulties associated with the assumptions behind the Cobb–Douglas function. Fig. 6.1 shows the estimated relationship between the level of manure use per hectare and the marginal return at different input levels based on data from Table 6.3. As may be seen, additional units of manure at very low levels of use per hectare produce very large increments in yield per hectare. As manuring levels rise, the marginal value of each extra unit will fall sharply and

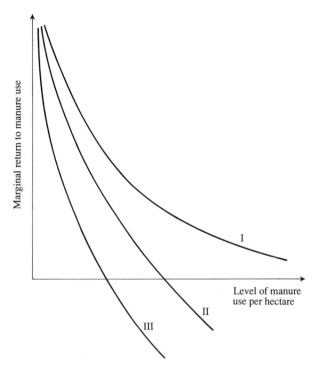

FIG. 6.1. Marginal returns to manure use

evidence suggests that above a certain level, marginal returns will become negative. The Cobb–Douglas function estimates a curve of type I, whereas types II and III are probably more realistic. The position and slope of the curve will depend on soil and rainfall conditions; where rainfall is low, the curve will follow the line of type III in which negative returns set in at a low level of manure use per hectare.

A second assumption behind the Cobb–Douglas function is that of a smooth, continuous relationship between the marginal returns to each factor and the level of factor use, as measured by the coefficient of elasticity for each factor, which remains at a constant value for all input levels. This coefficient is also independent of the ratio of factors used, that is it does not change with the level of other factors applied. Output changes only as a result of the independent action of changes in each of the inputs; interaction between inputs is not allowed for. The possibility of significant interaction between the different inputs is examined later. The assumption of a constant coefficient of elasticity for each input, whatever the level of input use, means that no allowance can be made for periods of increasing returns to a factor, followed by diminishing returns, nor, as noted above, the possibility that the marginal return to a factor may fall below zero.

Interaction between inputs can take the form of substitutability or complementarity. For inputs which are highly substitutable, output will remain unchanged even when factor ratios change considerably. At the extreme, perfect substitutes show a linear relationship with respect to any given level of output, implying that any input mix along that straight line will ensure a given level of output. In the case of Kala, there is some substitutability possible between the different factors. For bush-field millet, the two variables of interest are hand-weeding labour and plough-team inputs. A high plough-team input reduces the amount of weeding work which must subsequently be done by hand. Conversely, where land has not been ridged before sowing, weeding labour must be rapidly mobilized to maintain millet yields.

For village-field millet, the two variables of interest are manure and plough-team use, between which there may also be some substitutability. For example, farmers with limited access to manure are likely to make the most of this input by using a high level of plough-team work per hectare. However, there is no overall tendency for manure and plough-team use to be inversely correlated. Indeed, a low but positive correlation was found in the previous chapter, in Table 5.1, suggesting some complementarity between these two inputs. The complementary aspects of the relationship between plough-team and manure use stem from the role of the ridging plough in mixing dung into the soil and the contribution made by keeping down the heavy weed growth found on well-manured soils by the work of the weeding plough. A household with a large area per plough team of heavily manured land is unlikely to gain as much value from each unit of manure as another household with the same level of manuring but where a lower ratio of land per plough team is maintained. The effect of this complementarity will be examined more fully later in this chapter and in the following chapters where returns to investment in different productive assets are examined.

Comparing the marginal returns to factors between crops

Here, the marginal returns to each factor in bush- and village-field millet production are investigated and the much higher marginal returns to be gained in the short-cycle village-field crop during the two years studied are accounted for. Table 6.1 presents the estimated marginal value products for each factor input in production of the two millets in both years, taken from the full regression equations for 1980 and 1981 and for the pooled two-year data. In comparing returns in village- and bush-field production, only returns to labour and plough-team inputs can be looked at, since no manuring takes place on the bush fields.

TABLE 6.1. *Estimated marginal value productivities of main inputs* (in kilograms of threshed millet)

	Hand-weeding labour	Plough-team work	Manure use
1980			
Village-field millet	1.397	5.109[a]	1.102[b]
Bush-field millet	0.757[b]	0.491[b]	
1981			
Village-field millet	0.603	3.118[c]	1.976[a]
Bush-field millet	0.271	0.799[b]	
POOLED DATA			
Village-field millet	0.961	4.090[a]	1.556[a]
Bush-field millet	0.518[b]	0.610[a]	

[a] Statistically significant at the 99% confidence level.
[b] Significant at the 95% level.
[c] Significant at the 90% level.

Note: Values calculated at the geometric mean observation.

Plough-team inputs The coefficient on the plough-team variable was found to be significant for both crops and in both years. Comparing the marginal products (*MVP*) for the two millet crops within each year, it is clear that there is a very large gap in the value of plough-team work which must be explained. This gap was especially large for 1980, when the *MVP* of plough-team work in village-field millet was ten times that for bush-field millet. In 1981, the contrast was less marked but still represented a difference by a factor of nearly 4.0.

Hand-weeding labour The lack of significance for the hand-weeding coefficient has already been discussed above. The estimated marginal value products for this variable cannot therefore be treated with much confidence. The estimated *MVP*s in Table 6.1 would suggest that the value of labour use in bush-field millet was substantially less than its use in village-field millet in both 1980 and 1981. This is similar to the pattern found for the *MVP* for plough-team inputs, discussed above.

Accounting for differences in marginal factor returns

In static models of resource allocation, profit-maximizing behaviour on the part of producers would imply the use of a given factor in different activities up to the point where its marginal productivity is equalized across those uses. Thus, with two activities, bush-field millet (*B*) and village-field millet (V) production, it would be expected that farmers will allocate resource X between the two so that $MPX_B = MPX_V$. As was seen from Table 6.1, however, there are very substantial differences in the marginal products of different factors between the two crops, with much higher returns to factor use in village-field millet production. Non-equalization of the marginal conditions in any one year can be accounted for in a variety of ways, by introducing risk, interannual variability in returns, and by considering the constraints on production of each good.

Risk   Where producers are faced with some variability in the returns to a particular activity, their resource allocation decisions are likely to be modified. Taking the two crops grown, suppose that returns are more variable in village- than in bush-field millet. If producers are assumed to be risk averse, then a rational allocation of resources would be one in which MPX_B is less than MPX_V. The extent to which the marginal productivity in V exceeds that in B depends on the difference in riskiness of the two activities and on the degree of risk aversion of the producer. Evidence for a higher risk to the village-field crop comes from its lesser resistance to periods of drought during its growing-cycle, due in part to the heavy manuring of soils and in part to the less extensive root system developed by the shorter-cycle variety which makes it more vulnerable to lack of rainfall. However, it is unlikely that the wide difference in returns for the two millet varieties can be explained entirely in terms of risk.

Variability in returns from year to year   Crop production in semi-arid regions like the Sahel is marked by highly variable harvests from year to year as a result of fluctuations in the quantity and timing of rainfall received. Farmers must take production decisions on the basis of ex-pected returns to each crop. There are limited possibilities for reallocat-ing resources as the farming season progresses and as more information becomes available on the likely performance of each crop. This is be-cause, except in the case of a total failure of rainfall at the start of the farming season, yields of both crops often depend on whether or not rainfall is received in late August to mid-September, by which time resources will already have been invested and no further action can be taken in the light of new information. Farmers have to base their decisions on output expected at the start of the farming season. Only too often, fields which have been most carefully sown and weeded produce only a meagre harvest, due to insufficient rain falling at the crucial grain-filling stage in late August to mid-September, rendering almost worthless the work done in the field.

Thus, the performance of different crops and the marginal productivity of different factors in each crop will vary from one year to the next, depending on the volume and timing of rain received that farming season.

There are two possible scenarios for the behaviour of rainfall over time, each producing a different optimal strategy for resource allocation between bush- and village-field millet. The first scenario assumes that rainfall and expected yields of the two crops will fluctuate around a stable mean, characterized by their average performance over a long period of years. The marginal productivity conditions will not hold in a single year or even for a group of several years, since these are not likely to be a representative sample drawn from the larger population of rainfall and yields to be expected over a large number of years. However, over the long term, average $MPX_B = MPX_V$ and no shift in resources is indicated. The second scenario takes expected rainfall, and therefore yields, as following a particular trend, over the medium term, causing a shift in the relative returns to be gained from the two crops. In such a case, farmers are faced with the need to assess the likely direction of change and to respond to this change by reallocating resources in an appropriate fashion. The last twenty years have seen low and very variable rainfall throughout the Sahel to which farmers have tried to adapt by shifting resources towards shorter-cycle crops. With the benefit of hindsight, this reallocation of resources would have taken place more rapidly.

Constraints on production   The marginality conditions may also not hold where there are constraints on the production of a certain crop which limit the expansion or contraction of production beyond a certain level. These constraints are usually due to imperfect factor or product markets and to the technical requirements of each crop. The two main constraints on resource allocation between bush- and village-field millet in Kala are those imposed firstly by farmers' limited access to manure, an essential input to gaining high yields of this crop and, secondly, by the limited time period during which sowing of this crop can be done, if it is to complete its cycle to maturity before the end of the rains.

Increased supplies of manure come mainly from investment by a farmer in digging a well which then allows him to get more dung through the establishment of watering contracts with visiting herders. Wells are indivisible assets; a half-dug well yields nothing, there are no sharing arrangements by which several households can share a well, nor do well owners hire out the manuring services of their well. Manure is neither bought nor sold, being only obtainable in exchange for water. The cost of digging a well in terms of hiring labour or using the household's own work-force is considerable (see Chapter 8 for more detail), even for the largest and most wealthy households. For the smallest, poorest households these costs remain an insurmountable sum and no credit is available by which means those without the current capital could borrow against future earnings. These factors constrain a household's access to manure and consequently the scale of its village-field millet production.

The second constraint operating on expansion of village-field millet production is imposed by questions of timing within the short rainy season. Unlike bush-field millet which is often sown *paki* on the flat, unridged field, village land is always ridged before sowing. Ridging the soil cannot take place until there is a heavy enough rainfall for the plough to pass. Enough moisture must also be present in the soil to ensure full germination of seed, otherwise much resowing will have to take place. With a very large village-field holding, farmers must hope for several good rains while sowing this crop, as ridging work is quite slow and moisture leaves the soil two or three days after a medium shower. In addition, farmers must wait until the 'seventh' or 'eighth' month has been reached, before sowing, because by then they will be sure that the rainy season has truly arrived.[1] They did not consider, for example, the very heavy rainfall in early May 1981 to be part of the rainy season and so no sowing was done, despite 70 mm of rain having fallen. Farmers also consider it is not worth sowing short-cycle millet after the twentieth day of the eighth month, as it will not have time to mature before the rains come to an end.

Several other constraints on resource allocation by peasant farmers are discussed in farm-production studies and these will be looked at here to assess their significance in the Kala context. It has been widely argued that many farmers face a subsistence constraint which affects the way in which they allocate resources between their food and other crops (Lipton, 1968; Massel and Johnson, 1968). For reasons of food security, farmers have a target output which represents the minimum output of grain they need to satisfy their household's consumption requirements. As a result, they will devote a certain amount of land, labour, and other resources sufficient to achieve this target, which consequently constrains the amount of time and resources available to cultivate other crops. A related constraint on expansion of a certain crop may be imposed by there being limited marketing opportunities for sale of surplus output. Thus, for example, Massel and Johnson (1968) demonstrate in their study of small farmers in Zimbabwe that the marginal returns to land and other factors are higher in millet than in maize and groundnut production but, since farmers have little chance of being able to sell surplus millet, they limit their production of this crop and devote more of their resources to crops like maize, for which there is an active market.

Neither of the above constraints is likely to be important in the case of Kala, since the resource allocation question is concerned with two varieties of the same crop, rather than, say, with a food crop on the one hand and a cash crop on the other. The two millet varieties were con-

[1] The 'first' month is that in which the *dah* plants (*Hibiscus* species) are cut, sometime in November or December. The 'seventh' and 'eighth' months thus lie between late May and early August.

sidered close substitutes for each other as far as food is concerned. Each variety has slightly different characteristics which make it favoured for a particular dish; the short-cycle *souna* makes a sweeter *dege*, the afternoon meal of soured gruel, while the longer-cycle *sanyo* is said to make a more substantial *to*, the thick millet porridge. Neither can be said to be preferred overall to the other. Nevertheless, the longer-cycle bush-field millet is superior to that grown in the village fields in one important respect, which is the former's greater storage life. A granary of village-field millet is rarely kept for more than one year, it rapidly losing quality after this period. Bush-field millet can be stored for three or four years before it must either be eaten or sold. These differences would lead one to expect a slightly greater level of involvement in bush-field millet production than would be indicated by the equalization of marginal productivities between the two varieties, since the marginal product, measured here in grain, ignores the higher value placed on the storage qualities of one millet variety over the other. This consideration is not likely to play much part in accounting for the wide differences in marginal productivities in 1980 and 1981, since few farmers are able to hold stocks for more than a couple of years and, even these practise a rolling-over of stocks, selling the remaining grain as the new harvest comes in. More than half of all households in Kala had no grain stocks of any sort over the period studied.

Comparing marginal factor returns in 1980 and 1981

It was hoped that the analysis of farm data using a production function would provide estimates of the returns to factors which could be used to indicate the degree of variability in expected returns from year to year. Two years' data are obviously insufficient fully to identify the probability distribution of expected returns. For this, a run of data over 20 years or more would be required to approximate the probabilities involved and these would only be valid for determining future production strategies if it could be assumed that the future will follow the same pattern as the past. However, limited as it is, two years' data do throw light on the possible range in expected returns to different factors. Despite the great similarity in mean yields per hectare between the two years, with bush fields producing on average around 200 kg per ha and village fields around 1,000 kg per ha, there were nevertheless found to be considerable differences in estimated marginal value products of each factor at the mean from one year to the next. It is highly probable, over a longer period of years, that mean yields per hectare would show more variation than that found between 1980 and 1981, due to differences in rainfall patterns. This would lead one to predict a much wider variation in the marginal value products of factors than was found for the two years studied.

TABLE 6.2. *Estimated marginal value of one additional unit of main inputs at the mean* (in kilograms of threshed millet)

	Hand-weeding labour	Plough-team work	Manure use
1980			
Village-field millet	19.3	159.2[a]	24.2[b]
Bush-field millet	11.6[b]	27.6[b]	—
1981			
Village-field millet	10.5	132.7[c]	51.1[a]
Bush-field millet	5.2	55.6[b]	—
POOLED DATA			
Village-field millet	14.9	149.8[a]	37.0[a]
Bush-field millet	8.9[b]	38.9[a]	—
PRICES*	5.0	10.0	

* As explained later, these are the prices at which labour and plough teams are occasionally available to households for hire.

Notes: These values are derived from Table 6.1.
[a], [b], and [c] as Table 6.1.

The marginal value products and the value created by an additional unit of each factor were presented in Tables 6.1 and 6.2.

Weeding labour   As noted earlier, the coefficient on the labour variable cannot be treated with great confidence because of its non-significance in statistical terms in three out of the four cases analysed. The figures available would indicate higher returns to labour in both crops in 1980 when compared with 1981, a result which is the converse of that anticipated, given the overall lower levels of labour input into production of both millet varieties in the later year.

Plough-team work   Comparing the marginal value product of one plough-team day of work in the same crop from one year to the next raises significant differences. For bush-field millet, the marginal value product at the mean is higher in 1981 than in 1980, whereas for village-field millet the converse is the case. This pattern also shows up in Table 6.2, where the value of an additional plough-team day of work is compared for the two crops in 1980 and 1981. For bush-field millet, the value of an additional plough-team day in 1981 was double that of 1980. This is due first to the lower mean level of plough-team use per hectare in 1981, so that an additional unit of this input represents a higher percentage increase in its use, and secondly to the presence of five completely new bush fields in 1980 which required a high plough-team input but which gained low yields, partly as a result of late sowing dates, lowering the value of plough-team work in that year.

For village-field millet, the value of an additional plough-team day of work is somewhat lower in 1981 compared with 1980. It was seen from the results of the regression equations presented in Table 5.4 that the coefficient on the manuring variable was both substantially greater and of higher significance in 1981 and that on the plough-team variable of lower value and significance when compared with the previous year. There was also a positive partial correlation coefficient between manure use and plough-team input per hectare of higher value in 1981 when compared with that for 1980 (0.283 as against 0.134 for 1981 and 1980 respectively). As a result, the manuring variable may be capturing part of the plough-team variable's effect in the 1981 regression, attributing too great an influence to manure in this year. However, it is also the case that 1981 exhibited a better distribution of rainfall with respect to the flowering and grain-filling stages in the rapid-millet variety's development, which may have allowed the manure to exert a greater influence on final yield than in 1980.

Manure A comparison of the estimated response in output from the manuring variable between the two years shows the greater value and significance of the level of manuring in 1981. Table 6.1 shows that the marginal value product at the mean for the manuring variable was 70 per cent higher in 1981 and of greater statistical significance than the value for 1980. The data in Table 6.2 show that the value of an additional unit of manure at the mean observation in 1981 was more than double that in 1980. This large increase in the effect of an extra unit of dung in 1981 was the result both of the lower mean level of manuring per hectare in 1981, as compared with 1980, and of differences in the pattern of rainfall received in the two years. However, as noted above, there was also greater multi-collinearity between manure and plough-team use per hectare in 1981 (see Table 5.1) which may have biased upwards the coefficient on the manuring variable.

Variability in the marginal value of dung will be taken into account in calculating the returns to well investment in Chapter 8. The two years studied here provide strong evidence for the high returns to be gained from digging a well. The size of the potential returns to be obtained in years of good rainfall from getting access to more dung has been well recognized by farmers in Kala, as is shown by the growth in private wells from 16 in 1979 to 43 in 1983.

Comparing the marginal returns to factors with their prices

The purpose here is to compare the marginal returns to each factor with its price, and to show that the marginal return to most factors at the mean is far in excess of the price at which factors are sometimes available for hire. Several reasons will be put forward for this: 'price-setting' according to tradition rather than market-clearing forces, imperfections in the market due to technical or environmental factors, and the effects of production risks on the demand for purchased inputs. The consequences of the very limited development of markets will then be discussed in relation to household-investment strategies and the desire by households to ensure themselves secure access to labour, plough-team services, and dung.

In the following discussion of factor prices and productivities, kilograms of millet are used as the unit of account. Both weeding and harvesting labour are usually paid for in millet, while plough-team services are exchanged against labour time, the value of which can be calculated in terms of millet. Use of millet as the unit of account, instead of money, avoids problems arising from seasonal fluctuations in the price of millet and the question of the price at which to value it. However, there are also disadvantages to the use of millet to measure prices. The 'value' or shadow price of millet will vary considerably from harvest time to the farming season, especially for the poorest households where the main granary may be empty soon after the rains start. The seasonal change in the shadow price of grain will be only partially reflected in seasonal market-price fluctuations, as grain-deficit households are constrained by the lack both of disposable income and of credit with which to acquire millet during periods of shortage.

Table 6.2 presented estimates calculated at the mean observation of the marginal returns in terms of millet of 1 extra unit of labour, plough-team work, and dung for each crop and year. In order to compare the productivities of each factor with the price at which they are occasionally available, the cost of 1 man-day's work of weeding labour is also shown, equalling 5 kg of millet (the wage of 3 measures of millet, or 4.5 kg, plus grain for the midday meal). By tradition, the hire of 1 plough-team day's work is paid for by returning 2 man-days' of weeding work and thus costs the equivalent of 10 kg of millet. This is the 'price' when exchanges of these services are made between households. As discussed in the following chapter, plough teams are also hired for cash by individuals, particularly retired women. Old women usually have to pay 1,500 to 2,500 FCFA for a day's work (equivalent to between 25 and 35 kg of millet) depending on whether the team works a half or full day. They have to pay a higher price than do households because lesser social value is attached to helping private individuals gain extra income than to helping other village households grow enough food for their members.

The large differences between marginal product and price shown in Table 6.2 may also be due to the importance attached by villagers to the price of certain commodities remaining constant in volume terms. Thus, for example, 1 man-day's work in the farming season has long been exchanged for 3 measures of grain. The price of labour in cash terms has obviously risen over the years with the general rise in grain and other prices. When the price of farming labour is quoted in cash, it is calculated at the rainy-season price of millet (3 × 125 FCFA), equal in 1980 and 1981 to 375 FCFA per day. Similarly, milk is always exchanged against millet on a volume-to-volume basis, despite seasonal shifts in their relative availabilities (see Chapter 10). Having a common policy on prices within the village community is considered valuable, demonstrating both the desire to avoid strictly monetary relations between village households, held to be damaging to Bambara social principles of equality and reciprocity, and the ability of the village community to act together. In addition, given the high variability in yields and factor productivities from year to year, it would be very difficult for a farmer to fix on a price *ex ante* for hiring a factor that would necessarily be close to that of its marginal productivity *ex post*.

Weeding labour   Only in 1980 was the coefficient on the labour variable for bush-field millet statistically significant. In this case, the value in millet of an extra man-day of weeding was roughly twice the price at which labour was occasionally available for hire. This was not unexpected, given the difficulty with which farmers can get extra labour, due to the abundance of cultivable land in this area and the lack of a landless labouring class available for hire. While farmers in Kala do not actively go in search of labour to hire, they are usually willing to take on additional workers during the farming season should they present themselves. For example, households which have run out of millet will send one or two of their workers to earn grain elsewhere, thereby feeding the rest of the family. In 1981, neither of the two estimates were statistically significant due to the general difficulties associated with the labour variable, discussed earlier. Their relative values were, however, as anticipated with higher marginal labour productivity in village- as compared with bush-field millet.

Plough-team work   All four estimates for the value of one plough-team day's work were based on coefficients which were statistically significant at the 90 per cent level or above. Taking the cost of hiring a team for one day as 10 kg of millet, it can be seen that in all cases the value of one plough-team day was in excess of this price and, for village-field millet, very substantially so. Chapter 4 discussed the relatively limited development of factor markets and the possibilities for hiring a plough team for those households without their own equipment. It was shown that the few households without their own team could usually get help from others for the most essential task—the preparation of village-field land before sowing. However, hiring a plough team for other work was much more difficult, as the plough-team owner preferred to use the team on his own land, a preference amply justified by the data in Table 6.2. The figures would imply a large net loss at the mean observation were the plough team hired-out instead of being used in the owner's field; in the most extreme case of village-field millet in 1980, by hiring out the plough team for one day, the owner would lose between 120 and 150 kg of millet, depending on the value put on the receipt of two man-days' weeding work taken in exchange. The price paid for the hire of a plough team is very low and, as can be seen, bears little relationship to the estimated value of the two commodities exchanged, at least as far as village-field millet is concerned.

Some households without ploughs have been able to borrow a team from a neighbouring Fulani herder who is willing to make this exchange because he has access to very little household labour for weeding, due to small household size, the non-participation of Fulani women in agricultural work, and the conflicting demands on labour during the rainy season from livestock care and farming a millet field. Consequently, the value to Fulani fields from a couple of days of hand-weeding is probably considerably higher than that estimated here for the mean Bambara household.

Manure   The final row in Table 6.2 presents the estimated value at the mean of an extra unit of manure in kilograms of village-field millet. An additional unit of this input was worth twice as much in 1981 as compared with 1980, which is largely due to the rainfall distribution, as discussed above. No price exists for manure against which the value of an additional unit can be compared. Manure is neither bought nor sold, access to this factor depending on the ownership of livestock and of a private well. The following chapter investigates the costs and returns to manuring strategies, such as well-digging. It will be seen from this that investment in digging a well can provide a very high and rapid return on the capital invested, the implicit price of manure in terms of the cost of well-digging being low in comparison with the benefits to be reaped from this investment, in years of reasonable rainfall as in 1980 and 1981.

Accounting for the divergence between marginal value products and prices

The above comparison has shown the wide divergence existing between factor prices and their marginal productivities. Several explanations can be offered to account for these differences and the generally poor level of market development.

Traditional 'prices' Taking the example of plough-team services, it was seen that the return at the mean of an extra plough-team day was very much greater, especially in village-field millet production, than the 'price' at which plough teams could occasionally be hired by the household, set by tradition at the exchange of one plough-team day for two days of hand-weeding labour. The large gap between price and productivity means that those households without a team have a very strong incentive to borrow a team but find it hard to get more than a couple of days, usually to help them complete the ridging of the village fields. The market for plough-team services is controlled by rationing rather than prices. A household looking for a team to borrow must spend much time pursuing possible exchange relations in Kala and neighbouring settlements, using the power of kinship ties to support the case for help being given.

Value is attached by the community to the existence of stable exchange rates between commodities and the avoidance of monetized relations between households in the village. On the one hand, this cultural value probably accounts in part for the relative lack of economic and social hierarchy in Bambara communities, in comparison with Hausa society in northern Nigeria and southern Niger (P. Hill, 1972; Watts, 1983; Sutter, 1982). On the other hand, control of the market through rationing rather than realistic prices makes it more difficult for asset-less households to gain access to certain resources from which they would reap a high return.

Environmental and technical factors The constraints of the short rainy season in Kala and the consequent tight timing requirements for different operations further reduces the scope for a market in factor services to develop. Development of the plough-team market in particular is hampered by problems of timing. The value of one plough-team day of work depends crucially on its timing in relation to recent rainfall, especially where ridging of land before sowing is concerned, as farmers want to ensure that seed is in the ground before too much of the moisture from a shower has evaporated. A plough-less household may find it relatively easy to borrow a team five or six days after a shower but impossible to get one on the day following a heavy rainfall, as the team's value to its owner will be much greater in the latter case. As already noted, the generally low level of population density in this region and the abundance of land to cultivate explain the very limited development of a market in labour services.

Risk The presence of production risks may also account for the persistence of marginal value products in excess of each factor's market price. Where a factor X is hired, where there is some risk to production, and where producers are risk averse, it is likely that marginal productivities will be greater than factor prices and that:

$$MPX(1 - r) = P_X$$

where *MPX* is the marginal product of factor X and P_X is the unit price. The coefficient, r, represents the producer's degree of risk aversion; the larger its size, the further will be the marginal product from its value under conditions of no risk. Bliss and Stern (1982) argue that it is production risk and producers' risk aversion which is largely to blame for the considerable differences which they find between the estimated marginal value products and the prices of each factor. Farmers may have to borrow money to purchase certain inputs, like fertilizer, and when crops fail, those who cannot repay the loan may be faced with an irreversible worsening of their position involving further indebtedness and the possible loss of land. Faced with such a prospect, small, poor farmers prefer to keep their purchases of inputs to a minimum, to reduce the possibility of social and economic disaster, even at the cost of significantly reduced yields. In the case of Kala, there are certainly high risks to production and farmers are risk averse. However, no credit is currently available by which means poorer farmers could finance the purchase of productive assets, nor has land become a marketable or pledgeable asset through which credit markets could be developed.

However, in the past an analogous situation existed for Kala as that described by Bliss and Stern (1982), when in the 1940s and 1950s the colonial government established a credit scheme to help farmers purchase ploughs and work-oxen. The loans were to be repaid over three to five years and repayments were known to have been demanded with some force in other villages in order to set an example to farmers taking out new loans. Not a single farmer in Kala took out a loan for the purchase of a plough team, although they had seen the potential benefits to be derived from them. They argued that production risks made it impossible to be certain that they would be able to find the money to pay off the debt at the due date because harvests of millet invariably fluctuate from year to year. The consequences of becoming indebted to the state were known to be severe; to be in debt is to have a rope (*juru*) around one's neck, one's creditor being able to lead one as he likes. As a result, people in Kala waited until they had saved the money they needed to purchase oxen and a plough from their own resources rather than take out a loan, thereby freeing themselves from the fear of default.

Three explanations have been given for the imperfection of factor markets in Kala and the large gap which exists between the marginal product of a factor and the price at which it is sometimes available for hire. Poor market development creates a strong incentive for households to ensure themselves secure access to supplies of different factors used in crop production: dung, oxen plough teams, and labour.

Comparing the returns to different farmers of oxen plough teams and dung

The aim of this comparison is to investigate the extent to which there are large differences in the returns to each factor when farmers are compared amongst themselves. The last few pages have taken estimated factor productivities calculated at the mean observation. However, account should also be taken of the range of factor returns which are likely to accrue both from differing levels of input use per hectare and from differences in the mix of productive assets owned and inputs used. Variation in the returns to different factors from farmer to farmer is of especial importance when looking at the investment decisions faced by them. For example, it is probable that the return from purchase of a plough team by a household which formerly was without this equipment will be higher than for a similar household buying its third or fourth team. In like manner, the marginal return from the first private well dug by a household is likely to exceed that from second and subsequent wells for a household of equivalent size. However, farmers are partially able to counteract the tendency for marginal returns to investment to decline by increasing the land area they farm. The acquisition of a new plough team or the digging of a new well will be accompanied by an extension in area cultivated. This allows farmers to keep levels of input use per hectare low and thus to reap high marginal returns from the use of each factor in comparison with the returns which would obtain under conditions of land scarcity. However, a household must also have sufficient labour to manage and work with these additional factors.

  In order to compare returns between farmers, the estimated production function derived from the pooled input–output data was used to provide the marginal value product of a particular factor at various different factor mixtures. The results of this exercise are presented in Tables 6.3 and 6.5 and are then discussed.

Village-field millet

The general production function estimated for village-field millet was:
$$Q/ha = A(HWL/ha)^a(PTD/ha)^b(k + MN/ha)^c$$
Differentiating partially with respect to the manuring variables gives:

$$\frac{\delta(Q/ha)}{\delta(MN/ha)} = Ac(HWL/ha)^a(PTD/ha)^b(k + MN/ha)^{c-1}$$

  In order to investigate how the marginal product of manure changes at different levels of manure use and as plough-team inputs change,

TABLE 6.3. *Marginal returns to manure use at different levels of manure and plough-team use*

| Plough-team days per hectare (PTD/ha) | Manuring levels per ha | | | | |
	0.30	1.66	4.20	6.73	9.27
1.29	202.4	50.0	23.5	15.9	12.3
2.73	282.9	70.0	32.8	22.3	17.2
4.17	341.8	84.5	39.6	26.9	20.7

Notes: The levels of manuring use per hectare taken correspond, starting with the lowest value, to the constant term taken, the mean less one standard deviation, the mean, the mean plus one standard deviation, the mean plus two standard deviations.

The relationship between $\delta(Q/ha)/\delta(MN/ha)$ at each level of plough-team use is represented by the following:

$$\text{for 1.29 PTD/ha: } \delta(Q/ha)/\delta(MN/ha) = 75.66\ (MN + k)^{-0.817}$$
$$\text{for 2.73 PTD/ha: } \delta(Q/ha)/\delta(MN/ha) = 105.76\ (MN + k)^{-0.817}$$
$$\text{for 4.17 PTD/ha: } \delta(Q/ha)/\delta(MN/ha) = 127.76\ (MN + k)^{-0.817}$$

coefficients were taken from the estimated pooled-data production function shown in Table 5.4. The effect of changes in the hand-weeding variable has not been pursued because this variable was not found to be of any statistical significance; consequently, the mean value for this variable from the pooled data was substituted into the equation. Three levels of plough-team use were investigated, that of the mean value for plough-team days per hectare, and those of the mean plus or minus one standard deviation. The marginal product of manure use was examined at five different levels, as shown in the table above, the values taken representing most of the range found in use of this input per hectare in the two years studied.

The declining marginal returns to manure use as levels of this input rise per hectare can be seen from the table above. For a household digging its first well, raising manuring per hectare from a very low level, there are very high returns to the investment. The fall in the marginal return to rising manure use is very steep, so that the marginal benefit from raising manuring levels above the village mean of 4.20 units per ha is only around one-tenth of that gained at the lowest manuring level considered here. The very high marginal return to manure use at low levels of manuring explains why farmers usually accompany the digging of a new well with the cutting of a large new village-field plot. The well will be partly used to raise the level of fertility on existing fields, but mainly to fertilize the new field over a period of several years. A fairly light manuring policy is especially favoured by farmers who fear the effects of low rainfall on highly manured soils.

TABLE 6.4. *Well-ownership and levels of manure use per hectare, 1981*

No. of wells	No. of households	Mean MN/ha
0	7	2.35
		(2.55)
1	17	5.50
		(3.13)
2	5	9.18
		(5.12)
Village sample	29	5.37
		(3.95)

Note: Figures in brackets are the standard deviation of manure use in each class of household.

Table 6.3 also shows the considerable addition to marginal returns obtained by raising the level of plough-team use. For the three levels of use considered, the highest produces a marginal return some 70 per cent above that of the lowest. These returns diminish as plough-team use rates rise per hectare, which is to be expected given the general form of the production function estimated. It would also appear that the greatest marginal return can be gained by increasing plough-team use at the lowest manuring levels. This may be due to the benefit derived by careful land preparation and weeding of fields in order to maximize the returns to the limited amount of dung available. However, it is possible, given the significant correlation between plough-team and manuring variables, that the analysis has underestimated the value of a high plough-team input at high manuring levels, when heavy weed growth means that timely plough and hand-weeding work becomes crucial in achieving high millet yields.

Input use and asset ownership Table 6.4 shows the average use of manure by households according to the number of wells owned. As may be seen, levels of manuring rise as a first and second well is dug. This would indicate that, while farmers do expand the area they cultivate as they gain access to more dung, this area expansion is not sufficient to keep the level of manuring down to mean levels. However, the standard deviation within each class of households is high, especially so for the households with two wells apiece, one of which had the very high manuring level of 17.60 units per ha. Thus, in general, investment in a well raises the level of dung used per hectare, suggesting that there may be diminishing marginal returns to well-digging as the number of wells owned by a household rises. This possibility will be considered more fully within the context of expected returns from well-investment to different farmers in the following chapter.

Bush-field millet

The general production function estimated for bush-field millet was:

$$Q/ha = B(CTW/ha)^d(PTD/ha)^e PNB^f SOIL^g SWI^h RAIN^j$$

Differentiating partially with respect to the plough-team variable gives:

$$\frac{\delta(Q/ha)}{\delta(PTD/ha)} = Be(CTW/ha)^d(PTD/ha)^{e-1} PNB^f SOIL^g SWI^h RAIN^j$$

To investigate how the marginal return of plough-team work changes at different levels of plough-team use and as labour input per hectare changes, coefficients were taken from the estimated pooled-data production function shown in Table 5.5. The last three dummy variables were taken at their mean values for the pooled data, while the first, *PNB* or the proportion of newly cleared land in the bush field, was taken at three different values in order to assess its importance in the overall productivity of other factors. The *PNB* was taken at its mean value of 0.327, at a high value of 1.0, indicating an entirely new bush field, and at a low of 0.1, for a field very largely composed of land already cultivated for at least one farming season. Both the plough-team and the hand-weeding variables were taken at four different levels of use and the marginal productivity of plough-team use was estimated at each of these combinations, the results of which are presented in Table 6.5.

Several points emerge from this table. First, there is a sharp decline in the marginal return to plough-team use moving from the lowest level to the mean, after which the decline flattens out. This conforms with the general shape expected of the relationship between marginal factor returns and levels of factor use derived from a Cobb–Douglas production function. Secondly, the fall in marginal returns is somewhat dampened by the addition of more hand-weeding labour; within the range of observations taken, the highest level of labour input per hectare, in comparison with the lowest level, adds 27 per cent to the marginal return. The addition of extra labour, however, contributes less and less in absolute terms as plough-team use per hectare rises. Thirdly, taking account of the effect of varying the *PNB* variables increases considerably the range in marginal returns from the 27 per cent noted above to 78 per cent between the extreme values taken in each class of plough-team use per hectare. There is no general tendency for plough-team use per hectare to rise with rising *PNB*; having a bush field with a high proportion of newly cleared land requires a lot of plough-team work at the start of the farming season, when the land must be ridged before sowing, but much if not all of the subsequent weeding work will be done by hand.

TABLE 6.5. *Marginal returns at different levels of plough-team and labour use*

Hand-weeding labour (man-days/ha)	Plough-team use (PTD/ha)			
	0.50	1.57	2.36	3.14
	41.6	18.8	14.1	11.6
2.90	49.1	22.2	16.7	13.7
	58.4	26.4	19.8	16.3
	46.2	20.9	15.7	12.9
4.36	54.5	24.6	18.5	15.7
	64.8	29.3	22.1	18.1
	49.8	22.5	16.9	13.9
5.82	58.7	26.5	20.0	16.4
	69.9	31.6	23.8	19.5
	52.8	23.8	18.0	14.7
7.28	62.2	28.1	21.2	17.4
	74.1	33.4	25.2	20.6

Note: The levels taken for plough-team use per hectare refer from the lowest value to: a low plough-team use per hectare, the mean value of plough-team use, the mean plus half the standard deviation, the mean plus one standard deviation.

For the labour variable the input levels chosen refer to: the mean less two standard deviations, the mean less one standard deviation, the mean of 5.82 man-days per hectare, the mean plus one standard deviation respectively.

Variation in the PNB variables is shown taking three values, 0.327, 1.0, and 0.1, the marginal returns for which are as follows:

> PNB(1.0)
> PNB(0.327) for each combination of other input uses
> PNB(0.1)

Input use and asset ownership It was shown earlier in Table 6.4 that the level of manure use per hectare was positively correlated with the number of wells owned by the household. In the case of oxen plough teams, no clear relationship exists between the level of plough-team use per hectare and either the number of plough teams owned by the household or the ratio of plough teams per worker. This suggests that households keep the number of plough teams owned roughly in line with household size and area cultivated, so that there is less variation in input use per hectare than in the case of manuring. Only for those households without permanent access to a plough team are plough-team use rates per hectare very low. For example, of the two households without a plough team permanently at their disposal during the rainy season of 1981, one household used 0.38 plough-team days per hectare, compared with the village mean for that year of 1.40, while the second household was unable to borrow a plough team at all for its bush-field work and subsequently had to abandon this field because the weeds had taken over. For these households, investment in oxen plough teams should yield high returns as it would allow them to raise their rates of plough-team use from currently very low levels.

Conclusions

This chapter has presented an analysis of the returns to factors in production of the two millet varieties in 1980 and 1981 and has compared the marginal returns obtained by different farmers. It has also noted the very limited development of markets for goods and services in this village and has shown the great disparity which exists between estimated marginal returns to factors and the prices at which these are occasionally available.

The comparison of estimated factor returns for the two farming seasons showed the much higher returns to be gained in both years from cultivating the short-cycle village-field millet on manured soils. This explains the current farming strategy in Kala which is characterized by a gradual shift of resources towards this rapid-millet variety. However, farmers have not abandoned their bush fields, partly because they cannot afford to risk total dependence on a single-crop variety, given the high variability in rainfall distribution from one year to the next. In addition, there are relatively tight timing requirements for the sowing of village-field millet which limits the period within the rainy season during which it can profitably be sown. The main factor limiting village-field expansion, however, is the limited access for many farmers to supplies of manure, an input which for households without their own cattle herd must be derived entirely from establishing manure–water contracts with migrant pastoralists who visit the village for several months of the dry season.

PART III

FARM INVESTMENT

7

INTRODUCTION

An important aim of this research was to investigate changes in the pattern of investment in Kala over the past few decades, the range of variation in returns to the main productive farm assets, and the way these were related to different household characteristics. In this and the following chapters, we focus on three assets in particular—wells, oxen plough teams, and breeding cattle—and assess the variability in their returns from one type of investor to another, in relation to a variety of different assumptions. The main cause of variability to be examined here is that arising from farmers' differing access to resources, scales of operation, objectives, and constraints. Account is taken of how returns vary in relation to variations in rainfall, costs, and the strategies pursued by farmers in the period following the investment. Results from the previous chapter are used to explain both the changing pattern of asset holdings in the village and the allocation of substantial resources to the maintenance and expansion of the domestic group.

We begin, however, with a brief survey of how the investment literature deals with questions of risk and the derivation of criteria for comparing the flow of returns from alternative assets under conditions of uncertainty. This is followed by an examination of the reasons for variability in returns to investment from one farmer to another. In subsequent chapters we investigate the range of expected returns to each of the three main investments in wells, oxen plough teams, and breeding cattle before comparing returns to the different investments and showing how the changing pattern of asset holding in Kala has responded to changes in environmental and institutional factors over the last twenty to thirty years. We note, however, certain constraints on returns to these investments in the longer term.

INVESTMENT MODELS

The problem faced by any investor is that of choosing how to allocate current resources between different sectors and over different time periods, in order to maximize utility. This involves determining the optimum scale and timing of resource allocation among different yielding assets, given the investor's own preference over time for consumption and leisure.

Uncertainty about the future tends to put a high value on quick returns from any investment or, in the absence of this, on flexibility in asset holding (Hirshleifer, 1970). This flexibility can take the form of the asset's services being easily transferred from one sector to another, or of the asset being easily marketed. Flexibility in assets owned in Kala will be examined in later chapters, in the light of the risks to which each investment is subject.

A number of models exist for assessing different patterns of investment. The simplest decision-making models, such as the maximization of net present value or of the internal rate of return, derive criteria for choosing among different investments based on a comparison of the flow of net returns from alternative uses of funds. Partial account can be taken of capital-market imperfections and of uncertainty by the use of linear programming and of sensitivity analysis, respectively. The investor's utility function is assumed to be a linear function of the net return in each period, aggregated over the life of the project and discounted to take account of positive time preference. Explicit account of risk is taken in more sophisticated models which consider the probability distribution of returns in each time period.

Portfolio models similarly take risk as a central element in determining the optimal investment strategy. The decision to allocate resources to one asset will be determined not only by the asset's expected return and its variance, but also by the correlation between that asset's return and the return on other assets held. Investors reduce their exposure to risk, for any given expected return, by building up a portfolio of assets whose individual returns are less than perfectly correlated (Tobin, 1958; Markowitz, 1959).

A variety of approaches and criteria is used in the following three chapters for the comparison and appraisal of the three key investments made by farmers in Kala. Fairly simple criteria, involving net present value and the payback period are employed to compare the variability in returns across different farmers, according to their access to other resources. Following this comparison, account is taken of the risks associated with each asset and the extent to which farmers can reduce their overall vulnerability to risk by building up a portfolio of assets. For this, account must be taken of the expected return on each asset and its variability over time and of the correlation between returns on different assets and the dependence of one asset's return on the performance of all others. Each of the three assets will be described in turn and the following questions posed. What is the expected return and how does this vary from year to year, and from one producer to another? What form does risk take both to the capital value of the asset and to its flow of services? Can risk be controlled or reduced? Are the asset or its services marketable? How flexible is the asset, and consequently its value, to changing economic and technical conditions? It must also be asked not only what are the relative merits of investment in each asset, but also what are the consequences of not making a particular investment? The particularly vulnerable position of well-less households will be noted here and examined in greater detail later.

Variability in returns to investors

In examining the range in returns to different investors from the three main productive assets, we aim first to clarify the conditions under which high or low returns are obtained, investigate the complementarities between different assets, and show the strong correlation between high returns to investment and large household size.

The returns to investment vary across households in Kala as a result of a number of factors:

(i) Variable access to factors of production, combined with the poor development of factor markets through which farmers could gain access to the assets they do not own themselves (if they had the resources to do so). Households differ in their access to labour, manure, and plough-team services. Certain investments, particularly wells and plough teams, complement each other. For example, a household digging its first well will reap higher returns to this investment if it also has access to an oxen plough team, which allows it to expand considerably the area of manured land cultivated with village-field millet.

(ii) Differences in the scale on which farmers are operating, largely due to variation in the size of the domestic group, given the low significance of hired labour and other inputs in Bambara peasant production and the low degree of capital accumulation. Scale is important where assets are indivisible and relatively costly. In the absence of a credit market, certain households may be unable to mobilize a large enough investible surplus to purchase costly assets. In addition, capital investments like an oxen plough team may have an optimal level of operation in relation to the associated labour-force and area cultivated, below which returns fall significantly. Households cannot necessarily achieve this optimum level in the absence of a labour market.

(iii) The differing opportunity cost of resources between households, the monetary value of costs and returns being only an imperfect measure of the real cost and benefits accruing to the household. The marginal utility of a given sum of money is likely to be much greater for a household with very few resources, and consequently, the real cost of any investment outlay will be much higher in terms of forgone consumption than for a wealthier farmer. For example, a fairly large, rich household with ample stocks of grain will find it much easier to mobilize the sum needed to hire a labourer to dig a new well. For a small, poor household, the allocation of an equivalent sum of money will have severe implications for how household members will be fed over the coming year.

(iv) Farmers in Kala are faced by considerable risks, not only to returns from the current farming season, due to rainfall variability, but also to longer-term returns from their portfolio of assets—wells, cattle, and household members. Households vary in their vulnerability to these risks and their degree of risk aversion, depending on the size and composition of their asset holdings. Large households which have a diverse portfolio will be more tolerant of risk and better able to take advantage of new economic opportunities as they arise than smaller households. There is evidence from elsewhere in West Africa that larger households were the first to adopt oxen-drawn ploughs (Tiffen, 1976; Weil, 1970), having the investible surplus and, more importantly, being more able to bear the risk of uncertain returns in the investment's initial years. Producers taking up a new technology early in its cycle often face high risk but also reap high returns which accentuates economic differentiation among producers.

HOUSEHOLD TYPES

In order to compare the returns to each investment for different kinds of household, four household types have been taken, the characteristics of which are described below. The same four households are used in the analysis of each of the investments examined in the next three chapters, so that returns can be compared for the same investment between different households and between different investments for each household type. The choice of household types illustrates the range of domestic groups found in a Bambara village like Kala, the purpose being to show the variation in returns to investment which results from their differing scales of operation and access to other assets. The types do not represent particular classes of household defined in strict statistical terms, nor do they necessarily correspond to any one particular household from the village. However, they do follow the general pattern whereby the smallest households are those with the fewest assets, be they in the form of wells, oxen plough teams, or livestock holdings. Table 7.1 summarizes the main characteristics assumed for each of the four types examined, in terms of household size, assets owned, and areas under each millet variety.

Household A typifies the small, poor household in Kala. It owns neither oxen nor breeding cattle and must rely on borrowing plough animals and equipment from elsewhere. It owns no well and, because of its small work-force, must hire labour to dig the well-shaft were it to decide to invest in one. It has no supply of dung under its control and must depend on the occasional basketful of compound sweepings to

TABLE 7.1. *Assumed characteristics of four household types in pre-investment period*

	Households			
	A	B	C	D
Size	small	small	medium	large
No. of workers	2–4	2–4	7–10	15–20
Manure index	0	5	35	90
Asset ownership:				
wells	0	0	1	1
oxen plough team	0	1	2	3
total cattle	0	5	20	75
Initial area farmed (ha)				
village field	1.5	1.5	6.0	12.0
bush field	10.0	20.0	30.0	40.0

fertilize its small village-field holdings. If a well can be dug, however, the security of household food supplies is much improved and this has now become the priority investment for such households.

Household B is a small household which owns its own plough team and several head of cattle other than oxen. Even without a well, it gains access to a certain amount of dung from its own animals. Many of the households which have recently dug themselves a well are of this type. The well is dug primarily for exchange of its water against dung from visiting herds, allowing an expansion of the area which it cultivates with the short-cycle village-field millet. With its small work-force, the household must hire labour to dig the well-shaft, paying for this by the sale of one of its cattle.

Household C is typical of the mean village household, operating a couple of plough teams and owning a well of its own. It also has a non-oxen cattle holding of 15–16 head which supplements the manure received from its well. With a work-force of 7–10 workers, it has sufficient labour to dig its own well without resorting to hiring outsiders.

Household D represents one of the largest households in the village, with 15–20 workers. It runs three oxen plough teams and has a large non-oxen cattle holding of 65–70 head. Already owning one well, it can easily finance the digging of a second, either by using its own labour or by hiring a blacksmith for the job, in exchange for a young animal.

8

WELL-DIGGING

Wells have always played a role of great importance in this large arid zone north of the River Niger, as is seen in the abundance of oral legends relating to the discovery or drying-up of water sources. As explained in Chapter 2, until Malian Independence in 1960, only the village chief had the right to dig wells within the village territory, so households other than the chief's did not have their own private wells. Independence brought a change in the law whereby all Malians were entitled freely to exploit land and water resources and, as a result, well-digging by individual households in Kala gradually became established. As a result, many village households are now involved in manure–water exchange contracts with visiting pastoralists during the dry season.

The first well belonging to a household other than the chief's was dug in 1963, followed by several others over the next few years. By 1979, more than half of the village households (15 out of 29) had their own private wells and by 1982, 75 per cent of households (22 out of 29) had their own wells. This progression in private-well investment, including the large increase in 1983, can be seen from Fig. 8.1. In addition to private wells, there has always been a number of public wells, of which there are currently five, used for domestic-water supplies. One public well, the *kolonba*, or big well, to which the founding lineages have priority access for their herds, is deep enough to water several cattle herds throughout the dry season.

DISTRIBUTION OF WELLS

Data on the distribution of wells is presented in Table 8.1. It may be seen that by 1982, only 7 out of the 29 households in the village were still without a well of their own, these 7 being the smallest, poorest households in Kala. Key characteristics of these well-less households are presented later in Table 8.9 and discussed thereafter.

Table 8.1 shows that in the years 1980–1 the number of private wells grew by 69 per cent, from 16 to 27. While this growth in wells dug seemed very impressive during the period of research, the subsequent period has seen a further increase, with a total of 16 wells being dug in the single dry season of 1983—an increase of 60 per cent—from 27 to 43 private wells. Subsequently, following the appalling harvests of 1984, well-digging has slowed down greatly, with only 3 wells dug between 1984 and 1988.

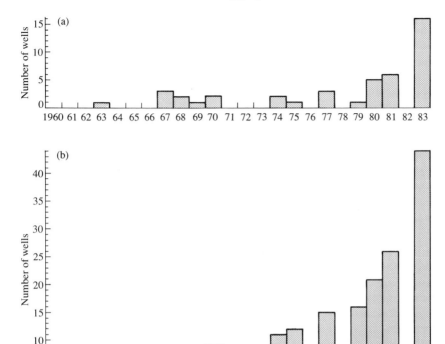

FIG. 8.1. Well-digging by households in Kala, 1960–1983.
(a) Number of wells dug by households per year
(b) Cumulative total of private wells dug

Four out of the 11 wells dug in 1980 and 1981 were second wells for households wishing to expand the area cultivated with village-field millet. Most of these households have their own cattle herd which takes much of the water from the existing well, thereby limiting the quantity available for establishing manure–water contracts with visiting pastoralists.

Table 8.2 presents data on the number of wells dug in the two dry seasons of 1980 and 1981, the status of households digging these wells, and the means with which the wells were dug. The data show that larger households used their own labour for well-digging, while smaller households had to hire labour for this task. Of the 16 wells dug in the dry season of 1983, only 2 were first wells, 10 were second wells, and 4 represented a third well for certain households.

Differences in the speed with which households have invested money and labour in digging a well are a result of:

TABLE 8.1. *Well-ownership in Kala, by the end of 1981*

	Households with			
	No well	One well	Two wells	Total
	7	17	5	27
Private wells:				
dug in 1980 (22% of total)		4	2	6
dug in 1981 (19% of total)		3	2	5

TABLE 8.2. *Well-digging in 1980 and 1981*

No. of wells	11
No. of households:	11
for whom first well	7
for whom second well	4
Financed by:	
household labour	7
(mean no. of workers 10.5)	
hired labour	4
(mean no. of workers 4.1)	
Paid for by:	
livestock sales	2
grain sales	2

The cost Well-digging requires an outlay of capital to finance the purchase of pickaxe, hire of a blacksmith to dig the well if household labour is not to be used, and to provide for the work-party which will reinforce the well-head. Details of these costs are laid out in Table 8.3. For the smallest, poorest households, the cost of well-digging has been insuperable. They lack the labour-force which could dig the well and they also lack those assets which could finance the hire of a blacksmith to do the work.

Livestock holdings and date of settlement Households differ in the date of their settlement in Kala. The earliest settlers (17 out of 29 households) have prior access for their herds at the one public well large enough to water stock. Households whose forefathers arrived later in the village, during the nineteenth century, must wait for the founders' cattle to be watered before their own herds can drink. For a later arrival with a large cattle holding, there are strong incentives to get a well dug early, as the herd can then be watered at dawn and spend the day at pasture.

Household size and political strength In the early years following Independence, a household digging a private well faced considerable hostility from the chiefly lineage, despite the change in the chief's legal position over control of water resources. The first well to be dug after 1960 was by the leading rival to the chief, belonging to one of the other two founding families. This man was able to act as a test case in the establishment of rights in this field of activity, not only because of the family's long settlement in the village but also because his household was sufficiently large and wealthy to withstand intimidation. The main households to follow this man's lead in the subsequent period of well-digging also belonged to the largest and strongest families in the village who could claim to have also been among the first settlers of the village.

THE PROFITABILITY OF WELL-DIGGING

Costs of well-digging

The cost of digging and maintaining a well over a five-year period is summarized in Table 8.3. The cost of digging the well-shaft varies from 15,000 to 25,000 FCFA, depending on whether household or hired labour is used for this task. Where household labour is available, the cash outlay for well-digging is much reduced, as the household does not pay its own members. There is, however, an opportunity cost to the use of household labour, as these workers could be earning cash on migration, equal to around 5,000 FCFA per month per worker, or a total sum of 15,000 FCFA for well-digging by three young men for a period of one month. Other costs from using household labour may also be considerable; for example, one household which dug a well in 1981 using its own work-force, saw the collapse and death of one of its young men, a youth in his early 20s, a death attributed to the very heavy work in which he had been engaged.

The cost of hiring labour to dig a well was 25,000 FCFA in the dry seasons of 1980 and 1981, this being either paid in cash or in the form of a young ox. The site fee is paid to a *marabout*, or holy man, who is paid to choose an appropriate place to dig the well. In fact, around Kala the choice of site is not very important, because of the large reservoir of underground water on which the village sits. The work party is made up of young men from one of the two village wards, hired to dig out the well-head and to block it in with wooden beams to prevent subsidence. While no fee is charged for this work, the new well owner must provide food for these workers—millet and meat—over the two days needed. A water trough from which cattle can drink must be bought every two years by the well owner, while the herd owner is responsible for providing equipment to draw water, such as a pulley, rope, and bucket. Maintenance costs

TABLE 8.3. *Costs of well-digging* (in FCFA)

Category of cost	Year 0	Year 1	Year 2	Year 3	Year 4	Year 5
Digging of well-shaft:						
using household labour	15,000	—	—	—	—	—
using hired labour	25,000	—	—	—	—	—
Fee for choosing site	2,500	—	—	—	—	—
Work-party for building						
well-head	6,250	—	—	—	—	—
Pickaxe	1,250	—	—	—	—	—
Water trough, replaced						
every two years	5,000	—	5,000	—	5,000	—
Maintenance: digging-out						
labour	—	3,000	3,000	3,000	3,000	3,000
Total discounted costs at 20% p.a.:						
using household						
labour = 44,850	30,000	2,500	5,550	1,750	3,850	1,200
using hired labour						
= 54,850	40,000	2,500	5,550	1,750	3,850	1,200

Note: A discount rate of 20% p.a. is taken and millet has been valued at its mid-dry season price of 50 FCFA per kg.

consist of wages for those who dig out the well each year, to remove sand that has fallen into the shaft during the rains.

The costs of well-digging vary relatively little across households, the main difference concerning whether hired or household labour is used for this task. However, even though the monetary costs do not vary greatly, as noted earlier in this chapter, the opportunity cost of resources devoted to well digging will differ from poor to rich households. One case in particular illustrates the very high cost to small, poor households of raising the cash needed to hire a worker.

This household sold a large part of its harvest in early 1980 to pay a blacksmith to dig a well in the dry season, leaving little grain for the household's own food needs. Members of the household pursued a hand-to-mouth existence in the following months, eating bush-fruit and begging millet and bran from other households in the village. The young man of the family was sent to work for others during the farming season, earning millet in return, which fed the other members of the household, enabling them to survive until the harvest was brought in. In such a case, where poverty is acute and where there are no assets which may be sold to raise cash, the burden of raising 25,000 FCFA is very much greater than for a household owning a herd of cattle, one of which may be sold with no effect on household food supplies.

1. An aerial view just after harvest shows conical stacks of millet, cattle grazing and trees dotted through the fields

2. Livestock graze the millet stubble after harvest

3. Ploughing the field at the start of the rains

4. Harvesting the village field millet: cut heads of millet are collected in a basket

6. Scything the fonio

5. Hand-held hoes are used to weed the field after passage of the weeding plough

8. During harvest time, visiting women reapers bring home their basket of millet as payment

7. Young men and boys thresh the millet

9. Women thresh and winnow grain from their private plots

10. A small plot of tobacco provides a supply of snuff and extra income

12. . . . and pounding millet

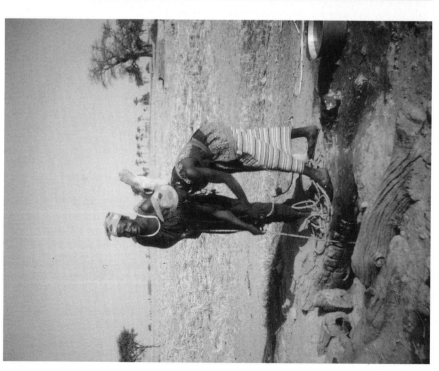

11. Women help each other to carry out many of their daily chores, such as drawing water

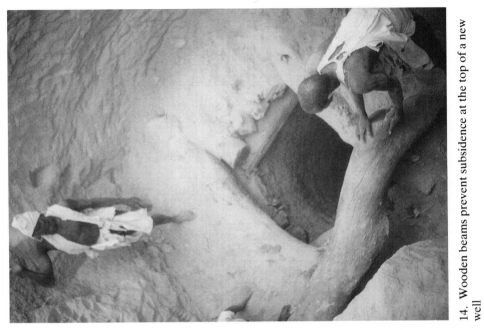

14. Wooden beams prevent subsidence at the top of a new well

13. Stored grain needs cleaning and winnowing before it can be ground into flour

15. Calves must wait, attached by a rope, until their mothers have been milked

16. Herders building their hut on the village lands once the harvest is over

Uses and value of well water

Wells are used for the watering of stock, for household needs, for irrigating small vegetable plots, and for various miscellaneous purposes, such as providing water for brick making. Livestock requirements receive priority with household and other needs taking second place, but as the hot dry season progresses, bringing increased difficulty in getting herds watered, some visiting herders will be told to move their animals elsewhere.

Watering village livestock   A cattle owner wants to have access to enough water in the village for his own animals for two reasons. Firstly, the owner then gets dung from his herd during the dry season, a valuable input for the next cropping season. Secondly, by having his animals close at hand, the stock owner is able to monitor their management and well-being. Animals are usually watered every day, either in the morning or in the evening, cattle being taken to the well where water is drawn by a team of three young men from those households with animals jointly herded together. Sheep and goats drink from a large pot in the household's courtyard, filled by women. Families from the founding lineages water their herds at the large village well, while others are watered at a well belonging to one of the members of the joint herding group. During the time that the joint herd is watering at the well of a particular household, the herd also passes the night on the fields of that same household, dung being received in exchange for water. Those households with no well of their own, but who own a few head of cattle, usually receive the joint herd onto their fields for a short period, in payment for the contribution made by their labour in the daily watering of the herd. The droppings of sheep and goats are women's property, since it is they who provide their drinking water and they carry this dung out regularly to fertilize their small plots of maize, millet, and vegetables.

Visiting herds   Visiting herds of cattle, sheep, and goats are brought to pass several months of the dry season at villages like Kala where there is an abundance of water and pasture. Most of the animals belong to Fulani and Maure pastoralists who spend the rainy season further north, but herds also come from neighbouring Bambara villages without enough water for their cattle. The herd owner makes a contract with a household owning a well whereby the herd is able to water at this well in exchange for passing the night on the fields of the well owner. The well owner may provide food for the herder, when the latter is not accompanied by his wife, and may send a son to help with watering the herd, although this work is usually paid for. As the dry season advances, the water-level sinks and wells begin to run dry, forcing some visitors to go elsewhere.

The peak number of animals in the dry season of 1981 was reached in the month of February when around 1,800 cattle (of which 1,100 were visitors') and 1,950 small stock (of which 1,250 were visitors') were watering at the village's wells. With the harvest of the rice fields around Niono, some 80 km away, completed in early March, several herds left to go in this direction to graze the stubble.

Conflicts arise occasionally between the two parties to the water–dung contract when, for instance, the herd owner takes his stock to graze during the night. Animals regain their appetite at cooler night-time temperatures but this practice deprives the well owner of dung for his field. In other cases, the herd owner may complain that the water is insufficient and demand that the well be kept for his exclusive use. Village women will be warned not to draw water from this well, at the risk of incurring the well-owner's wrath.

Household-water requirements Women spend several hours each day drawing and carrying water for household purposes, water to drink, for cooking and washing-up, for small stock, and for people to wash with. However, women in Kala are less hard-worked than those in many other villages who must queue through the night to fulfil the most basic household needs.

Having good water-supply has several advantages. Women do not have to spend long hours waiting for the well slowly to refill and consequently can spend more time on income-earning activities, such as cotton spinning. Women will also be more eager to marry into a community where water is in good supply, and the health of the community benefits when water is no longer drawn from rain-filled ponds, as the incidence of guinea-worm infection and of bacterial disease is reduced.

Irrigated gardens During the rainy season and early dry season, small fenced gardens are kept irrigated from nearby wells. In these gardens, retired women grow tomatoes and okra, while men grow tobacco. However, these irrigated plots are of only minor importance, both in terms of their output and the quantity of water used. A typical plot measures 4 m by 4 m. Only in villages closer to markets and where water is very abundant, such as along the irrigation canals of the Office du Niger, do vegetable gardens become a significant source of income.

ASSESSING RETURNS TO WELL-DIGGING

In a village like Kala, the main reason why a household digs a well is to gain access to the dung of animals watering there. An extra well around the village will also improve the supply of water for other purposes, particularly domestic-water supplies, but the main benefit to be captured by the individual household is derived from the increase in yields gained with higher levels of fertilization and from improved watering facilities for the household's cattle. The calculation of returns to well-digging presented here is based on the manuring component alone, although the benefits from reducing constraints on women's time should also be remembered.

Returns to well-digging will vary both from year to year and from one farmer to another. The significance of such variation is investigated below for each of the household types described earlier in Chapter 7. A range of assumptions is taken on which the calculation of returns is based concerning:

(i) the response of village-field millet to a particular level of manure, which will be strongly affected by the amount and distribution of rainfall during the growing season;

(ii) changes in the area cultivated, following the well being dug, some farmers greatly expanding village-field area whereas others opt for a more intensive application of manure after the new well is dug; and

(iii) changes in the level of input use per hectare following the investment, given the possibility of shifting resources from bush- to village-field millet cultivation.

Crop response The returns to well investment are based on the crop response equations estimated in Chapter 5 covering the farming seasons of 1980 and 1981. Problems with the data collection and limitations of this analysis were discussed in that chapter. Estimated coefficients for the manuring and plough-team variables, on which the analysis of this chapter depends, were subject to fewer difficulties and can be treated with greater confidence than those relating to the labour variable. The use of production coefficients derived from more than one year's data provides some indication of the variation in returns from one year to the next. However, as noted in Chapter 5, returns for the two years actually studied probably represent only a small range within the distribution of expected factor returns over a longer series of years. In the absence of detailed information on input levels and crop yields from other years, one cannot accurately assess where 1980 and 1981 lie within the expected probability distribution of returns. However, farmers themselves thought that in both years village-field millet yields were above and bush-field yields below expected 'normal' levels.

Changes in the area cultivated Table 8.4 outlines the assumed changes in village-field area following investment in a new well. A household digging a new well is assumed to expand only its village field, as the manure gained from the well is not used in the cultivation of bush-field millet. A_0 refers to the area each household is assumed to cultivate in the

Farm Investment

TABLE 8.4. *Assumed changes in village-field area following well-investment* (hectares)

Household	Initial area	Alternative assumptions	
	A_0	A_1	A_2
A	1.5	2.0	3.6
B	1.5	3.6	6.0
C	6.0	8.0	10.0
D	12.0	15.0	18.0

Note: See Chapter 7 for details of assumptions regarding the different households.

pre-investment period and is based on the average area cultivated per working household member in the village as a whole.

All those households digging a new well in the dry seasons of 1980 and 1981 subsequently cut a new village-field plot, increasing the area they cultivated with this millet variety by a varying amount, ranging from 30 per cent to 200 per cent. A_1 and A_2 represent alternative assumptions made about increases in village-field area after the well has been dug, A_2 representing the larger of the two increases in areas.

A wider range and greater proportionate increase in village-field growth has been assumed for households A and B, than for C and D, in order to assess the sensitivity of returns for the smallest households and to investigate, in particular, whether high returns to well-digging depend on having access to a plough team. Household A is assumed to lack an oxen plough team and thus cannot increase the area it farms with village-field millet by the same amount as household B. For this latter household, assumption A_2 is taken to represent an extreme strategy involving a very large increase in village-field area which requires a substantial shift in resources from bush-field millet production, if total labour and plough-team inputs available to the household are assumed to remain at their former levels. Households C and D are assumed to expand their village fields by a smaller proportion following well investment but, because of their larger scale of operation, these involve a larger absolute increase in area than for the first two households.

Changes in the level of input use per hectare   In order to calculate yields of village-field millet after a well has been dug, assumptions must be made about changes in levels of manure, plough team, and labour use per hectare. Tables 8.5–8.7 present the assumptions made about levels of each input used in the pre- and post-investment period.

TABLE 8.5. *Assumed changes in input use, pre- and post-well investment* (in manuring units)

Household	Change in area	Level of manuring per village-field ha					
		Year 0	Year 1	Year 2	Year 3	Year 4	Year 5
A	A_1	0.30[a]	2.80	5.30	7.80	7.80	7.80
	A_2	0.30[a]	1.69	3.08	4.47	4.47	4.47
B	A_1	3.63	3.08	4.47	5.85	5.85	5.85
	A_2	3.63	1.97	2.80	3.63	3.63	3.63
C	A_1	6.13	5.30	5.90	6.55	6.55	6.55
	A_2	6.13	4.30	4.80	5.30	5.30	5.30
D	A_1	7.80	6.66	6.96	7.30	7.30	7.30
	A_2	7.80	5.57	5.85	6.13	6.13	6.13

[a] A constant of 0.3 manuring units per hectare is attributed to household A to represent the residual fertility of the soil in the absence of any manure being applied, as described in Chapter 5.

TABLE 8.6. *Assumed changes in input use, pre- and post-well investment* (in plough-team days spent per village-field hectare)

Household	Change in area	Initial	Alternative assumptions	
			P_1	P_2
A	A_1	1.33	1.50	2.50
	A_2	1.33	0.83	1.39
B	A_1	2.35	0.98	2.35
	A_2	2.35	0.59	2.35
C	A_1	2.35	1.76	2.35
	A_2	2.35	1.41	2.35
D	A_1	2.35	1.88	2.35
	A_2	2.35	1.57	2.35

Manure (see Table 8.5)   A household's access to manure increases when a new well is dug, the household's manuring index being assumed to grow over the first three years of its operation by 5, 10, and 15 units respectively, after which the manuring capacity of the well stabilizes at 15 units for all subsequent years (as described in Chapter 5). Assuming a single increase in village-field area following the digging of a new well, the level of manuring per hectare will increase over the first three years before stabilizing.

TABLE 8.7. *Assumed changes in input use pre- and post-well investment* (in hand-weeding labour days per village-field hectare)

Household	Change in area	Initial	Alternative assumptions	
			L_1	L_2
A	A_1	5.74	4.31	5.74
	A_2	5.74	2.39	5.74
B	A_1	5.74	2.39	5.74
	A_2	5.74	1.44	5.74
C	A_1	5.74	4.31	5.74
	A_2	5.74	3.44	5.74
D	A_1	5.74	4.59	5.74
	A_2	5.74	3.83	5.74

Plough-team use (see Table 8.6)   Households B, C, and D are assumed to be operating in the pre-investment period at the mean level for all farm households of 2.35 plough-team days (PTD) per village-field ha. Following the digging of a well and the consequent expansion of village-field area, two alternative assumptions are considered:

(i) the first (P_1) in which the total number of plough-team days spent in the village fields remains at the pre-investment level but is now spread over a larger area, giving a lower input level per hectare, and

(ii) the second (P_2) in which the level of plough-team use per hectare is maintained at the mean level of 2.35 PTD per ha by shifting some plough-team work from the bush to the village field.

In the latter case, the cost of this shift in plough team work in terms of bush-field millet forgone can be estimated and subtracted from the extra village-field millet output obtained. In the case of household A, which has no oxen of its own, it is assumed that it can hire a total of 2 PTD for work in the village field in the pre-investment period and can hire either one (P_2) or three (P_3) extra days after having dug the well and expanded its village-field holding. The price it must pay for each PTD hired is taken as 21 kg of millet, as described under Table 6.2.

Hand-weeding labour (see Table 8.7)   This is assumed to lie in the pre-investment period at the mean level for the village for all four of the households considered here, equal to 5.74 man-days per village-field hectare. Following the digging of a well and the subsequent expansion of village-field area, two alternative cases are investigated. The first (L_1) involves the total number of man-days spent remaining the same as in the pre-investment period, but being spread over a larger area and yielding a lower level of weeding per hectare. The second (L_2) involves maintaining hand-weeding labour at the mean level per hectare by hiring labour at the going wage of 4 to 5 kg of millet per day.

NET RETURNS FROM WELL-INVESTMENT

The flow of output over a five-year period following the well being dug is calculated for each of the assumptions considered above, based on the crop-response equations estimated in Chapter 5, the limitations of which have already been noted. The two highest and two lowest values have been taken for each of the four household types in order to demonstrate the degree of variation in returns to investment gained by making different assumptions. These values are presented in Table 8.8 in the form of the present value of millet output produced over a five-year period, having taken account of the cost of hiring factors or of shifting resources from one field to the other. The value of additional millet produced as a result of the well investment is discounted at the rate of 20 per cent per annum and is given a cash value of 50 FCFA per kg, the mid-dry-season price in 1981. This relatively high discount rate is used for all three of the investments considered here and is justified by the high marginal utility of current consumption attributed to producers in this region of low incomes and high risks.

Table 8.8 shows the wide range in net present values (NPV) for different households digging a well, according to the different assumptions made. The increasing size of returns from household A to D can also be seen, attributable to the declining costs associated with larger household size and to the large quantity of complementary inputs available to larger and richer households.

The pattern of assumptions providing the lowest and highest returns to well investment is very similar between households. The lowest returns accrue when the crop-response equation for 1980 is used, which may be explained by the lower estimated marginal value product of manure in this year (see Table 6.1). Conversely, use of production coefficients from 1981, a year in which the marginal value product of manure was double that of 1980, gives the highest returns to the investment. In all cases, the lowest NPVs are found under assumption P_1, that is where no additional plough-team inputs are allocated to the village field despite the expansion in area undertaken. Conversely, the highest values are found where sufficient plough-team days have been transferred from bush to village fields to maintain this input at the mean level of 2.35 PTD per ha. This pattern of returns is due to the greater value of plough-team work in the village as opposed to the bush field and to the high marginal value product of an additional plough-team day's work when the overall input

TABLE 8.8. *Well-investment: Present value of additional output, costs, and net returns* (in FCFA)

Household	Present value output	Present value costs	Net present value (NPV)	NPV/Costs	Payback period (years)	Assumptions
A	82,800	54,850	27,950	0.51	3	1980, A_1, P_1, L_1
	86,550	54,850	31,700	0.58	2	1980, A_1, P_1, L_2
	273,600	54,850	218,750	3.99	1	1981, A_2, P_2, L_1
	287,000	54,850	232,150	4.23	1	1981, A_2, P_2, L_2
B	52,350	54,850	−2,500	−0.05	—	1980, A_1, P_1, L_1
	71,250	54,850	16,400	0.30	3	1980, A_2, P_1, L_1
	461,150	54,850	406,300	7.41	1	1981, A_2, P_2, L_1
	509,050	54,850	454,200	8.28	1	1981, A_2, P_2, L_2
C	57,150	44,850	12,300	0.27	4	1980, A_1, P_1, L_1
	83,300	44,850	38,450	0.86	2	1980, A_1, P_1, L_2
	457,050	44,850	412,200	9.19	1	1981, A_2, P_2, L_1
	487,300	44,850	442,450	9.87	1	1981, A_2, P_2, L_2
D	72,650	44,850	27,800	0.62	2	1980, A_1, P_1, L_1
	114,200	44,850	69,350	1.55	2	1980, A_1, P_1, L_2
	673,450	44,850	628,600	14.02	1	1981, A_2, P_2, L_1
	719,000	44,850	674,150	15.03	1	1981, A_2, P_2, L_2

level per hectare is low. Adjustment of the hand-weeding labour variable by hiring additional labour, following the increase in cultivated area, does not affect returns so significantly.

Household B shows the only case in which a negative NPV is found. This occurs where low input levels and a low value attributed to manure lead to a fall in predicted output per hectare following the investment which is not compensated for by a sufficiently large increase in area.

Household A exhibits a relatively high minimum NPV. This is due to the assumption P_1, in which one extra plough-team day is hired, so that the fall in plough-team input per hectare after expansion of its village field is moderated, falling from 1.33 to 1.20 PTD per ha. Assuming it is either less easy or more costly to hire a plough team, the returns to household A from well investment will be correspondingly lower. For example, if under P_1 an extra plough-team day could not be hired, this input level would fall from 1.33 to 1.0 PTD per ha, and a negative NPV of −4,200 FCFA would be obtained. Overall, the returns to investment in a well for household A are limited by the relatively small area of land which it can farm, as it lacks its own plough team. Thus, the maximum NPV for A is only 30–50 per cent of the maximum for the other three households.

The higher maximum NPV for household B in comparison with household C is explained by the very large area expansion that has been assumed for the former household under assumption A_2, village-field area in this case rising from 1.5 to 6.0 ha. While the overall level of manuring per hectare is low as a result, it has a high marginal value product, given the Cobb–Douglas form of the crop-response equations estimated in Chapter 5.

The highest NPV of all in Table 8.8 accrues to household D, for whom the digging of a new well permits a marginal increase in the level of manure use over a very large hectarage. Its large holding of work-oxen also allows it to transfer oxen plough-team resources from the bush to village field at a relatively low opportunity cost.

Additional sources of variability in returns

The calculations performed above demonstrate that returns to well investment depend on various assumptions regarding household size, the response of yields to levels of manuring and changes in levels of input use per hectare. Returns to this investment will also vary as a result of other less systematic factors, described briefly below.

The number of animals received by well owners varies from year to year due to differences in the pattern of rainfall. An early end to the rains means that ponds in the bush dry up early and herders must seek a reliable water-supply for their herds from November onwards, while an early start to the rainy season will prompt herds to leave their dry-season watering site in May. The herders' own farming activities also affect their time of arrival in Kala. In the dry season of 1982, for example, Maure herders were a month late in arriving in Kala as they had been occupied with cutting and storing their unusually large grain harvest.

Wells vary in their productivity, due to differences in depth and the nature of the water supply tapped. The depth of the well is a function of its position—how deep it must be dug before reaching water—and the time and money devoted to digging. Most wells in Kala are between 15 and 25 m deep, depending on their location. Wells dug on the upper slopes of the saucer-like depression within which Kala sits must go deeper before hitting the water-table, whereas those in the centre of the saucer are shallower. The difference between the two represents only a few days' work, as the extra depth passes through light, sandy strata which are easy to dig.

Most wells are dug until a reasonable supply of water is reached. In the case of one well dug in 1975, however, the household continued digging for several more metres, enabling the well to draw far more water than others. As a result this well can water a larger number of animals than any other in the village and provides its owner with a larger quantity of dung. Wells also differ in the quality of their water. One household has a well yielding very salty water which is said to cause sickness and occasional deaths among animals watering there. Consequently this well owner has not been able to attract many stock and started digging a new well in 1983 to compensate for the lack of success with his first well. These sources of variation contribute to some uncertainty regarding the size of returns expected by a household following a well being dug.

RISK TO THE WELL'S CAPITAL VALUE

The physical integrity of wells in Kala is fairly invulnerable to risk, because of the stable strata through which the shaft is dug and the care with which the well-head is supported with wooden beams. In sandier zones, wells are especially prone to collapse and must be lined with concrete rings, adding greatly to the cost of construction. Near the neighbouring village of Dofinena, shallow wells are re-dug every few years because the sandy soils where water is found mean that the well-shaft collapses after two or three years. Elsewhere in the region water is often only found at great depth and through a thick layer of sand, which must be reinforced with concrete rings. Sometimes a well subsides during digging, trapping the well-digger and a substantial investment in concrete within it.

Control or reduction of risk

Risks to returns from well investment stem from variation in the value of services received from the well: the amount of dung received and its value within the farmer's cropping strategy. These are only partially under the control of the well owner.

The number of livestock received and the length of their stay at the well depend partly on the characteristics of the well owner. The majority of well owners receive different herders on their land from one year to the next and there is also considerable movement of animals from well to well during the dry season. This would suggest that as yet well owners do not feel the need or are not able to establish a long-term contract with a single herd owner which would ensure the former a secure supply of dung and the latter a sure place to bring his herd. Herders may want to keep their options open in this respect and therefore be unwilling to make such a commitment.

The other risk to returns from the well comes from climatic variability. While there is little that an investor can do to affect the climate, he can try to moderate its impact. Fields which are on heavy clay soils have been abandoned and manuring kept to a minimum on drier ridges and less-sandy areas where there is a greater risk of 'burning' from the manure if rainfall is low. New village fields have been cleared away from the south-west of the village where the soils are dry and gravelly with most expansion towards the north and east, on light sands.

Flexibility of well investment

In Kala, wells only have value within a cropping system which requires dung. Water is exchanged exclusively for dung and in no case was it bought for any other commodity during the two years of research. Neighbouring villages in the region practise a similar system of exchange, although elsewhere in the Sahel water is often also sold for cash, and dung obtained either with cash or in exchange for grain. In the case of Kala, the return from a well depends on the well owner being involved in farming, and at present dung is only used for short-cycle millet. The significance of other returns to well investment could grow were circumstances to change; for example, if marketing of fresh vegetables to urban centres became easier, irrigated gardens would be of greater value.

Wells lack flexibility as a form of investment because they contribute to a single specific sector and they are also not marketable assets. Wells have never been bought or sold; a household which wants to own a well digs one on its village lands. However, some well owners in 1984 said they were considering selling water to herders for cash rather than in

TABLE 8.9. *Characteristics of well-less households*

	Well-less households	Average village households
Household size:		
no. of people	6.9	18.2
no. of workers	3.5	7.5
Cattle per household	1.7	20.8
Total millet production:		
VFM per worker 1981 (kg)	538	807
BFM per worker 1981 (kg)	478	634
TOTAL (kg)	1,016	1,541

exchange for dung, given the harsh effects on village-field harvests from low rainfall on heavily manured land.

Consequences of not owning a well

Table 8.9 presents the characteristics of those households in Kala without their own well. The figures reflect both the causes and consequences for well-less households of having little dung to boost yields of the short-cycle millet. Households when considering whether to dig a well must take into account not only the relative returns to wells as opposed to other assets but also the longer-term consequences for the household of persistently low grain production if it fails to get a well dug.

9

OXEN PLOUGH TEAMS

Heavy mouldboard ploughs were first introduced into this region in the 1930s with the instalment of the Office du Niger cotton-growing irrigation scheme, and the first ones were bought by farmers in Kala in the early 1950s. Wider adoption followed the fabrication by local blacksmiths of a lighter ridging plough, all that is required for sandy soils and light enough to be pulled by local oxen. Ploughs were first bought to prepare land for sowing groundnuts and village-field millet. They could ridge land much faster than the hoe so that a larger area could be sown within the limited time available. Weeding ploughs are a more recent development and are used to break up the soil between the lines of millet, speeding up the work of weeding the extensive area farmed with this crop. These weeders are similar to a single-bladed ridging plough.

DISTRIBUTION OF OXEN PLOUGH TEAMS

Table 9.1 presents data on those households with permanent access to plough-team equipment and animals in the farming season of 1981 and thus include those households where oxen have been borrowed for the entire rainy season.

Only one household had neither a plough nor animals. One household had invested in a plough that could be lent to another household, loan of the plough being repaid by the loan of oxen. The third household without permanent access to a complete plough team had bought a plough in early 1981 and was loaned a young ox for its use, in return for help in watering stock during the dry season. The vast majority of households had at least two oxen and a plough at their disposal during the farming season of 1981, and many had several oxen teams as may be seen below. Most households in Kala have one or two plough teams, but the largest three households operated four or five plough teams at the height of the weeding season. As may be seen from Table 9.2, the number of plough teams operated is strongly related to the size of the work-force.

In the period 1980–2 there were 63 transactions involving male cattle in Kala, of which 28 were purchases and 35 sales. Only three cases involved sales of animals between households in Kala, all others taking place with outsiders. As may be seen from Table 9.3, the animals purchased were predominantly aged less than three years while sales were mainly of mature and old animals. Male animals were used exclusively for animal

TABLE 9.1. *Distribution of plough-team holdings, Kala, 1981*

	Households	
	No.	%
At least 2 oxen and plough	26	91
1 ox and plough	1	3
1 plough	1	3
Nothing	1	3
All households	29	100

TABLE 9.2. *Distribution of households by number of oxen owned in 1980 and 1981*

Households	No. of oxen owned			
	0	1–4	5–8	9–12
in 1980	3	19	4	3
in 1981	3	18	5	3
Mean household size (no. of workers, 1981)	2.6	5.3	13.0	16.3

Note: In 1980, of 109 oxen used, 8 (7.3%) were on loan from other households and, in 1981, of 120 oxen used, 11 (9.2%) were on loan from elsewhere.

TABLE 9.3. *Sales and purchases of male cattle, Kala, January 1980–1982 (in FCFA)*

	Age of animal (years)					TOTALS
	<2	2–3	3–4	Mature	Old	
Sales:						
No. of cases	1	5	4	21	4	35
Mean price	11,250	18,300	28,125	58,900	33,750	
Price range	11,250	17–20,000	22–40,000	35–72,500	16–35,000	
Purchases:						
No. of cases	8	12	4	4	—	28
Mean price	11,475	17,400	30,000	47,800	—	
Price range	10–12,500	12–20,000	20–35,000	40–52,500	—	
TOTALS	9	17	8	25	4	63

TABLE 9.5. *Yields of millet for three households without oxen teams, 1981* (kilograms per hectare)

	Millet	
	Bush-field	Village-field
Mean for village	215	1,010
Household x	97	1,088
Household y	262	—
Household z	144	665

Note: Household y had no well and hence a very poorly manured village field, abandoned in 1981.

because the oxen are busy at work in the field of the owner, and it may be worth little to get the team at any other time.

Bush-field millet is usually sown on unridged land, so it is not essential for a household to gain access to a plough team in order to cultivate this crop. Plough teams are of especial value in preparing land for village-field millet and where teams have been hired, it is this crop which takes priority.

Consequences of not investing in an oxen plough team

A household in Kala when deciding whether to invest in its first oxen plough team must consider not only the flow of costs and benefits from the whole investment, but also the speed at which the investment should be made (given the possibility of borrowing a spare ox from another household) and the possibilities of hiring a plough team from others if no part of the investment is made. Table 9.5 presents data on yields of millet for households without permanent access to a plough team. Their low village-field yields are mainly due to their also lacking a well and therefore having no dung for fertilizing these fields. Low yields per hectare of the bush-field millet are due to slow and incomplete weeding of these fields. In one case, in 1981, the bush field was abandoned to weeds after sowing and the working couple spent all their time on the village lands.

COSTS OF ACQUIRING AND MAINTAINING A PLOUGH TEAM

The flow of costs associated with the purchase and maintenance of an oxen plough team is shown in Table 9.6.

TABLE 9.6. *Flow of purchase and maintenance costs of an oxen plough team for different households* (in FCFA)

Category of cost	Year 0	Year 1	Year 2	Year 3	Year 4	Year 5
Oxen purchase of 2 animals aged 2–3 years	35,100	—	—	—	—	—
Castration fee		4,000	—	—	—	—
Training (2 months' household labour time)		5,000	—	—	—	—
Herding fees	1,500	1,500	1,500	1,500	1,500	1,500
Salt, tax, and equipment	900	900	900	900	900	900
Plough purchase (1 ridger and 1 weeder)	—	20,000	—	—	—	—
Plough maintenance	—	—	4,000	4,000	4,000	4,000
Watering labour per oxen pair:						
Household A (2 head of cattle)	12,500	12,500	12,500	12,500	12,500	12,500
Household B (7 head of cattle)	3,550	3,550	3,550	3,550	3,550	3,550
Household C (22 head of cattle)	1,150	1,150	1,150	1,150	1,150	1,150
Household D (77 head of cattle)	650	650	650	650	650	650
Total discounted costs at r = 20% p.a.:						
Household A	50,000	36,550	13,150	10,950	9,100	7,550 = 127,300
Household B	41,050	29,100	6,900	5,750	4,800	4,000 = 91,600
Household C	38,650	27,100	5,250	4,350	3,650	3,000 = 82,000
Household D	38,150	26,700	4,900	4,100	3,400	2,800 = 80,050

Purchase of animals It is assumed that animals are purchased at the age of 2–3 years, at a cost of 35,000 FCFA a pair, although the owner must wait for more than a year before they are ready to start work.

Maintenance of animals The main components of oxen maintenance costs are the provision of watering labour during the dry season, payment of herding fees and taxes, and purchase of other inputs, such as salt, watering equipment, ropes, etc. The largest of these costs is that of providing labour to water the animals for the seven or eight months of the year when stock must be brought to the village wells to drink. All owners of cattle must provide someone to take part in the team which draws water for the joint herd, regardless of the number of animals owned. This makes a demand on the young men of the household during the dry season, a time when they could be away on migration earning cash. A household head expects to receive around 5,000 FCFA from a young man for each month spent away on migration. One half of this sum is taken to represent the opportunity cost of one month's watering labour, since this job is done early in the morning, after which the worker is also available for other household tasks. Oxen must be watered for seven to eight months of the year, from early November until the beginning of June. However, for the months of November and December, the household is occupied with harvesting, threshing, and transporting grain and it is only from the end of December that a large number of young men start to leave for the towns. The total cost of watering labour is therefore taken as 2,500 FCFA × 5 months, equalling 12,500 FCFA per year.

The cost of watering labour per animal depends on the number of cattle owned. A household considering purchase of their first oxen plough team is unlikely to have a non-oxen cattle holding and thus watering costs per ox will be high. For a household with a herd of 20 or more cattle, in addition to an oxen team, the unit cost of watering each ox is very much lower. In practice, the unit cost of watering labour varies less systematically than this would suggest. This is because households provide labour of differing quality to draw water and this labour is consequently of differing value. This tends to reduce the actual cost faced by many households. Who is sent to draw water depends on the labour available to the household, the number of animals owned, and the number of other households in the herding group. Some send a middle-aged man who controls the herd as it is brought to water, but who rarely pulls the heavy bucket of water. Those with a large number of animals generally send two young men while those with a single ox send someone only every other day and may be granted leave of absence while this young man goes on migration to earn cash for the household's taxes.

Training of animals Before the oxen can be used, they must be castrated and trained. These operations are undertaken in the fourth year of the animal's life, over a period of a month, during which the beast is accustomed to being handled and to drawing weights. Assuming the pair of oxen are trained in consecutive months, at a monthly cost of 2,500 FCFA, the training cost will be 5,000 FCFA per pair of oxen. A castration fee of 2,000 FCFA per animal is paid to a local Fulani herder who carries out the operation.

Miscellaneous expenses   Herding fees, salt rations, taxes, and equipment costs must also be met, estimates of which are laid out in Table 9.6.

RETURNS TO OXEN PLOUGH-TEAM INVESTMENT

The main return to investment in an oxen plough team comes from the role played by this equipment in expanding the area which the household can cultivate and in raising use of this input per hectare. Variability in this return stems from the effect of fluctuations in rainfall on harvests of the two millet varieties. Returns will also vary between farmers given differences in their access to the complementary inputs of labour and dung and in the areas cultivated with each variety. Variation in returns to plough-team investment are investigated below using the four household types described in Chapter 7. The returns are calculated on the basis of several alternative assumptions concerning the following:

Crop response. The returns to this investment are based on the crop-production functions estimated in Chapter 4 covering the farming seasons of 1980 and 1981, as was done for well investment.

Changes in area cultivated. Where an additional plough team has been acquired, both bush and village fields are assumed to increase in area as this asset is used in the cultivation of both millet varieties. The overall increase in area cultivated is assumed to bring each household to the mean land-holding per plough team of 16.5 ha. Two alternative distributions of the addition to cultivated land are investigated (see Table 9.7), the first A_1 in which a higher proportion is allocated to bush-field millet and the second A_2 in which a higher proportion is allocated to the village-field crop.

Change in input use per hectare. In order to calculate the yield of each millet variety following investment in a plough team, assumptions must be made about levels of input use per hectare in the pre- and post-investment period. Tables 9.8–9.10 summarize these assumptions.

Manure use. Acquisition of an oxen pair increases the household's supply of dung, the value of which depends on access by the household to other sources of dung and on the existing level of manure use on its village field. Two additional units on the manure index are attributed to

TABLE 9.7. *Assumed changes in village- and bush-field areas following oxen plough-team investment*

	Initial area	Alternative assumptions	
	A_0	A_1	A_2
Village-field area (ha):			
Household A	1.5	2.0	3.6
Household B	1.5	3.6	6.0
Household C	6.0	8.0	10.0
Household D	12.0	15.0	18.0
Bush-field area (ha):			
Household A	10.0	14.5	12.9
Household B	20.0	29.4	27.0
Household C	30.0	41.5	39.5
Household D	40.0	51.0	48.0

TABLE 9.8. *Assumed changes in input use, pre- and post-investment in an oxen plough team* (in manuring units per village-field hectare)

Household	Initial	Alternative area assumptions	
	A_0	A_1	A_2
A	0.30	1.30	0.85
B	3.63	2.24	1.47
C	6.13	4.93	4.00
D	7.80	6.43	5.41

each household following purchase of an oxen team, giving new levels of input use as shown in Table 9.8.

Plough-team use. Households B, C, and D are assumed to operate in both the pre- and post-investment period at levels of plough-team use which lie close to the mean for Kala (see Table 9.9); in 1981, these were at 2.35 PTD per ha in the village fields and 1.40 PTD per ha in the bush fields. This constancy in the level of plough-team use per hectare is achieved by assuming that the total area cultivated following purchase of the new plough team increases sufficiently to maintain the area per team for each household at the mean level of 16.5 ha. For household A, it is assumed that in the pre-investment period it can hire a total of 5 PTD, of

TABLE 9.9. *Assumed changes in input use pre- and post-investment in an oxen plough team* (in plough-team days per hectare)

Household	Change in area	Village field		Bush field	
		Initial	Post-investment	Initial	Post-investment
A	A_1	1.33	2.50	0.30	1.38
	A_2	1.33	2.36	0.30	1.40
B	A_1	2.35	2.36	1.28	1.39
	A_2	2.35	2.33	1.28	1.41
C	A_1	2.35	2.37	1.47	1.40
	A_2	2.35	2.35	1.47	1.41
D	A_1	2.35	2.33	1.48	1.40
	A_2	2.35	2.33	1.48	1.40

TABLE 9.10. *Assumed changes in input use pre- and post-investment in an oxen plough team* (in man-days of hand-weeding labour per hectare)

Household	Change in area	Village field			Bush field		
		Initial	Alternative assumptions		Initial	Alternative assumptions	
			L_1	L_2		L_1	L_2
A	A_1	5.74	4.31	5.74	5.18	3.57	5.18
	A_2	5.74	2.39	5.74	5.18	4.02	5.18
B	A_1	5.74	2.39	5.74	5.18	3.52	5.18
	A_2	5.74	1.44	5.74	5.18	3.84	5.18
C	A_1	5.74	4.31	5.74	5.18	3.74	5.18
	A_2	5.74	3.44	5.74	5.18	3.93	5.18
D	A_1	5.74	4.59	5.74	5.18	4.06	5.18
	A_2	5.74	3.83	5.74	5.18	4.32	5.18

which 2 are spent in the village and 3 in the bush field. This is sufficient to enable all village land and some new bush field to be ridged before sowing. Following purchase of an oxen plough team, the level of plough-team use per hectare is assumed to rise to the mean levels for each field, as for the other three households.

Hand-weeding labour. This is assumed to lie in the pre-investment period at the mean level for all four households considered here, equal to

TABLE 9.11. *Oxen plough-team investment: Present value of additional output, costs, and net returns* (in FCFA)

Household	Present value output	Present value costs	Net present value (NPV)	NPV/Costs	Payback period (years)	Assumptions
A	286,100	127,300	158,800	1.25	2	1981, A_1, L_2
	292,500	127,300	165,200	1.30	2	1981, A_1, L_1
	402,900	127,300	275,600	2.16	1	1981, A_2, L_2
	445,500	127,300	318,200	2.50	1	1980, A_2, L_2
B	354,950	96,600	263,350	2.88	1	1980, A_1, L_1
	369,850	96,600	278,250	3.04	1	1981, A_2, L_2
	563,700	96,600	471,400	5.15	1	1981, A_2, L_2
	617,800	96,600	521,200	5.69	1	1980, A_2, L_2
C	380,750	82,000	298,750	3.64	1	1980, A_1, L_1
	390,000	82,000	308,000	3.76	1	1981, A_1, L_2
	585,700	82,000	503,700	6.14	1	1981, A_2, L_2
	637,000	82,000	555,000	6.77	1	1980, A_2, L_2
D	501,700	80,500	421,650	5.27	1	1981, A_1, L_2
	502,400	80,500	422,350	5.28	1	1981, A_1, L_1
	819,150	80,500	739,100	9.23	1	1981, A_2, L_2
	861,400	80,500	781,350	9.76	1	1980, A_2, L_2

5.74 man-days per ha of village field and 5.18 man-days per ha of bush field. Following the purchase of a new plough team and the subsequent expansion of village- and bush-field areas, two alternative cases are investigated, shown in Table 9.10. The first (L_1) involves the total number of man-days spent by the household remaining the same as in the pre-investment period but being spread over a larger area and yielding a lower level of weeding per hectare. The second (L_2) involves maintaining hand-weeding labour at the mean level by hiring labour at the going wage of 4–5 kg of millet per day.

NET RETURNS FROM PLOUGH-TEAM INVESTMENT

Table 9.11 summarizes the range of returns and costs between the four household types according to the different assumptions taken, based on the crop-response equations estimated in Chapter 5. The two lowest and two highest net present values (NPVs) are presented in this table to indicate the degree of variation in returns. In all cases returns to the investment are positive. They also increase with increases in household size, the largest NPV for A being less than 40 per cent of the maximum NPV for household D. The difference in returns between households A and D is only partly due to the higher unit cost of maintaining the oxen faced by a small household. Much of the increase in output for D is the result of expansion in village-field area following purchase of a new plough team and the subsequent spread of its substantial manure supply over a larger area.

The two highest NPVs occur for all households under the following assumptions—1980, A_2, L_2, and 1981, A_2, L_2. A_2 refers to the strategy in which village-field area expands by a relatively larger and bush-field area by a relatively smaller amount. Thus, the highest returns to oxen plough-teams are found where a larger proportion of plough team inputs are allocated to expanding village- as opposed to bush-field millet production. This is not surprising given that the marginal value product of plough-team work was estimated to be much higher in village-field millet pro-duction (see Table 6.1). The highest NPV is obtained using the 1980 crop-response equation, due to the marginal value product of plough-team work being especially high in this year. No consistent ranking emerges for the assumptions producing the lowest NPVs for different households. Most cases, however, involve assumption A_1, in which much of the expan-sion in area cultivated is devoted to bush-field millet in which plough-team work has a relatively low value.

The ratio of NPV to cost indicates the rate of return on this investment over the five-year period. It can be seen that this ratio rises steadily in moving from household A to D, the largest household gaining between a five- and ninefold return on capital depending on the assumptions taken. Differences in the length of payback period show the same tendency, with the small household A being the only case in which the investment takes longer than one year to repay its initial costs.

JOINT INVESTMENT IN A WELL AND OXEN PLOUGH TEAM

This and the previous chapter have presented evidence on how returns vary between households when each investment is undertaken singly. Table 9.12 presents comparable data on the flow of costs and benefits over five years when investment in both assets takes place in a single year. A similar pattern of returns is found for the joint investment as for each taken singly, with the size of net returns increasing as household size rises from A to D. As expected, the discounted flow of benefits is greater for the joint investment than for either of the two taken singly. However, the joint investment produces net returns which are far less than the sum of net returns gained from each separate investment. This may be accounted for by the following considerations. Investment in both assets

TABLE 9.12. *Joint investment in well and oxen plough teams: Present value of additional output, costs, and net returns* (in FCFA)

Household	Present value output	Present value costs	Net present value (NPV)	NPV/Costs	Payback period (years)	Assumptions
A	309,450	182,150	177,550	0.97	3	1980, A_1, L_1
	335,550	182,150	203,650	1.12	2	1981, A_1, L_2
	479,750	182,150	347,850	1.91	2	1981, A_2, L_1
	492,450	182,150	360,550	1.98	2	1981, A_2, L_2
B	377,750	146,450	231,600	1.58	2	1980, A_1, L_1
	411,150	146,450	314,950	2.15	2	1981, A_1, L_1
	626,300	146,450	530,100	3.62	1	1980, A_2, L_2
	646,100	146,500	549,900	3.75	1	1981, A_2, L_2
C	358,850	126,850	282,250	2.23	2	1980, A_1, L_1
	408,100	126,850	331,500	2.61	1	1981, A_1, L_2
	615,600	126,850	539,000	4.25	1	1981, A_2, L_2
	626,500	126,850	549,900	4.34	1	1980, A_2, L_2
D	484,600	124,900	409,950	3.28	1	1980, A_1, L_1
	510,450	124,900	435,800	3.49	1	1981, A_1, L_2
	336,000	124,900	761,350	6.10	1	1981, A_2, L_2
	840,400	124,900	765,750	6.13	1	1980, A_2, L_2

permits the household to attain higher total levels of input use per hectare than when either investment is undertaken singly. The production function estimated in Chapter 5 assumed that the marginal product of each input declines as input levels rise. With the same expansion in area assumed under both the single- and joint-investment cases examined here, there will inevitably be diminishing returns to the joint investment. Only where investment in both assets was accompanied by a larger increase in village- and bush-field area would investors be able to maintain lower input levels and thus to gain higher marginal returns.

Joint investment moderates the minimum return obtained from well investment using the least favourable assumptions, so that no negative NPVs are obtained for any household. However, the high discount rate used means that the heavy initial costs of joint investment have a strong influence on net returns which helps account for the low ratio of NPV to cost.

RISK TO CAPITAL VALUES

The major source of risk to the capital value of an oxen plough team lies in the loss of an ox. Such a loss may arise from injury, death, or theft but these are fairly infrequent. For example, over the two farming seasons of 1980 and 1981, of the 29 households in Kala only three suffered the loss of a total of four oxen, out of a village work-oxen population of 120. Two of these were badly gored in a fight and had to be sold for slaughter, while two died of disease just at the start of the rainy season. While the incidence of loss is very low, at less than 2 per cent per year, the effects of loss are harsh for the individual household that owns only a single pair of animals. One small, fairly poor household had the misfortune to lose an ox in each of the two farming seasons, the first from disease and the second from goring.

Theft of cattle occurs mainly at the start of the rainy season before livestock herding begins, when animals can be trekked through the bush without needing to be brought to village wells for water. Several cases of theft occurred during 1980–2, but these concerned mainly female and young stock (see Chapter 10 for more details). In the farming season, work-oxen are being used during the day and kept in the village at night so that the risk of theft to these animals is lower than to the rest of the herd.

The risk of damage to plough equipment is restricted to the blade. This is replaced every year but may also need repair during the farming season. Most repairs are done late in the farming season and have little impact on the household's ability to continue weeding. Typically, one worker takes the plough to the neighbouring blacksmith's hamlet, and works in the latter's field until the repair is done and returns at the end of the day.

There is little the farmer can do to reduce the risk due to rainfall variation faced by investment in an oxen plough team. Some security in return comes from the cultivation of two millet varieties, since yields of the two varieties exhibit no clear correlation. Risk from injury to oxen can be reduced by careful handling of the beasts, while attempts are made to prevent the loss of an animal through death by the regular sale of work-oxen before they reach the age of 10–12 years. Little can be done to limit loss from disease or theft. Effective prophylaxis is not available for the former and only year-round herding would prevent the latter. The incidence of theft is not sufficiently high for this to have been adopted yet, although in other areas continuous herding throughout the dry season has been adopted for this reason (World Bank, 1989).

Flexibility of oxen plough-team investment

Originally introduced to ridge land for groundnuts, plough teams continue to make a crucial contribution to the farming system despite the abandonment of this crop. This is because the plough team is also used to ridge village fields before sowing and because weeding of both millet varieties is much speeded up by use of a single-blade weeding plough. Local blacksmiths have adapted the heavy equipment originally introduced and now fabricate much lighter ploughs that can be pulled by medium-weight, often poorly nourished, village oxen. The abundance of cultivable land has enabled farmers to take advantage of the area-increasing possibilities of plough-team use.

Both ploughs and oxen are relatively easy to market with little or no loss. It is rare for a household to sell its plough but one case did occur in 1980 where a millet-deficit household without its own work-oxen was able to exchange its plough for grain. Oxen are easily marketed and fetch a good price as meat animals. The only problem households face in selling oxen is if they are in desperate need for cash and must find a buyer fast. This was not the case for any household during the period of study so far as mature oxen were concerned. Households plan the marketing of stock over several weeks in the early dry season and will find a buyer during that period from among the traders that visit the village.

The investment has additional flexibility due to the separability of its components. Households do not have to find the entire sum needed to pay for two animals and ploughs in a single year. Typically, the purchase of an oxen pair and plough takes place over several years, the household borrowing an animal in the interim.

Oxen can also be used for pulling carts and, in the past, they were widely used for this. However, most households now have opted for a light donkey-cart, which is both less expensive and also easier to manœuvre than the heavy, iron-wheeled ox-carts available.

10

INVESTMENT IN CATTLE-BREEDING STOCK

The region to the north of the River Niger at Ségou has long been a zone for cattle raising, due to its light density of settlement and extensive areas of grazing. The villagers of Kala claim a long ancestry for their cattle holdings although these were, and remain, concentrated in a few households. Many herds were gravely depleted in the 1920s and 1930s, following several years of crop devastation due to locust plagues, but during the 1950s, rebuilding of herds gradually took place with the profits from groundnut cultivation.

Ownership of animals within the herd is complex. Some animals are owned at the level of the household as a whole, for example, work-oxen or heifers bought with surplus from the communal millet field. Some cattle are the property of men belonging to a smaller unit within the household, who either purchased these animals with the proceeds of groundnut cultivation or inherited them from their mother. In other cases, a few cattle may be owned by individuals, having been bought with the proceeds from trade or migration.

DISTRIBUTION OF CATTLE HOLDINGS

Table 10.1 shows the very unequal distribution of cattle holdings between households and the proportion of herds made up by work-oxen. Two-thirds, or 19, of the 29 households had 10 cattle or less and three of these owned no cattle at all. A few households have very large herds, seen in the mean herd size of nearly 80 animals for those with a holding of more than 40 animals. The proportion of herds made up by work-oxen declines very rapidly from 72 per cent among the smallest holdings of 1–10 cattle that are largely made up of this class of animal, to 13 per cent among the largest herds, which are similar in size and structure to the breeding herds of many pastoral groups.

This table also shows the strong positive relationship between herd and household size. All three cattle-less households have 10 or fewer members. More than half of all households (16 out of 29) fall into the class holding 1–10 cattle with a mean household size of 9.7, their cattle holdings composed largely of work-oxen. All households with more than 40 cattle have more than 20 members. Not only is large herd and household

TABLE 10.1. *Distribution of cattle holdings by household in Kala, 1981*

	Cattle holdings				
	>40	21–40	11–20	1–10	0
Mean herd size	78.4	31.3	20.0	4.1	0
Percentage of total village herd	65	21	3	11	0
Percentage as work-oxen	13	19	20	72	0
No. of households	5	4	1	16	3
Mean household size[a]	31.1	22.0	11.5	9.7	4.0
Percentage of households	17	14	3	55	10
Cattle per household member	2.52	1.57	1.74	0.42	0

[a] Household size has been measured here in adult equivalents, taking those over 15 years of age as equal to 1.0 those of 15 and younger as 0.5 units.

size correlated, but larger households also have absolutely greater cattle wealth, as demonstrated in the last column of the table, where it can be seen that there is a positive correlation between cattle wealth per person and household size.

This strong tendency for household and herd size to be positively related will be looked at in greater detail in Chapters 12–14 in which the process of household growth and development is described. Here it will just be noted that the line of causation between the two variables runs in both directions. On the one hand, large household size favours the production of an agricultural surplus and generation of income from non-farm activities which can then be converted into livestock wealth. On the other hand, livestock wealth can be used to increase household size through payment of bride-wealth, the early marriage of men, and more frequent second marriages for men. In addition, wealthier households can retain greater control over their own members, as will be seen in later chapters.

Table 10.2 presents data on sales and purchases of female cattle in the period 1980–2. Comparative data for male cattle are given in brackets to show the difference in both the number of animals involved and their prices.

A comparison of the data for male and female cattle shows, first, that far fewer transactions involve the latter. This is because females are rarely sold until they have reached old age and are no longer likely to calve again. Only one household was forced to sell a heifer because it was faced with tax and wedding expenditures after a relatively poor millet harvest. Secondly, a comparison of prices shows the premium placed on young females bought as breeding stock. Thirdly, purchases of female

Farm Investment

TABLE 10.2. *Sales and purchases of female cattle, January 1980–1982*

	Age of animal (years)					TOTALS
	<2	2–3	3–4	Mature	Old	
Sales:						
No. of cases	— (1)	— (5)	1 (4)	— (21)	8 (4)	9 (35)
No. of households	—	—	1	—	7	8
Purchases:						
No. of cases	1 (8)	9 (12)	— (4)	— (4)	— (—)	10
No. of households	1	2	—	—	—	3
Mean prices for Sales and Purchases (FCFA)	15,250 (11,450)	31,100 (17,550)	38,750 (29,550)	(58,400)	17,800 (27,100)	
TOTALS	1 (9)	9 (17)	1 (18)		8 (4)	19 (63)

Note: Figures in brackets refer to male cattle, presented here for purposes of comparison.

stock are limited to very few households. During this period, only three households bought heifers, two of which bought a single animal while the third bought eight heifers over the two dry seasons. For the two households buying a single animal each, the purchase was financed in one case by selling millet from a good harvest and in the other case by investing profits from the household's trading business. The household that bought eight heifers has two plough teams and one well with which it produces a regular large millet surplus from extensive village fields manured by visiting stock at its deep well. Several of the animals from this herd have now been sold to finance a series of marriages for the sons of the family.

PROFITABILITY OF BREEDING-CATTLE INVESTMENT

Purchase and maintenance costs   Table 10.2 presented the prices paid for female cattle in Kala during the period of research. For assessing the returns to investment in breeding cattle, the calculation will be based on taking a heifer aged three years, most breeding animals being bought by this age, and costing 30,000 FCFA. The flow of services derived from her are estimated over the following five years, to maintain comparability with estimated returns from well and oxen plough-team investments presented earlier.

The cost of maintaining cattle in Kala comprises four elements which are shown in Table 10.3. Firstly, the stock owner must pay a herding fee on work-oxen and on all females which have produced at least one calf. The hired herder receives this fee in the form of millet, 10 measures (or

TABLE 10.3. *Costs of investment in breeding cattle* (in FCFA)

Category of cash flow	Year 0	Year 1	Year 2	Year 3	Year 4	Year 5	TOTALS (FCFA)
Purchase of heifer aged 2–3 years	30,000	—	—	—	—	—	
Salt, tax, and equipment	450	450	450	450	450	450	
Herding fees	750	750	750	750	750	750	
Watering labour:							
Household A	12,500	12,500	12,500	12,500	12,500	12,500	
Household B	2,100	2,100	2,100	2,100	2,100	2,100	
Household C	600	600	600	600	600	600	
Household D	350	350	350	350	350	350	
Total discounted costs at $r =$ 25% p.a.:							
Household A	43,700	10,950	8,750	7,000	5,600	4,500	161,000
Household B	33,300	2,650	2,100	1,700	1,350	1,100	84,400
Household C	21,800	1,450	1,150	900	750	600	73,300
Household D	21,550	1,250	1,000	800	650	500	71,500

Notes: Assumed cattle holdings for each household: household A (1), household B (6), household C (21), and household D (76).

Costs are discounted at 25% p.a. which combines a time discount rate of 20% p.a. with an adult cow mortality rate of 5% p.a..

15 kg) being paid per head of stock cared for. Secondly, the herd owner must supply labour to the joint watering team for the six to seven months when cattle must be watered at the well. Every household with animals in a joint herding unit must normally contribute at least one worker to this team, depending on the number of cattle owners making up the joint unit. Details of the variation in watering costs per animal were discussed in Chapter 9, in relation to the watering requirements for plough oxen, which showed that unit watering costs fall greatly with an increase in the number of cattle owned. Thirdly, all cattle owners must spend some money on cattle-related expenditures, such as salt, a pulley for the well-rope, a watering skin, a rope for drawing water, ropes for attaching the new calves, and so on. Some of these expenses are shared, households taking it in turns to provide equipment needed by the water-drawing team. Fourthly, all animals liable for herding fees are also liable for tax. The government carries out a census every few years on human and livestock populations. The figures for stock on which taxes must be paid rarely bear much relation to the actual holdings of the household, the

villager's conservative estimate of this livestock wealth being liberally added to by the census officer. Although the cattle tax per capita was only 200 FCFA in 1981, for the largest herd owners this amounted to a considerable sum.

RETURNS TO CATTLE INVESTMENT

Returns from investment in cattle come from three sources:

(i) the natural increase of the herd provides calves to be sold or to be kept in the herd as work-oxen and breeding stock, and elderly animals that are sold or slaughtered for meat;

(ii) milk is a small but much appreciated part of the Bambara diet; and

(iii) for some households, their own cattle holdings provide a substantial part of their total manure supply with which to fertilize their village fields.

Each of these outputs will be discussed in turn and data put forward on which to base estimates of overall herd productivity and returns to investment in cattle.

Income flows from each of these elements are shown in Table 10.4. Costs and benefits from investment in cattle for different household types are compared in Tables 10.3 and 10.4. Details of the differing costs and returns are discussed over the following pages.

Calf production and herd offtake

The rate of calf production from female cattle is determined by three factors—the cow-survival rate, the calving rate, and the rate of calf survival.

The cow-survival rate depends on age and on the incidence of drought and disease. Age-related mortality rates among livestock follow a U-shaped curve. Deaths are particularly high in the first year of life, thereafter declining to a low for most of the animal's adult life, then rising rapidly as the normal length of life is approached. The survival rate for cows is consequently very high (at around 0.95 per cent per year) through most of their productive lifetime except in times of drought or epidemic and only falls significantly after the age of 8–10 years.

The calving rate refers to the number of calves born into the herd as a proportion of the potential female breeding population, and this rate varies considerably between different production and management systems. Nutritional factors play an important role in affecting how often cows calve and in particular the age of first calving. Better nutrition can be achieved by careful herding of animals towards favoured pastures. Regular rations of salt throughout the rainy season encourage the animals

TABLE 10.4. *Returns to investment in breeding cattle*

	Year 0	Year 1	Year 2	Year 3	Year 4	Year 5	TOTALS (FCFA)
Calf production and dung Assumed benefit flow:							
(i)	1,650	5,625	5,625	5,625	5,625	5,625	
(ii)	1,650	7,720	7,720	7,720	7,720	7,720	
(iii)	3,500	10,405	10,405	10,405	10,405	10,405	
Milk		2,363	2,363	2,363	2,363	2,363	
Terminal value aged 8 years						25,000	
Total discounted returns at $r =$ 25% p.a.:							
(i)	1,650	6,390	5,112	4,090	3,272	10,810	31,325
(ii)	1,650	8,065	6,452	5,162	4,130	11,497	36,956
(iii)	3,500	10,215	8,170	6,537	5,230	12,375	46,027

Note: Benefits and returns from investment in breeding-cattle are calculated for three different assumptions regarding the value of calf production and of dung. Estimated values under these differing assumptions are taken from the two central rows of Table 10.7 as below:

	Calf survival rate	Value of dung
(i)	low	medium
(ii)	medium	medium
(iii)	high	high

These assumptions have been chosen to represent the most frequent values for calf survival and for dung from amongst households in Kala during the period of field-work.

to eat more and quicken the rate at which they put on weight. Salt was the only regular input given to livestock in Kala. In sahelian conditions, the mean age at first calving lies between four and five years. Some cows produce a calf every year, conception occurring some 50 days after the last birth. Many cows, however, calve only every other year, giving an overall calving interval of around 18–20 months. Conception is most likely to occur during the few months of the wet season when cows regain their weight and condition. Cows that fail to conceive in one wet season will probably not conceive again until the next season. Because of the highly seasonal distribution of conceptions, calving is also highly concentrated with more than 50 per cent of all calf births occurring in the three months of April, May, and June.

TABLE 10.5. *Reproductive performance for cattle in central Mali*

Age (years)	No. of animals observed	No. of calves born	Standard deviation
10	36	5.0	1.40
9	30	4.0	0.98
8	47	3.3	1.05
7	50	2.6	1.09
6	44	2.2	1.60
5	69	1.3	0.84
4	61	0.8	0.71

Source: Table 66, p. 143, 'Carrière des réproductrices dans le système pastoral', in Wilson *et al.*, 1983.

Table 10.5 presents data on the reproductive performance of cows for several pastoral herds in central Mali (Wilson *et al.*, 1983: 143). From this may be seen that by the age of eight years, a cow can be expected to have produced 3.3 calves (standard deviation 1.05), which is equivalent to a calving rate of 66.7 per cent, over five breeding-cow years.

The calving performance of three herds in Kala was followed for the rainy season of 1981. Of 72 cattle of breeding age, there were 48 pregnancies, giving a calving rate of 66 per cent. This figure, so very close to that in the table above, will be used here in calculating returns to investment in breeding cattle.

Calf-survival rates   The rate of calf survival is taken as the proportion of pregnancies that produce a calf still living at one year of age. It usually includes losses due to miscarriage and stillbirth as well as deaths among animals in their first year of life. Mortality among calves is high in regions like the Sahel where there is a long dry season during which the quality of pasture is low and cows are producing little milk. Data on calf mortality rates for a pastoral herd in central Mali shows death rates varying from 20 per cent to 40 per cent in the first year of life (Wilson *et al.*, 1983). During times of drought, rates are likely to be much higher than this, as calves are especially vulnerable to stress. Calf deaths are also related to the amount of milk to which calves had access in their early months of life, a period during which calves must compete with humans for milk supplies. All livestock suffer some weight loss in the dry season, as a result of poor pasture quality, and it is only the better nourished calves that can survive this period. Parasites and other internal disorders account for some deaths in the first two years of a calf's life, striking in particular the poorly nourished. Calf mortality is a subject of great discussion and dispute between herd owners and their contract herders in Kala since it focuses on the conflicting interests and aims of the two parties. The herd owner wants to see many calves survive to swell herd numbers while the herder sees his own short-term interest as maximizing current milk supplies to his household.

The factor considered of primary importance in affecting calf mortality by herd owners themselves is the level of milk offtake from cows and consequently the quantity left for the calf to drink. The division of milk between the herd owner, contract herder and calf causes constant dispute and in the three-cornered struggle for milk, the calf tends to come off worst. For example, one cattle owner lost all 12 of the calves born in the 1981 rainy season during the following months, which he attributed to very heavy milking by his hired herder, who was subsequently sacked.

In calculating returns to investment in breeding cattle in Kala, several different values for the calf-survival rate will be taken to assess the variability in returns due to this factor.

Herd offtake The pattern of purchases and sales for male and female cattle was presented in Table 10.2. The potential offtake from investment in a heifer consists of the value of calves produced and brought to a saleable age and the slaughter value of the cow after the age of 8–10 years. These values are taken from the above table in which a calf at 18–24 months is worth 11,450 FCFA if male and 15,250 FCFA if female and the value of an 8-year old cow is taken as 25,000 FCFA. This latter figure is slightly above that for 'old' cows in Table 10.2, since a cow of 8 years still has some chance of producing a calf and will bear more meat than a cow that is 10 years old or more.

Value of returns from calf production and herd offtake

The value of annual calf production from a cow of reproductive age can be calculated from the following:

$$SR^{cow} \times CR \times SR^{calf} \times \text{Value}^{calf}$$

where:

SR^{cow} is the survival rate for a cow in her reproductive years, taken here as 0.95 per annum.

CR is the calving rate, estimated earlier to have a mean of 66 per cent.

SR^{calf} is the survival rate of the calf to its sale age of 18 months (taken as one minus the calf-mortality rate for calves in their first year of life minus half the mortality of calves in their second year). Several different values are taken for calf mortality from 0 to 12 months while the rate for calves aged 12 to 24 months is taken as 5 per cent.

Value^{calf} is the monetary value of a calf at 18 months. Assuming an equal likelihood of male and female calves, this will be $\frac{1}{2}(11,450 + 15,250) =$ 13,350 FCFA.

Taking a calf survival rate in the first year of 0.75 and the above values for the other variables, the average expected value of calf production per year can be calculated as:

$$(0.95 \times 0.66 \times 0.725 \times 13{,}350)\,\text{FCFA} = 6{,}069\,\text{FCFA}.$$

Milk production

Output of milk from cattle holdings in Kala is low, highly variable, and concentrated in the few months of the rainy season. Of all the cows in the herd, only a certain proportion calve every year and of those cows that do calve, some are barely milked if, for example, it is their first calf. A high proportion of calves are born at the start of the rains and, with the plentiful fodder available at this time of year, this means that milk supplies, both per animal and for the herd as a whole, are at their peak in the months of July to September as seen in Table 10.6. The terms of the herding contract only entitle a cattle owner to milk from his animals for the three months that the herd is at the rainy-season encampment, from July to September, the herder having absolute control over milk outside this period. Nor does the herd owner have access to milk from all cows, several being set aside for the exclusive use of the herder. In addition, milk from all the animals on Mondays and Fridays is usually the herder's alone.

Data on milk offtake from three herds were collected in the rainy season of 1981 and these figures are shown in Table 10.6. This milk was shared in roughly equal parts by herder and herd owner, giving the owner a total mean yield over the three months of 51.15 litres.

Calculating the value of milk received

It was shown above that a herd owner could expect to receive 51.15 litres of milk from each cow that calves. However, since calving rates are around 66 per cent the likely yield of milk of a fertile cow will only be 51.15×0.66 litres in any year. Almost all milk was bought and sold within the village, at the ratio of one volume of milk to one of millet. This gives a low value of milk of around 70 FCFA per litre when millet is valued at its rainy season price of 87.5 FCFA per kg. The millet–milk exchange rate in the village is set by tradition and does not vary during the year, despite the increasing scarcity of milk in the dry season when the price of millet is low. The reason given for the low fixed price at which villagers can buy milk is that most of the cattle actually belong to the villagers and herders should not, therefore, be able to negotiate its price.

Valuing milk at 70 FCFA per litre gives a cash value to annual expected milk yield received by the herd owner of:

$$51.15 \times 0.66 \times 70\,\text{FCFA, equal to } 2{,}367.5\,\text{FCFA}.$$

TABLE 10.6. *Average daily offtake of milk per cow from three herds in Kala* (in litres)

Month	Litres of milk	Av. no. milked
June	0.85	11
July	1.45	23
August	1.80	28
September	1.40	31
October	0.45	16

Note: Mean yield for July to September received by the herd owner will be (1.45 + 1.80 + 1.40) litres × 22 days, since Mondays and Fridays are excluded from each month, equalling 102.30 litres per cow milked.

Dung

Dung from animals herded together is available to the cattle owner in roughly the proportion represented by his holding in the herd. Out of the twelve months of the year, the cattle pass four months in the rainy season encampment, six to eight weeks on the field of the herder, and the remaining six to seven months on the village-field holdings belonging to those households which make up the joint-herding unit. Once the dry season starts, dung is carted from the rainy-season camp to be spread on the household's fields. During the dry season the herd is moved between the plots of a number of households. Alternatively, where the number of herd owners is small, each household receives the herd for the entire dry season in turn.

The marginal return to dung for a household depends on the level of manuring on its village fields and the household's access to other complementary factors, in particular plough-team inputs. The variation in marginal returns to dung between households was investigated in Chapter 6 in which it was seen that at the mean level of plough-team use per hectare, the estimated marginal return to a unit of dung varied from 283 kg of millet at the lowest level of manure use (0.30 manuring units per hectare) to 17 kg of millet at the high level of 9.27 manuring units per hectare. Thus, the value to be attributed to the dung gained by investing in breeding cattle must take this high variability in estimated marginal returns into account. Four alternative scenarios are presented in Table 10.7 from which the returns to cattle investment will be calculated.

Variability in yields from breeding stock

Rainfall Yields from cattle vary from year to year due to variations in rainfall and livestock prices. The two parameters of herd productivity

most affected by rainfall in Kala are the calving rate and the rate of calf
survival. The strongly seasonal pattern to calving, noted earlier, is due to
the single short rainy season during which conception takes place. The
rate and speed of conception in one wet season will affect the calving rate
of the following year, while conditions during pregnancy will determine
the number of abortions and stillborn calves. Typically, a cow becomes
pregnant in the mid-rainy season (July or August) and gives birth at the
start of the following rains (April or May). If pasture conditions are good,
the cow will conceive again in the following three months, producing a
calf every rainy season. Where animals do not conceive until the end of
the rains, the calf will be born in the middle of the following rainy season,
leaving little time for the cow to conceive again before pasture conditions
worsen and animals start to lose weight and condition. Late conception
will produce a lower overall rate of calving and consequently a lower rate
of herd productivity. Calf-mortality rates are also affected by rainfall and
its impact on grazing conditions. The dry season is a period of particular
stress during which mortality can be as high as 50 per cent for young
calves. An early rainfall in May reduces the risk of calf deaths by producing high quality pasture for the young animals and their mothers,
following which milk production will start to rise. Cattle in Kala are not
nearly so mobile as those kept in a completely nomadic system, where
animals can be trekked from one area to another as water and grass
become available, thus reducing the risk to herd productivity from
pasture shortfall in any specific area. Animals tend to stay within an area
of 10–15 km radius around Kala. However, it is not unknown for herds to
be taken considerably further when local pastures are very poor and
better conditions exist not too far away. In June 1981, for example, most
cattle were taken up to 50 km away for a week at the start of the rains to
take advantage of new grass growth towards the west.

Prices Prices of livestock vary seasonally, reaching a low point at the
end of the rains when animals must be sold before the rigours of the long
dry season ahead. The incidence of the major Islamic festivals also causes
a temporary peak in livestock prices given the strong demand for meat to
celebrate these feasts. Fluctuations in cattle prices from year to year are
usually caused by climatic factors, such as a major drought, which reduces
the productivity of herds and forces pastoralists to sell stock to buy grain.
The animals are usually in poor condition because of pasture scarcity and
fetch a low price. During a drought, the relative prices of grain and
livestock swing sharply against the latter, putting pressure on herders to
sell more animals in order to pay for the grain they need to survive.
Villages like Kala have usually benefited from such swings in relative
prices of millet and cattle, buying animals from distressed herders in
times of drought in exchange for grain stocked by the household. Several

households added to their herds considerably in this way during the drought of the early 1970s.

Variability in returns from breeding stock from one farmer to another

The main factors determining the flow of net returns have been outlined above. Here, the range of variation in returns will be investigated, taking several values for the two major determinants of overall yields—the calf-survival rate and the value of an extra unit of dung. The various combinations of low and high values for each of these elements are shown in Table 10.7. The marginal values of dung at different levels of manuring are taken from the middle column of Table 6.3, while the effects on returns of varying the calf-survival rate are found by substituting different values in the equation for the value of calf production presented earlier in this section. Table 10.7 shows that annual returns, excluding milk, from investment in a heifer can vary from a low of 4,825 FCFA to a high of 21,055 FCFA depending on the assumptions taken. One way for a herd owner to achieve a higher rate of calf survival is to forgo the collection of milk. It is interesting to note that the mean expected value of milk (estimated to be 2,362.5 FCFA) is approximately equal to the difference in values between columns (1) and (2) in Table 10.7. This would suggest that the value to the herd owner of a calf-mortality rate of 0.50 plus the receipt of milk is equivalent in value to a lower calf-mortality rate of 0.25 and no milk received. The relatively narrow gap in values between columns (2) and (3) (of around 850 FCFA) indicates that it would not be worth the herd owner giving up his rights to collect milk in exchange for an improvement in calf-survival rates from 0.75 to 0.85. However, were the herd owner also able to improve calving rates, from say 66 per cent to 80 per cent, then the improvement in returns would be sufficient to compensate the owner for the loss of milk. Such improvements in calving performance are not, however, costless and require higher inputs of herding-labour care and the provision of more regular rations of salt.

In calculation of discounted returns to cattle investment, three values from the centre of Table 10.6 have been taken—5,625 FCFA, 7,720 FCFA, and 10,405 FCFA. Tables 10.3 and 10.4 showed the range in costs and returns which may be expected from investment in a heifer under different assumptions, using the four household types described earlier in this chapter. The net present values for investment in breeding cattle are presented in Table 10.8, followed by the ratio of net present value to total investment cost and the length of the payback period.

Investment by households

Investment by household A yields a negative return on capital used to buy a heifer under all three of the assumed benefit flows taken here. This

TABLE 10.7. *Variation in the annual returns from calf production and dung* (in FCFA)

| | Calf Survival Rate | | |
	Low (CSR = 0.50)	Medium (CSR = 0.75)	High (CSR = 0.85)
Marginal value of dung			
Low (MVD = 17 kg)	4,825	6,920	7,755
Medium (MVD = 33 kg)	5,625*	7,720*	8,550
High (MVD = 70 kg)	7,475	9,570	10,405*
Very high (MVD = 283 kg)	18,125	20,220	21,055

Notes: Values in the table are in FCFA, millet being valued at its mid-dry season price of 1 kg = 50 FCFA. These returns exclude the annual value of milk production, estimated at 2,365 FCFA. MVD is the marginal value of dung, taken from Table 6.3, the four manuring levels taken being 9.27, 4.20, 1.66, and 0.30 manuring units per hectare.

The three starred elements in the table are those used in Table 10.4 to calculate alternative flows of benefits and returns stemming from breeding cattle.

is due to the high unit cost of providing watering labour for this small household which owns very few cattle. For household B, the investment is unprofitable under assumptions (i) and (ii) but yields a small net return under (iii). The position for household C is slightly better, with the investment breaking even under assumption (ii) and making a net return of 9,400 FCFA under (iii). Household D gains a negative return on assumption (i), like all the other households, makes a small margin on assumption (ii) and gains a net return of 10,300 FCFA on (iii). The difference between assumptions (i) and (ii) lies in the figure taken for the calf-mortality rate; in case (i), 50 per cent of all calves are assumed to die in their first year of life while in case (ii), only 25 per cent of calves are assumed to die. This difference in calf-mortality rates is worth a discounted value of 5,600 FCFA over the five years of the investment. The difference between cases (ii) and (iii) rests both on an improvement in the calf mortality rate from 25 per cent to 15 per cent in the first year of life and on a higher value attributed to an additional unit of dung. The net present value of these two elements over the life of the investment is worth 9,100 FCFA, of which 75 per cent is attributable to the higher value of dung and the remaining 25 per cent to the fall in calf mortality.

Using the above figures, it can be seen that returns to investment in breeding cattle are low in comparison with the other two investments examined in the two preceding chapters, with small, livestock-poor households like A reaping negative returns from buying a heifer. Even for those assumptions under which the net present value is positive in

TABLE 10.8. *Performance of investment in breeding cattle for different households (in FCFA)*

Household	Assumed benefit flow	Present value benefits	Present value costs	Net present value (NPV)	NPV/Costs	Payback period (years)
A	(i)	31,350	80,500	−49,150	—	—
	(ii)	36,950	80,500	−43,550	—	—
	(iii)	46,500	80,500	−34,450	—	—
B	(i)	31,350	42,200	−10,850	—	—
	(ii)	36,950	42,200	−5,250	—	—
	(iii)	46,500	42,200	3,850	0.09	end Year 5
C	(i)	31,350	36,650	−5,300	—	—
	(ii)	36,950	36,650	300	0.01	end Year 5
	(iii)	46,500	36,650	9,400	0.26	end Year 5
D	(i)	31,350	35,750	−4,400	—	—
	(ii)	36,950	35,750	1,200	0.03	end Year 5
	(iii)	46,500	35,750	10,300	0.29	end Year 5

Note: Refer to note below Table 10.4.

Table 10.8, the speed at which the returns are paid back is very slow, in every case all costs not being paid back until the end of year 5, when the cow is finally sold. With a calf-mortality rate of 50 per cent, the investment is not profitable for any herd owner, which explains the importance placed by cattle owners on the question of milk offtake from the herd. The inability of cattle owners to monitor effectively the milking behaviour of their herders underlies the general lack of confidence which exists between many herd owners and their contract herders and puts in jeopardy the profitability of investing in cattle.

Throughout the calculations of expected returns to investment in breeding cattle, the probability of death among adult stock of 5 per cent per annum has been taken to discount the value of benefits in each subsequent year. However, it is arguable whether the use of survival probabilities is very helpful when considering investment in a single animal. So far as the small herd owner is concerned, either the heifer lives and reproduces, or she dies; in the latter case, all the capital invested in the animal is lost. Only in the case of a large herd owner is the use of survival probabilities to discount expected returns a reasonable reflection of reality.

RISK TO CAPITAL VALUES

Variation in returns from cattle and their sensitivity to different calf-mortality rates were examined above. Cattle are also subject to risk of damage to their capital value through neglect, illness, injury, death, or theft. The main effects of neglect are in the flow of services from the animal, particularly its reproductive performance, described earlier.

Illness in animals is common. The main diseases found in the Sahel include anthrax and bovine pleuropneumonia. Rinderpest was largely controlled throughout the Sahel due to long vaccination campaigns in the 1950s and 1960s but is now re-emerging in many areas while trypanosomiasis does not pose a problem here because this zone is to the north of the main centres of tsetse fly infestation. Internal parasites are widespread and may prove fatal where the animal is already malnourished. Calves are often struck by diarrhoea in their first few months and some will die of this. Stock are occasionally injured, especially bulls and work-oxen, and three animals in Kala which had been gored in fights had to be slaughtered over the two years of research. Others suffered from sores or cuts but these could be treated and were usually of negligible importance.

Cattle rarely lose their entire value through death. An animal which looks as though it will soon die, either from illness or old age, is usually slaughtered and the meat sold within the village. The cash received from such forced slaughterings is however much less than the value of an undamaged beast and represents what the owner can salvage from his asset, given the animal's plight.

Animals are occasionally stolen. In 1980, 5 cattle (including 2 young oxen) and more than 20 sheep and goats were lost in this way, while in 1981, 12 cattle (including 5 oxen) were stolen, of which 9 were subsequently found and returned to the owner. The incidence of theft is said to be rising and has led elsewhere to the adoption of herding all through the year, rather than being limited to the cultivation season.

Thus, cattle are subject to some risk. While the control of major epidemics has reduced the incidence of the most devastating diseases, cattle are still vulnerable to risk from other diseases that cause occasional death, from injury, and from loss through theft. In this section, the adult mortality rate for cattle has been taken as 5 per cent per annum which represents the likelihood of death under 'normal' conditions. An outbreak of disease or a period of drought will raise this rate very greatly.

Reducing the risk to capital and to income flows

Cattle owners can reduce some of the risks they face from investing in cattle. Of particular importance is the nature of the relationship the herd owner builds up with his contract herder. Not only will this affect calf-mortality rates as a result of milking practices but also the existence of a mutually beneficial long-term contract between the two parties will reduce the attraction for the herder of selling-off animals secretly and claiming they have been stolen, an event which usually results in his being sacked regardless of any proof of involvement in the theft. Herd owners try to minimize over-milking by herders in a number of ways. First, some try to hire a herder whom they think will be conscientious and have only moderate consumption needs to satisfy; for example a herder who himself owns a few cattle or one with a small family. Secondly, some herd owners limit the demands they make on milk supplies so that there is less competition for the little milk available. Thirdly, many herd owners start paying out the herder's fees in the rainy season so that herders are not forced, through lack of grain, into over-milking the cows in their care. Fourthly, control is exercised by regular and careful monitoring of the herder's work, the owner visiting the animals at dawn and dusk each day. Fifthly, herders are also given land on which to farm on the edge of the village fields, which is manured by the animals in the herder's care. However, these strategies are only partially successful in controlling milking practices, and are more easily followed by large herd owners whose animals comprise the major part of a joint-herding unit. Those owning only a few head are less able to influence the herder's behaviour.

Relations between herd owner and herder necessarily involve a large element of trust due to difficulty in monitoring the herder. Only one herd owner in Kala appeared to have established a long-term relationship of trust with his hired herder. This herd owner made few demands on milk for himself, helped the herder cut and manure a large millet field and acted as his patron, with gifts of kola-nuts and snuff. In return, the herder kept his own milk demands to a minimum, milking a few animals once a day, which was enough for his small nuclear family.

Herd owners are limited in their ability to protect their animals against other risks. Effective veterinary services are not available to herd owners who are distant from urban centres and who do not have contacts with the administration. A herd owner's only protection from total loss through the death of animals from illness or old age is to slaughter or sell them early enough to gain some remaining value from them.

Flexibility of investment in cattle

The investment of capital in cattle is both more flexible and more reversible than investment in digging a well. Cattle produce a number of products—offspring, milk, dung—and can be sold when desired to realize a cash sum. The value attached to their different products varies within different production systems and economic environments. Near market towns, for example, milk is of great economic value and revenue from its sale supplies the greater part of the investment's return. Milk is of relatively low value in the case of Kala because the market is limited to consumers in the village. By contrast, dung from cattle is of high value and represents around half the annual returns gained from this investment under the assumptions made here.

The sale of cattle is relatively easy, they being sold either locally for slaughter or to cattle traders. Livestock sales are usually planned, and most villagers can afford to wait for a better offer if one trader's prices are too low.

A herd of breeding cattle is not essential to the continued existence of the Bambara household in the same way as is a plough team or a well. The products cattle provide can be got by other means, unlike the services of a plough team or a well. Milk is sold in the village throughout the wet season by the wives of contract herders and of local Fulani residents. Dung is obtainable by digging a well. Young oxen can be bought from neighbouring herds or visiting dry-season visitors. This is in contrast to the services of a plough team or well, access to which depends on the household having made an investment in this asset.

It is the value of cattle as a readily marketable asset which is stressed by farmers in Kala. They are well aware that returns to this form of investment are low and may be negative in years when calf deaths are high. However, they argue that cattle are important to them as a store of value and as a source of realizable income, for meeting marriage costs, and emergency expenditures.

11

FARM-INVESTMENT STRATEGIES

This chapter considers the longer-term strategies pursued by farmers in Kala regarding the different investments open to them and the broader constraints within which they live. Table 11.1 summarizes the differences between the three assets examined in the previous three chapters. There is considerable variability in the returns to all three of the investments examined, due to fluctuations in yearly rainfall and to differences in household size, strategy, and access to complementary inputs. For each of the three assets, returns are consistently greater for the larger households. This is because of their access to other productive factors and the scale of their farming operations. The latter factor means first, that marginal returns to each investment are high as their services are spread over a large area and second, that the maintenance costs of livestock-related investments are low, as watering costs can be spread over a large number of animals.

Both wells and plough-teams produce a very rapid return on capital under most of the assumptions taken here. Investment in breeding cattle is much slower to repay the capital outlay under all assumptions considered and it is not until the elderly animal has been sold at the end of five years that the initial capital is retrieved. When the net present value of each investment is compared with the initial capital outlay, both wells and plough-teams are seen to produce high rates of return under most assumptions. The return on capital invested in breeding stock is very much lower, and in several cases returns do not cover costs.

Returns to the three assets are not perfectly correlated, although all rely in large part on the volume and timing of rainfall in the short wet season. The main risk to the return from investment in a well comes from variability in the short-cycle millet harvest, which is determined by the amount and pattern of rainfall in the two central wet-season months of July and August, while returns to plough-team investment depend on both millet harvests. The respective sizes of these harvests exhibit a lack of correlation, it being rare for both crops to fail in a given year. This reduces the variation in returns from investment in an oxen plough team in contrast to returns from well investment. Returns to investment in cattle depend on pasture conditions throughout the year and particularly

TABLE 11.1. *A Comparison of the three assets: Wells, plough teams and breeding cattle* (in FCFA)

	Wells	Oxen plough teams	Breeding cattle
Net Present Value over five years	−2,500 to 674,000	158,800 to 781,350	−49,150 to 10,300
Returns between households	Highest returns to household D, due to larger scale on which it operates, so that services from each asset gain high marginal return, plus low maintenance costs for D with respect to livestock care		
	Low returns to household A because it lacks oxen plough team	Lower returns to household A due to higher costs of maintaining livestock (dry-season watering labour)	
Return in form of:	Higher millet yields, improved herd productivity, better domestic water supplies	Increased millet yields, dung from oxen, oxen resale value	Calves, milk, dung, cow's resale value
NPV/costs	Wide variation from −0.05 to 15.03	Lesser variation from 1.25 to 9.76	Little variation and low in value, from −0.59 to 0.2
Payback period	End of year 1 if high value attributed to manure and high plough-team input assured	Over 1 or 2 years under all assumptions taken	At least 5 years under any assumption, in many cases costs not recouped
Initial costs	30,000–40,000 for well-digging	68,900 to purchase young oxen and equipment	30,000 for 3-year old heifer
Form of payment	Forgone earnings of household labour, or hired labour paid in cash or livestock	Millet or cash	Millet or cash

	Indivisible outlay	Divisible outlay, oxen and tools bought over several years	Indivisible outlay
Divisibility initial costs	Indivisible outlay	Divisible outlay, oxen and tools bought over several years	Indivisible outlay
Maintenance requirements	Yearly digging out of shaft, replace trough	Watering labour, herding fees, salt, tax, renew plough blades	Watering labour, herding fees, salt, tax
Maintenance done by:	Household or hired labour	Bambara watering labour, Fulani herding labour, blacksmith repairs	Bambara watering labour, Fulani herding labour
Risks: services	Rainfall in July and August affecting short-cycle millet yields, number of livestock visiting in dry season	Rainfall throughout rainy season affecting both millet varieties	Impact of rainfall on pastures throughout rainy season affects calving rate and calf mortality, over-milking causes high calf deaths, value of dung depends on short-cycle millet yields
: capital	Little or no risk	Risk of losses through death, theft, or injury, 5% p.a. for adults	Risk of losses through death, theft, or injury, taken at approximately
Length of useful life	Indefinite if maintained, otherwise water supplies reduced and eventual collapse	Death in 10–12 years, declining productivity with increasing age	Death in 10–12 years, lower calving rate with increasing age
Resale value	No resale value	Resale after 5–8 years for more than 50,000 as meat animal	Resale after 5–8 years for 25,000 as meat animal
Consequences of non-investment	Only source of dung for households without own cattle, low millet yields	Limited possibilities for hiring or borrowing plough team, low millet yields	All products obtainable from elsewhere, low household liquidity

on the length of the dry season. If this is prolonged by a late start to the rains, deaths among calves and other vulnerable stock will rise.

Purchase of a complete oxen plough team requires a much larger sum than is needed to buy either of the other two assets. In fact, households rarely make such an outlay in a single year, relying on borrowing a second ox for a number of years. Animals are sold for meat after they have worked for five or six years providing more than 50,000 FCFA per ox, which is enough to finance the purchase of new animals, with surplus cash to spare for other needs. Thus, once acquired, the oxen plough team pays for itself.

All three investments require little cash outlay and can be carried out largely within a barter economy (except for the purchase of a few items of equipment, such as a pickaxe), and therefore require minimal involvement of the household in outside markets or travel to urban centres. This is in contrast to the early ploughs introduced which were only available in the larger market towns. Investment in digging a well has a particularly low cash outlay when using household labour although such labour has an opportunity cost in forgone cash earnings.

Both wells and cattle are indivisible investments, requiring a single major outlay. Investors have not developed a system whereby they can share the costs and returns from these investments. However, in 1983, two small households planned to join forces to help each other dig a well in the following two dry seasons. There were no known cases where households had jointly invested in a plough team.

The maintenance requirements for oxen and breeding cattle vary with the size of holding. This is because the provision of watering labour is a relatively fixed cost, regardless of the number of animals owned. Watering costs per head of cattle are particularly high for small households with few animals but decrease greatly as the number of animals increases. The cost of well maintenance does not differ across households in a systematic way.

The three assets differ in their marketability. Oxen, plough equipment, and breeding stock can be sold if necessary. Wells, by contrast, are not assets that have ever been sold in this area. Research among the Rimaibe of the Gourma has found that these agro-pastoralists regularly dig and sell for cash rights of access to shallow wells to herd owners looking for dry-season water-supplies (Hesse, 1984). However, these transactions involve only a temporary transfer of ownership rather than the permanent sale of the well.

Wells in Kala face almost no risk to their capital value, whilst cattle may be lost through theft or death; cattle owners do not as yet have access to veterinary inputs which could reduce the latter risk.

The three assets vary according to the complementary inputs they require to produce a return. Their productivity also rests on different institutional factors.

Wells   The value of a well in Kala depends on a number of factors. First, only Bambara households in the village are allowed to dig wells. If herders were allowed to settle and dig their own wells, the attractive power of Bambara wells would decrease and the high village-field millet yields resulting from well ownership would decline. Secondly, the yields of short-cycle millet achieved by farmers in Kala depend not only on the availability of dung but also on the characteristics of the soils around this village. Thirdly, wells in themselves are not saleable assets, nor is the water from them sold. Reaping the yield from investment in a well requires the involvement of the well owner in making use of the dung acquired within his own farming strategy. Households best able to do this will be those that have access to a large supply of labour and plough teams.

Oxen plough teams   As with wells, plough teams only become high-yielding assets when put to work in farming, since no market currently exists for the sale of their services. Land and labour must be provided as complementary inputs; where land is in short supply and dry-season labour has a high opportunity cost, the profitability of investment in an oxen plough team will be much lower, as shown by Delgado (1979) for his case-study in Burkina Faso. The availability of other complementary inputs, such as donkey-carts to transport larger harvests, and blacksmith skills close at hand, further contributes to the rise in agricultural productivity associated with the adoption of this technology.

Cattle as breeding stock   The surprisingly low level of herd productivity and slow return on investment in breeding cattle needs to be seen within the total production and investment strategy of households in Kala. For example, the return on capital invested in cattle might be higher were it cared for by a member of the herd owner's own household, rather than by contract herders. However, the opportunity cost of this household labour would be high in terms of forgone earnings in millet production. Similarly, where cattle investment is considered in isolation from the cultivation systems with which they interact, their dung is taken as of little or no value. But, in cases like Kala, dung plays a major role in raising grain yields and improving the food security of village households. The relatively low rate of return on capital invested in cattle as breeding stock should also be considered in the light of alternative forms of holding wealth. Female cattle represent a long-term asset that requires little extra direct labour input above that needed to maintain a work-oxen holding and they remain a saleable asset, disposal of which does not significantly affect levels of agricultural productivity, unlike, say, sale of work-oxen or plough equipment. Other avenues for surplus investment, such as a trading business, produce high rates of return on capital but require the regular involvement of at least one household member to manage the business.

The consequences of not owning one of these three assets differ. Investment in a well is crucial for households without their own cattle, since dung is not bought or exchanged for goods other than water. Investment in an oxen plough team is not so crucial to farm production as is digging a well, since a household without a plough may be able to borrow or hire one for the few days needed to ridge its village fields. However, this dependence on other households for borrowing a plough team does mean getting it at a time which is not optimal so far as rainfall is concerned. As for breeding cattle, their physical products can all be obtained from other sources, but they do provide a form in which surplus can be held, keeping pace with inflation and yielding a small return.

THE PATTERN OF ASSET-HOLDING AND INVESTMENT BY HOUSEHOLDS

Wells and plough teams are currently of central importance to household-investment strategies since these assets allow households to maintain and raise their millet yields. Only once these assets have been acquired, do households turn to investing surplus in breeding stock. However, the pattern of asset holdings must be seen not only in terms of the current returns and risks to different assets but also against the background of changing economic and technical conditions. Historically, cattle were the main form in which surplus could be held and wealth in cattle was limited to a few households in the village. In the 1940s the introduction of groundnut cultivation provided a means to generate a surplus, enabling many to finance the purchase of oxen plough teams and to build up cattle herds. Since the 1970s, short-cycle crops have become crucial in supplying grain for household needs and a surplus for investment in livestock. High yields are dependent on a regular supply of dung. Wells have therefore become the latest productive asset in which households want to invest, since these allow them to maintain and expand the area they farm with short-cycle millet. The growth in well investment is extremely recent: between 1979 and 1981, the number of wells grew from 16 to 27, and in 1983 as many as 16 wells were dug, representing an increase of 60 per cent on the number owned in 1982.

Table 11.2 presents the distribution of households in terms of their asset-holdings and demonstrates the strong positive correlation between

TABLE 11.2. *Distribution of wells, work-oxen, and breeding-cattle holdings, Kala, 1981*

Holdings of work-oxen	Breeding-cattle holding				
	0	1–10	11–20	21–40	40
0	$2^a\,1^b$ (2.6)				
1–4	$4^a\,5^b$ (4.9)	$1^a\,5^b\,1^c$ (5.1)		$1^b\,1^c$ (7.9)	
5–8			2^b (10.7)	1^b (11.6)	1^c (14.9)
9–12					$1^b\,1^c$ (16.1)
13–16					$1^b\,1^c$ (16.9)

[a] Households with no well.
[b] Households with one well.
[c] Households with two wells.

Notes: Figures in the matrix refer to the number of households.

Figures in brackets are the mean number of household workers for that element in the matrix.

ownership of different assets. At one extreme are households without wells and few cattle apart from a pair of work-oxen, while at the other extreme are households all of which have at least one well and keep large holdings of both work-oxen and breeding cattle. The strong association between livestock holdings and household size can also be seen from the average size of household for each column and row of the table.

There are important relations between holdings of the different assets, from which certain patterns emerge.

Cattle and work-oxen   The importance of work-oxen in livestock invest-ment can be seen from the fact that there are no households with a cattle holding that does not include work-oxen. Investment in breeding stock comes only after the household's work-oxen requirements have been fulfilled. The largest cattle owners run several plough teams, since these are the largest households in the village with abundant supplies of dom-estic labour to use in farming.

Work-oxen and wells   The most common work-oxen holding is of one to four head, 18 out of the 29 households falling into this class, and most of these are associated with a non-oxen cattle holding of ten head or less. This group has a mixed experience with respect to well-digging; five households have no well, ten have a single well and three have a couple of wells each. Of those five without a well, four also have no cattle other than work-oxen. These small, poor households are unable to dig a well using their own domestic labour; they are equally unable to pay a well-digger since they lack saleable assets and must keep their work-oxen in order to continue farming. The fifth household without a well has a cattle holding containing more than just work-oxen which could have been sold to finance digging a well; but this had not been done because of the need to use these animals to help finance the household head's forthcoming marriage. Three households own no work-oxen at all, two of which also have no well. In both the latter cases, the households are very small with five or fewer members, an aged head, and no young adult males who could either dig a well or finance from migration earnings the hire of labour for this task. The third household with neither oxen nor cattle managed to dig a well in the dry season of 1980, its head hoping by this means to be assured of a regular harvest. While without a plough team of its own, the household was able to borrow a team from various sources, as shown in Table 9.4 (case x), repaying the team owner in labour. Almost one-third of households (9 out of 29) have one to four work-oxen and a single well; six of these wells are very recent investments, having been dug in the dry seasons of 1980 and 1981.

Cattle and wells   Of the eight largest herd owners, four have a single well and four have two wells each. All of these households were among the earliest to dig a private well, needing to provide their herds with an independent water supply as well as making it possible to exchange water for manure. The second wells have been dug explicitly for getting access to more manure and this investment has been accompanied by an expansion of area farmed with village-field millet. The relationship between holdings of wells and of cattle is complex, involving elements of complementarity and of substitution. On the one hand, households with large cattle holdings initially dug a well in order to provide enough water for their herds during the dry season. In this context, wells and cattle holdings can be thought of as complementary assets. On the other hand, households with very few cattle have recently started to dig wells and this investment has been explicitly to obtain supplies of dung, so that the household does not have to depend exclusively on its own few cattle for supplies of this input. In this case, wells represent a substitute for cattle.

Investment in wells has itself contributed to a further growth in cattle holdings in the village. Although initially a household may have to sell an animal to finance digging a well, in subsequent years, the dung received from visiting herds will raise productivity and increase the investible surplus. For a few households, ownership of a well and a large manured area has provided the basis for regular purchases of female stock that have enabled them to establish a self-generating herd of cattle. In less extreme cases, the high yields of village-field millet have contributed to meeting household food needs and expenses that might otherwise have required the sale of stock.

Changes in asset ownership over time

The position of a household at any one time in terms of the composition of its assets represents a point reached within a dynamic process, the result of past performance in agriculture and of decisions to convert assets from one form to another. Over time a household will hope to move towards the lower right-hand end of Table 11.2, investment in productive farm assets—work-oxen and wells—providing a surplus to invest in breeding cattle. Household size plays a crucial role in this process of accumulation. Larger units are better able to generate the investment sum required for well-digging and the purchase of ploughs and oxen, thereby overcoming any problems posed by indivisibility. Larger households can also diversify their production activities and take risks with new technologies early in the 'adoption cycle'. A large and diverse labour-force is itself an asset of value and part of a household's income, and capital is devoted to expanding the size and work-force of the domestic group, as will be seen in the following chapters.

Households at the upper left-hand end of the table are handicapped not only by their lack of assets, but also by their small size. For them, diagonal movement in the table is constrained by their inability to generate sufficient surplus to invest in raising farm productivity. With their chronic grain deficits, the cohesion of the domestic unit is threatened each year once the household granary is empty and individuals are left to their own resources. Digging a well has been essential for enabling these households to produce enough millet for their domestic needs, as they lack their own cattle to provide them with dung. Households with a plough team but no well have generally not been able to produce a regular supply of millet, depending as they must on lower and more variable yields of longer-cycle millet for the bulk of their needs. Some of these households have seen a progressive worsening of their fortunes, shown by their movement towards the left-hand end of the table, as cattle have been sold to pay for grain.

RETURNS TO INVESTMENT IN THE LONGER TERM

The high returns gained by households in Kala from their current crop production and investment strategies depend upon several factors of which climate, land availability, and village control over land and water rights are the most important. An adverse change in one of these would have adverse implications in particular for returns to village-field millet and well-digging, and would endanger the longer term sustainability of current production systems.

Climate

Detailed data on rainfall was presented in Chapter 3 where it was shown that rainfall levels since the end of the 1960s have been substantially below the long-term mean for the region as a whole. Rainfall in Kala averaged 375 mm per annum over the five years of 1980–4, a level far below that which had been anticipated before field research began. Were rainfall trends to improve in future, pressure on cultivable land would grow fast, with the movement into this region of farmers from further south. This immigration of households would ultimately affect the sustainability of the present system which relies on there being a large land area around the village both for the expansion of fields and for the pasturing of livestock, a constraint examined in more detail below.

On the other hand, were rainfall to decline further such as to the 200–250 mm received in 1984, households in Kala would be forced to reappraise radically their crop and investment strategies. Years such as 1984 do not provide sufficient grain for the household's subsistence needs, let alone payments for tax and bride-wealth and investment in assets. Under such low rainfall conditions, some households might choose to migrate elsewhere while those remaining would have substantially to change their patterns of household organization and income-earning, probably involving a much higher rate of male and female migration to urban areas in both the dry and the farming season.

Land availability

The present system of cultivation and crop manuring depends on there being a large area of bush around the village, both for maintaining extensive bush fields under long fallow and for supporting the large herds of village and visiting livestock used for providing dung.

Bush-field fallowing   The large size of bush fields and their long fallowing period were described in Chapter 4, where it was seen that farm land is not at present in short supply around Kala. This can be seen from the very long periods of fallow practised, often for 30 years or more, and the movement of some fields into areas that are not known to have been cultivated before. Large tracts of land to the north of the village have never been farmed because of the lack of ponds, from which the work force could get drinking water during the cultivation season. However, with the widespread ownership of donkey-carts, these areas are potentially cultivable, as drums of water can be transported out to the field. Population growth within this and neighbouring villages and the continuous movement into this area of farmers from zones further south will gradually check the current land-use system, by reducing the length of time for which land can be fallowed before its re-use. However, unless there are a large number of immigrant households, this point must still be several decades away.

Village-field manuring   A more immediate threat to the sustainability of the current cropping system is the limited pasture available for the very large number of animals brought to water at village wells in the dry season and providing dung for village fields. There are both short- and longer-term constraints on the continued growth of these water–manure exchanges.

In the short term, there are limits to the number of animals which can be supported over the long dry season on the grass available within a reasonable distance of the village. As will be seen from the calculation performed below, the recent rapid growth in well-digging has brought the system close to its limits.

Assuming that cattle can be taken up to 7 km from the village for a day's grazing, there is a potential area of pasture of 154 sq. km, equal to 15,400 ha, most of which is natural pasture with a few hundred hectares of millet-field stubble. Each Tropical Livestock Unit (TLU) requires, on average, 8–10 ha of pasture for its annual fodder needs. Thus, the estimated grazing area around Kala of 15,400 ha can support an annual charge of 1,540–900 TLU, each unit equivalent to an adult cow (averaging 250 kg liveweight) or 8–10 head of small stock.

The resident livestock population of Kala in 1981 totalled around 800 TLUs, leaving surplus grazing available for 740–1,000 TLUs on an annual basis, or double this number for a 6-month period (or 1,480–2,200 TLU). In the dry season of 1981, at the peak watering period, there were 1,100 cattle, and 1,250 sheep and goats belonging to visitors, equal to 1,225 TLUs. Given the short stay of many of these animals, less than a month in some cases, there was no problem of pasture shortage in this year. However, by 1983, an additional 16 private wells had been dug, each able to water an average of 60 head of cattle over 3 months (equivalent to 30 head over a 6-month period) thereby adding 480 TLUs over 6 months to the pressure on grazing. If this inflow of animals is added to the number of visiting stock watering at Kala in 1981, a total of 1,700 TLUs is reached, a figure which lies above the lower estimated limit of carrying capacity.

Thus, it is not surprising that several villagers had become worried by

1984 about the heavy pressure of livestock on dry-season pastures and the consequences of this pressure for the productivity and condition of village-owned cattle, particularly in a drought year. It was recognized that there had been an adverse effect on village herds from the large inflow of visiting stock following the increase in private-well ownership. The calculation performed above would support the view that the growth in manuring contracts has brought the system close to the limits in terms of the number of animals which can be supported by pastures around the village. While a larger area of grazing would be available by taking stock a greater distance, this would cut down the time available for grazing. Thus, while well-digging continues to provide high returns to farmers from the manure they receive, these are increasingly gained at the expense of returns to village-cattle holdings. Calves are particularly sensitive to fodder shortages in the dry season as they cannot be taken long distances from the village and it can be predicted that calf-mortality rates will rise as well investment, and the number of dry-season visiting herds, increase further.

There are longer-term constraints on the sustainability of the present manuring system. The fertility of village fields is maintained by transferring nutrients from natural pastures to farmland by means of grazing animals. Such a fertility transfer will become unsustainable when the pressure of grazing is so high as to lead to a decline in pasture productivity. Under such circumstances, a given area of village-field land would demand a steadily increasing area of natural pasture in order to maintain a certain level of fertility. It is unclear precisely at what level of grazing pressure this situation would be reached. It is likely to be higher than that stocking rate calculated above, of 1,500–2,000 TLUs at which livestock productivity starts to be adversely affected by fodder shortages which was based on an assumed 40 per cent consumption of available grazing and 8–10 ha per TLU.

Control over land and water

The third key factor permitting high returns to village-field cultivation and well investment is the continued power held by local Bambara communities over access to land and water within their village's territory. Although control over these resources has in theory passed to the state, following Independence in 1960, in practice villages continue to exercise much of their traditional power in this respect. A recent case of land dispute illustrates how such power is maintained.

In 1978, a Fulani herder who had been living and working in Kala for 30 years was told to leave the village. The ostensible reason for his eviction was that the man's brother had abused a village woman. However, it became clear from subsequent conversations with all parties that the underlying reason for wanting the man to leave was the latter's intention to settle permanently on the edge of the village and to dig a well. When the dispute was brought before the *Chef d'Arrondissement*, the Fulani was granted the right to stay, in line with his legal position. However, the villagers of Kala took the dispute further by travelling to Bamako whence they obtained (in exchange for an undisclosed large sum) a decision overturning that made at the *Arrondissement* level. Thus, the herder was finally forced to leave and is now working in a neighbouring village.

A second case from a nearby village provides a contrasting example. Here, a long-time Fulani resident decided to dig a well and when brought before the *Chef d'Arrondissement*, he was granted the right to continue with the work and to go on living in the village, despite the protests of the Bambara community. In this case, the villagers lacked the money to take the dispute further and they argued that even were they to do so, the Fulani was himself sufficiently wealthy to be able to ensure a subsequent ruling would also be made in his favour.

In both cases, the Bambara villagers were bitterly hostile to the prospect of a permanent Fulani settlement being established alongside their village. As noted in Chapter 2, this is due partly to historical antagonism between the two groups, partly to fear of damage to standing crops from the presence of large cattle herds around the village, and partly from the fear that a Fulani settlement might come to rival the Bambara community in size and wealth. In addition, the Bambara want to continue to control land and water resources so that herders are forced to bring their animals to Bambara-owned wells, enabling the latter to benefit from the herd's manure and to set the terms of these water–manure exchanges.

The high returns to digging a well depend therefore on the Bambara retaining the sole rights to exploit land and water around their village. Given the distance of other dry-season water sources from villages like Kala, whether at neighbouring settlements or along the Canal du Sahel, control over wells also gives the villagers effective control over use of village pastures in the dry season. In addition, by refusing the Fulani the right to settle and farm within the village's territory, the Bambara assure themselves a supply of herding labour on the terms they desire.

Thus, were land and water to be freely available to all, as is supposed to be the case by law, there would be substantial changes to the production system of villages like Kala. Firstly, there would be rising pressure on farm land as immigrant farmers took land into cultivation, by their temporary or permanent settlement in the region. Secondly, well owners would lose the monopoly they currently hold over water and grazing resources and would consequently reap lower returns from well investment. Thirdly, the bargaining power of Fulani herders would be strengthened, *vis-à-vis* their potential employers, since the former would no longer be subject to eviction from the village on their dismissal at the end of a herding contract.

PART IV
MANAGING THE FAMILY

12

FERTILITY AND CHILD-REARING

INTRODUCTION

The following three chapters analyse the factors affecting fertility, marriage, and household size and structure. The analysis is based on the assumption that decisions in these fields have a major economic component, despite their relative neglect by economists. It will be shown that not only is there a strong economic rationale behind the pursuit of particular domestic strategies, but also there are important complementarities between successful demographic performance and the pursuit by households of a diversified, surplus-generating crop and livestock production strategy.

The high average level of fertility found among the Bambara (of more than eight births per woman) is linked to the household's need to generate and control its own work-force, in this labour-scarce economy where labour for hire is in very limited supply. The returns from child-rearing are shown to be high, given the low costs of child care and education, the contribution made by children to the household economy from an early age and the common pattern by which sons remain under the control of their parents until the latter's death. However, there are substantial risks to child survival, with nearly 40 per cent of children dying before the age of five. Parents also face the risk of a son or daughter refusing to conform to their expectations. While the latter risk is dealt with by a mixture of threats and incentives, risks to health remain acute given the long distance of Kala from medical centres and the high costs of treatment once there.

Households invest considerable resources in marriage since it is only through the production of legitimate offspring that a household can ensure its future and the lineage is enabled to gain descendants. The costs of marriage have been rising over the past few decades and constitute a major outlay of funds for the man and his household. In order to safeguard the large expenditure involved, households establish and maintain marital alliances with other lineages. These alliances involve the regular flow of women as wives in each direction, often over several generations, contributing to the interest each lineage has in preserving the stability and harmony of each union.

The domestic group within which people live, work, and reproduce is not purely the result of demographic forces. Both its size and internal organization are variables which shift in response to changing external circumstances and internal tensions. Household size and structure have important consequences for levels of productivity on and off the farm, investment strategies, and the security of the individual. Members of the household are drawn together by the advantages reaped by belonging to a large domestic group. Tendencies towards household division are moderated first by the known vulnerability of smaller units and second, by the flexibility of internal household structure which makes possible renegotiation of the rights and obligations tying the individual member to the joint household estate.

The significance of risk and market failure in decision-making has been discussed in previous chapters within the context of annual grain production and long-term investment strategies. It was seen, for example, that resource allocation between long- and short-cycle millet must be understood by the farmer's need to ensure some grain is harvested each year. Similarly, the pattern and timing of investment in different assets was shown to respond in part to the changing returns and risks associated with different activities and in part to the absence of effective markets through which capital can be mobilized and labour and other services hired. The discussion of 'domestic decision-making' in this chapter continues to emphasize the role of risk and market failure in explaining patterns of fertility, marriage, and domestic organization.

The three areas of domestic decision-making examined in this and following chapters have important effects on the crop production and asset investment strategies which households are able to pursue. On the one hand, decisions made in the domestic sphere can reinforce or endanger particular patterns of crop and livestock production as, for example, where investment of surplus must be diverted from farm investment (e.g. a new oxen plough) to domestic capital (e.g. finance of a wedding). Conversely, the success of a household's production and investment performance feeds back into its capacity to satisfy obligations to its members and into the consequent willingness of the latter to live and produce within that domestic group.

Thus, domestic decision-making is not only subject to risk in itself but can also modify or compound the household's vulnerability to production and investment risks. At one end of the scale lies the large domestic group, able to diversify its production and income-earning activities, benefiting from economies of scale in the generation of surplus and maintenance of productive assets, while at the same time spreading demographic risk over a large number of individuals. Such large groups have a solidity and strength which reinforce the desire of their members to remain and contribute to the joint estate. At the other end of the scale lies the small domestic group, consisting of a nuclear household or one composed of unmarried brothers and their widowed mother. With a labour-force of two or three adults, the household is much more vulnerable to the ill-health or death of one of its members and there is little room for specialization and division of labour apart from the basic gender division of tasks. Investment in a new well, oxen plough team, or cow places a heavy burden on the household's available surplus. In the case of livestock investment, there is also a heavy cost in terms of providing dry-season watering labour, which restricts the pursuit of dry-season migration earnings by the household's adult males. The household's poverty leads to first marriage at a later age for men and thus a less assured line of descent. With only one or two couples producing children within the domestic group, the household is less resistant to failure in its marital and child investments, and experiences greater variation in its dependency ratios.

This and the following chapter examine fertility and marriage decisions. Each is discussed with respect to the costs and returns from alternative strategies, the nature of risks faced and how far these vary across households in a systematic manner. The consequences for the individual and for the household of a failure in these investments is then investigated. Chapter 14 discusses patterns of household organization and the advantages of large household size for successful farm and demographic performance. It also examines the internal structures which enable the large household to balance the rights and obligations of members against the demands of the joint-household estate.

ECONOMIC DETERMINANTS OF HUMAN FERTILITY

Recent work in economic demography has sought to analyse changing levels of human fertility and to explain different absolute levels of fertility between sample populations, using as its main explanatory factors the calculation of costs and benefits from reproduction. Economic theorists such as Becker and Lewis (1973) or demographers like Caldwell (1977) aim to show that fertility is an important area of human decision-making which responds closely to changes in the relevant economic variables. Becker and Lewis (1973), for example, relate changes in fertility to changing economic parameters, such as the level of household income or the opportunity cost of women's time. Thus as the value of women's time increases, through an increase in their income-earning opportunities, the relative cost of child-rearing rises and there will tend to be a fall in the number of children desired for a given level of returns per child.

The demographic transition

The passage of human society from a state of high fertility and high mortality to one with low fertility and mortality, the 'demographic transition', has been followed by many countries in the past and its timing is usually accounted for by general improvements in the standard of living, the impact of improved medical care, and changes within family structures and social values. Caldwell's (1977) analysis of this transition is perhaps the best known description of the factors accounting for the change in demographic behaviour. He identifies the crucial determinant of the switch from high to low fertility as being the change in direction of income flows between parents and children. In general, high fertility is associated with production systems in which children provide a positive flow of services to their parents over time, both in terms of current income and by ensuring the parents' security in old age, a situation typified by peasant societies in many developing countries. Caldwell accounts for a reduction in the level of fertility undergone by countries in the process of modernization by a change in value systems, whereby children no longer provide net economic benefits to their parents. The industrial society of developed countries is seen to typify the latter case, in which the rearing of children is a major economic burden, children do not contribute their earnings to their parents for any length of time, and many old people live out their last days in economic independence from their offspring. The continued production of children under such circumstances is explained in terms of the emotional satisfaction which parents derive from them.

Studies of child productivity

Most writers accept the importance of economic factors in determining fertility rates in developing countries. Researchers have gone on to try to quantify the size of income flows accruing to parents from their children so that the effect of changes in these can be related to changing demographic behaviour. Time allocation studies of children's labour have been carried out in Bangladesh, Java, and Nepal (see Binswanger *et al.*, 1980) which demonstrate the long hours worked by children in peasant households from an early age.

In assessing the value of child and female labour to household income, most writers make an important distinction between directly productive labour which brings in an identifiable product or income, and the work of household maintenance. The latter form of labour consists of the regular necessary round of housework—child care, fetching fuel and water, food preparation, washing and cleaning, care of sick—essential to the continued operation of the household as a unit. Even if children are not directly employed in earning an income, child labour can make a major contribution to household maintenance—by looking after smaller children, fetching water and fuel, etc.—which then frees more productive adult labour to enter the labour market.

Mead Cain (1980) attempts to calculate the returns to child production by estimating the 'payback period', that length of time needed for investment in a child to be paid back to the parents in the form of income from the child's labour. He concludes from his study of a Bangladesh village that a male child is a net producer by the age of 13, bringing into the household more than he consumes, and that by the age of 15 he will have repaid the entire costs of his feeding and upbringing to that age. After the age of 15, his parents begin to reap positive returns on the investment made in that child. Thus, the net benefits to be derived from male children depend on how long parents can maintain some degree of control over their sons' labour. Where the son leaves his parent's home early to establish his own independent production unit, the benefits from rearing children will be lower than where male children continue to live and work for longer under the authority of their father. However, even if the son does establish a separate production unit, his father may nevertheless have access to his son's labour for particular tasks, only partially losing control on his son's departure.

Nag *et al.* (1980) come to similar conclusions about the positive returns to be expected from male children in their comparative study of Java and Nepal. However, both these writers and Cain stress that the value of children to their parents differs between households according to their ownership of assets. Landless households in the areas they studied typically have little remunerative employment to engage their offspring who are still too young themselves to enter the labour market. By contrast, in richer households, especially those owning livestock, children can be employed profitably in caring for animals from an early age, leaving adults free for more productive tasks.

THE ECONOMICS OF HUMAN FERTILITY IN KALA

The various costs and benefits that are faced by parents in Kala with regard to their children are shown in the following equations and discussed below. Table 12.1 presents estimates of the values which may be attributed to different costs and benefits for children by age and sex.

> Net benefits from child rearing = Total benefits less costs
> Total Benefits = *PCL* × *DoC* × *MR* × *FR*

PCL is the productivity of child labour by age and sex
DoC is the degree of control which parents can exercise over their children by age and sex

TABLE 12.1. *Estimated costs and benefits from child production*

Age of child (years)	Costs and benefits	Millet equivalent p.a. (kg)	Total for age-class (kg)
	COSTS		
<2	Food 0.1 consumption units (c.u.'s)	55	110
	Mother's time	100	200
	Medicine and clothing[a]	25	50
	TOTAL	180	360
2–5	Food 0.5 c.u.s	275	1,100
	Mother's time	100	400
	Medicine and clothing[a]	25	100
	TOTAL	400	1,600
6–15	Food 0.8 c.u.s	440	4,400
	Medicine and clothing[a]	25	250
	TOTAL	465	4,650
>15	Food 1.0 c.u.s[b]	550	550[c]
	BENEFITS		
0–5	Nothing	0	0
6–11	Care of siblings, small stock, etc., equal to 0.25 W	250–375	1,750–2,625
12–15	Work in farming, etc., equal to 0.7 W	700–1,050	2,800–4,200
>15	Male children equal to 1.0 W	1,000–1,500[c]	
	Female children equal to 0.6 W in farming	600–900[c]	

[a] Costs at 1,250 FCFA.
[b] Plus marriage costs. (See Table 13.2.)
[c] And in each subsequent year.

Notes: Consumption units are based on the estimated intake of people of different ages, based on observations in the village. The average daily allowance of millet in Kala was 1.5 kg per adult male, or approximately 550 kg p.a.

W refers to the worker index described in Chapter 3, an adult male taking a value of 1.0. The size of the worker index attributed to children aged 5 to 11 years is based on the amount of time they work, often as much as 5 or 6 hours a day, and the cost in terms of adult labour is the time taken by the latter to perform these tasks. For example, by having children care for sheep and goats, adults can leave for the bush field earlier in the morning and do not need to wait for the small stock-herd to be taken to pasture, usually at around 11 a.m. during the cultivation season.

The annual farm output per worker (W) is taken at two levels: 1,000 and 1,500 kg of millet. In Kala, over the two years studied, average output per worker was 1,150–1,450 kg p.a. However, large differences exist between households, ranging from below 500 kg per worker for the smallest, least productive household to more than 2,500 kg per worker for the most productive households.

MR is the mortality rate for children by age and sex

FR is the 'failure rate' or the non-fulfilment of expectations for children by age and sex.

Total costs = Food costs by age and sex + Opportunity cost of
mother's time by age and sex + Marriage costs by
age and sex + Miscellaneous expenses by age and sex

Each of the vectors making up the costs and benefits from child-rearing are examined in turn below. Costs and benefits are likely to vary both between households (wealthier households, for example, spending more on a child's marriage) and between children within the same household, depending on the number of other children in the household, the child's birth order, the sex of the child, and the spacing between him/her and previous and succeeding children.

Costs

Food costs   Table 12.1 shows the estimated value of children's food costs for different age-groups using the consumption weights stated in the table. The infant relies almost entirely on breast milk until the age of 9 to 12 months, though this may be supplemented by cow's or goat's milk if the breast runs dry. The child continues to have access to the breast until aged between two and three years of age because of being carried on the mother's back for much of the day. From this position, the child can reach round for the breast and pull it towards the mouth.

Children are weaned on to the common household millet porridge and are not given much special food. If there are small quantities of milk and meat available, children are usually given a large share of these, but otherwise their food consists of whatever is cooked for the household. Food costs are met largely by the household granary from which millet is measured each day. Each household has a wooden container used for measuring the daily millet allowance, which contains approximately 1.5 kg of millet and is the average amount allocated per adult man per day. In addition to household meals, women often prepare a dish for their own children and husband, using grain from their small private granary. These meals act both as a supplement to household food and as an opportunity to vary the diet with a dish requiring more careful preparation and special ingredients.

There is no evidence of differences in food consumption between children of different sexes. Data presented by Randall (1984) indicate that child mortality is, if anything, slightly higher amongst male as compared with female children in the first five years of life. Typically, each meal is served into several bowls—one for men, one for women, one for children, one for special guests, and so on—depending on the size and composition of the household. Children of both sexes either eat from a common bowl or join the parent of their respective sex at mealtimes. The value of female children, both as domestic labour and within the system of marriage alliances, accounts for the lack of sexual discrimination in access to food in contrast, for example, to parts of the Indian sub-continent.

Women receive little special food either during pregnancy or once having given birth. While they probably eat more at this time, household heads said they would not make an adjustment in the amount of grain measured out each day for common meals. Thus, women probably satisfy their hunger either by eating a greater share from the common pot (from which there are often leftovers, given to the dogs) or by preparing food from their own stores.

Opportunity cost of women's time   Women in Kala continue to work till the day that they give birth and are only given a fortnight's freedom from work after the child is born. Households in Kala give women a much shorter period of rest before and after childbirth than those in many neighbouring villages. For example, elsewhere, women were often allowed to abandon work in the field when five or six months pregnant and did not return until three or four months after the birth. In case of her own or her child's illness, women in Kala were not expected to work in the field, but there were few cases where women did not return within 15 to 20 days after having given birth. There is considerable pressure on households to abide by the 'rules' regarding the absence of women at childbirth, as in other areas of personnel management, it being felt necessary to maintain a common policy across households. Change in practice by one household would set a precedent which other women could then use to demand similar rights.

There was one exception to the above rule in which a woman was let off work in the field for the last two or three months of her pregnancy. This involved the sole woman of working age in a very small, poor household who had had a series of infant deaths and was now in her late thirties. Despite the value of the woman's labour in farming, the household head decided that it was more important to gain a fourth living child, given the little time left to his wife to bear further children.

It is probable that the heavy work-load demanded of women in this village imposes a cost in the form of higher infant and child mortality. Indeed, some confirmation of this comes from Randall's (1984) fertility study among the Bambara which found that Kala had a relatively high child-mortality rate in comparison with other villages (see Table 12.3). This high mortality rate was surprising given Kala's relatively favourable crop and livestock economy.

The opportunity cost of a woman's time will vary between households depending on the number of other workers (particularly female) in the household. Where there are several other women of working age, the reduction in work efficiency of a pregnant woman, or one with a small infant, will have less impact on the household economy than where only one working woman is present. For many tasks, the child is strapped to the mother's back, which allows her to continue with even the most demanding chores, such as pounding grain. For farming, the infant is left in the shade of a tree under the eye of an older child while the mother is out weeding in the sun. From time to time, the mother returns to let the child suckle, but otherwise works alongside the other members of the household.

Table 12.1 takes the opportunity costs of a woman's time as equal to 100 kg per year, an arbitrary figure which is meant to capture the partial reduction in her efficiency over the first six years of her child's life. After the age of five, the child is assumed to impose no net cost on the mother, since by this age they start to contribute to her working ability by caring for younger siblings.

The opportunity cost of a woman's time will be greatest for the first two or three children she bears if there are no other children in the household to look after the infant. However, in such cases it is common for the mother to hire a child from elsewhere to look after the infant, especially during the farming season, in order to minimize the loss of working time. The marginal costs of child production for a given woman are likely to follow a U-shaped curve, falling for the second and subsequent births, until a certain point is reached after which costs will start to rise again. First babies tend to have a high cost due to the mother's inexperience and the absence of older children over which costs can be spread and who can be used to care for a younger sibling. The marginal costs of subsequent children will decline as the mother gains practice and as economies of scale come into play. However, as the woman reaches her mid-thirties and her seventh or eighth parity, the marginal cost of each extra child will probably start to rise, the woman becoming more exhausted by each pregnancy as she ages. Support for a U-shaped curve to marginal costs is provided by recent demographic work among the Bambara of this farming region (Randall, 1984). As Table 12.2 shows, child survival rates rise considerably after the first parity until the sixth child has been reached, after which survival rates start to decline, suggesting that later children are associated with both higher costs and higher risks.

Children's marriage and dowry costs By the time that a man marries, aged between 25 and 35, his household will have spent a considerable sum of money on bride-wealth and other costs associated with his wedding (discussed in greater detail in the next chapter). Girls are usually given some gift from their natal household, in the form of kitchen equip-

TABLE 12.2. *Survival rates for infants and children by parity*

Birth order	Percentage surviving to the age of:	
	6 months	18 months
1	77.5	69.1
2–3	84.6	77.0
4–6	87.5	78.5
7+	83.2	73.7
All	83.9	75.4
TOTAL BIRTHS	(6,033)	(5,045)

Source: Table 7, p. 24, Hill *et al.*, 1983.

ment, a pair of goats, or even a young ox in the case of the wealthier households, when they are married at age 16 to 18. This is in addition to the presents of cloth, soap, and jewellery a girl receives from her mother, aunts, and other relatives. The girl's household must also provide a feast for relatives and neighbours to come and see the girl sent off. Marriage costs vary between households, wealthier ones being able to afford a larger and more ostentatious wedding, providing rice, plenty of meat, and perhaps a singer for a night's entertainment.

Other expenses Young children receive clothes and shoes from their parents, but the costs are low because little clothing is necessary and from about the age of 12 they will be expected to help in acquiring these by doing some weaving. Medical expenses tend to be very low, because of the distance from hospital care; parents tend to limit their expenses to the cost of equipping a child with a large number of relatively low-cost charms to protect them against a variety of complaints and dangers. During the period of field-work, children received no schooling, either secular or Koranic, so this was no drain on the household's resources. Even now that a classroom has been built for literacy classes, these tend to take place either in the evening or during the afternoons in the dry season when there is little else that needs to be done.

Costs will vary between households, since women with access to fewer resources will be less able, for example, to provide many clothes for their children. In general, women in large households are better able to provide for the needs of their children, as they have more free time to cultivate a plot of their own and to earn money from spinning and hair-plaiting. In addition, larger households with access to more productive assets (in the form of wells, cattle, and oxen plough teams), tend to be less vulnerable to chronic grain shortages and thus women are able to conserve their millet stocks, rather than having to use these for feeding their husbands and children when the household granary is empty. However, young wives in all households are under considerable pressure from the multiple demands of work and child-bearing, so that much of the burden of providing shoes and clothing falls on the child's grandmother.

Thus, overall, the average costs of child-rearing in Kala are low, in comparison with many other societies where women leave their employment for months, or even years, to care for their small children and where there are high costs to clothing, feeding, and educating the young. While the costs of marriage are high, not only will sons and daughters have contributed to these costs, but also marriage yields its own returns, as will be seen in the next chapter.

Benefits

Against the costs of child-rearing outlined above must be balanced the benefits reaped by their parents. This discussion will concentrate on the material benefits to be derived from children while the less strictly economic advantages will be discussed later. There are several components making up the returns from children; first, the regular contribution they make to household income, either directly, by their employment in a productive activity or indirectly, by their freeing a more productive household member to become so employed; secondly, the long-term security that children represent to their parents, especially during the latter's old age; and thirdly, in the case of female children, the value they represent to their fathers as the means to form marriage alliances with other lineages.

The relative magnitudes of these three benefits depend on the ease with which an extra child can contribute to household income, the length of time during which the child is under the authority of his parents, alternative sources and costs of labour available to the household, and the availability of other income-earning assets.

The value of children's labour   The value gained by the household from the labour of children will vary with the age and sex of the child, with the household's own economic position, and with the number of other children present. The main contribution made by children of both sexes until they reach the age of 16 to 18 years is composed of the value of their labour to farm, livestock, domestic, and other activities. This contribution will depend on the household's income-earning opportunities, its ownership of assets, and the extent to which labour can be profitably employed outside the household. For the crop-production analysis in Chapter 5, a weighted index was used for aggregating the labour input of different categories of worker according to their sex and age. The weights taken for each class of worker depend both on the average time spent in the field and on the intensity of work during that time. The work of children aged 12 to 15 was taken as equivalent to 0.70 man-days. Children aged 12 to 15 are particularly valuable for their work in leading the plough oxen, leaving an older worker free to hoe, a physically more demanding task. Apart from their input into the annual production of grain, children also work hard in other areas. Unmarried girls help their mothers with domestic tasks and help them spin cotton, weed their fields, care for sheep and goats and for their smaller siblings. Young boys from an early age spend considerable amounts of time caring for small stock, cutting grass for the horse and donkey, and performing all manner of small jobs for their fathers and elder brothers.

Having reached adulthood, male children make an additional contribution to the household's finances with earnings from dry-season migration. These are especially important in meeting tax payments for poorer households without a grain surplus available for sale. For a male child, the contribution made to his parents' welfare continues until the latter's death, barring the death or out-migration of the young man.

The benefit derived from an adult son's labour also depends on the age at which he marries. Men are considered to be at their most productive in their late teens and twenties before they marry. The greater energy exhibited by unmarried men in farming is attributed to their sexual frustration and their lack of a comfortable home to which to return at the end of the day. Thus, households have an incentive to postpone the marriage of their sons in order to benefit as long as possible from their most productive working period and to delay the acquisition of new dependants. The risk of such postponement lies in the young man withdrawing his labour from the household by his prolonged migration to town and his possible permanent departure from the household of his birth.

A female child makes a much briefer contribution to household production than her brothers, leaving her natal household at 16 to 18 years of age. However, girls are valued by their fathers within a system of alliance and woman-exchange built-up between different lineages over several generations. Within this system, a man when looking for a marriageable girl will find himself in a stronger position if he himself has several daughters or sisters who can be promised in turn to those from whom he is asking for a wife. Rarely is an explicit exchange made between the two girls. Nevertheless, both parties to the marriage agreement are well aware of the position of each with respect to their access to unmarried girls and several men said that it would be much more difficult to arrange a marriage where a man had no sister or daughter to offer in return.

In Table 12.1, a range of values has been attributed to the contribution made by child and adult labour. This is based on the average annual farm output per worker in Kala in 1980 and 1981. On the basis of these figures, it can be seen that by the time a child reaches the age of 16, total costs will have reached 6,610 kg of millet. Total returns by this age vary from 4,550 to 6,825 kg depending on the assumed output per worker. For the lower value of output per worker returns do not exceed costs until the age of 21 is reached, in contrast to the much faster returns found by Cain (1980) noted earlier, unless earnings from migration or other sources are also considered. For the higher value of output per worker of 1,500 kg per annum, by the age of 16 the returns gained will have exceeded the costs. In both cases, the assumed values for annual costs and returns are such as to mean that children from the age of 12 onwards are contributing more than they consume.

Taking the lower value for output per worker, the returns from a girl's labour do not exceed the costs of care in childhood as she will marry by the age of 18 or 19 years. Taking the higher value of output per worker, female children provide a payback on their investment equivalent to those of males, with net benefits accruing after the age of 15.

In fact, output per worker varies much more than the above figures would imply, with the least productive households, which own no well nor a plough team, yielding less than 500 kg per worker, while the most productive household in Kala had a yield of more than 2,500 kg per worker in 1981. However, although children yield much lower returns from farm production for the poorer household, they are especially important in such cases as a source of security for parents in old age.

The marginal contribution made by each child is likely to vary as the number of children increases. Three possible forms to this relationship are shown in Fig. 12.1 in association with various marginal cost functions (discussed in greater detail below). Marginal output may be a negative, constant, or positive function of the number of children in the household:

(a) Where employment opportunities are limited, either within or outside the household, one would expect marginal product to be a negative function of the number of children produced, the household increasingly lacking complementary assets that can productively occupy each extra child.

(b) Constant returns to each additional child will exist where the household has access to resources and employment opportunities in sufficient quantity for their household members.

(c) Where there are significant economies of scale in production and where diversification of household labour among a variety of income-earning activities helps to reduce income fluctuations, the acquisition of an extra child will contribute an increasing amount to household income.

The debate about the relationship between household size and economic status (see, for example, Lipton, 1983) has not identified in sufficient detail the conditions under which one would expect the relationship to take on one of the above three forms and it is usually assumed that the first of the three is the most typical. In high-density agricultural areas with slack labour markets and little non-farm activity, it may well be the case for land-less households with few or no livestock that extra children beyond the first or second are unable to contribute significantly to household income, especially in their early years, and that each one represents an increasing drain on the household's limited income and on the time of the mother. However, in Kala, where land is relatively abundant, where a variety of activities is carried out and where young children can be usefully employed in numerous household chores—cutting grass, looking after sheep and goats, caring for younger siblings, etc.—there are grounds for assuming that marginal output is a constant or increasing function of the number of children in the household.

The length of time during which, and extent to which parents can control the labour of their children   The economic benefits to be derived from children depend not only on the size of their potential contribution to household income but also on how completely and until what age the household head can continue to control the child's labour and output. Societies differ in the form taken by the household-development cycle. In most western industrial societies, children reach independence in their late teens or early twenties, most having contributed little or nothing to their parents' income. In many West African farming and pastoral communities, sons may continue to work for their parents until they marry, say in their late twenties, after which the father has little call on his son's labour (Stenning, 1958; P. Hill, 1972).

In the case of many Bambara communities, sons remain under the control of their elders for much of their life and only gain independent control of the household estate at a late age. Many men in Kala never achieve this if they remain in the household led by a healthy elder brother who outlives them in age; out of the six elderly men who died over the five years from 1980 to 1984, only three were heads of household. The 'normal' pattern in Kala is for a son to remain in the household of his birth, at least until his father's death, and often beyond. Only in the event of a dispute or if the young man leaves the village permanently does his father completely lose control over his son's labour. Girls, as noted earlier, leave their natal household on their marriage, aged 16 to 18 years.

Alternative forms of labour   The importance of family labour depends on what other sources of labour can be tapped and their relative cost. Non-household labour may be obtained by hiring labour, by extracting labour services from a dependent group, or by controlling the labour of an enslaved population. Slave-based systems of production in the Sahel have declined since the turn of the century, and the agricultural labour market is very poorly developed in the Kala region. Nor is there much in the way of a dependent class that relies on others for its subsistence, although relations between village herd owners and Fulani contract herding labour have elements of dependency. In this case, herders are hired for a season by Bambara cattle owners and are given rights to farm land around the village during their period of employment. However, they have no job security and are forced to leave the village if in dispute with their employer, being refused permission to farm in Kala once the contract has ended. Control by the Bambara of cultivation rights gives them the power to obtain herding labour on relatively favourable terms, although as was seen in Chapter 10, there are also a number of problems associated with these herding contracts.

The absence of established relations of dependence between Bambara households is due to the abundance of cultivable land, the highly variable rainfall in the region, and the relatively low capital requirements needed for farming which makes it difficult for any one household to establish a permanent relationship of patronage *vis-à-vis* other households. High human fertility[1] and the attempt to maintain control over household labour are obvious strategies for farmers to follow in the absence of alternative sources of labour.

Alternative forms of assets and their returns It has been widely noted that children play an important role in assuring their parents some security in old age, when the latter will be too weak to be able to provide themselves with food and shelter. Cain (1983) in his study of a Bangladeshi village thinks that the security function may be paramount in reproductive decision-making, given the lack of alternative assets that could provide a steady income. He takes the example of land as an alternative asset and shows that even this is a fairly imperfect investment, requiring a heavy management input in order to produce a yield and subject to capital loss through expropriation in the absence of grown sons who can provide protection. Stark (1981) pursues a similar vein, arguing that children are highly flexible assets providing by far the best defence against changing economic circumstances. In times of harvest failure, for example, the household's offspring can disperse into a variety of occupations, diversification of activities reducing the vulnerability of household

---

[1] The Bambara high-fertility strategy is contrasted by Randall (1984) with lower rates of child production among noble women in pastoral Tuareg communities in central and eastern Mali. In the latter case, less emphasis is placed on producing a large number of children, partly because of the lower labour requirements of a pastoral as opposed to a farming economy, and partly because many 'noble' Tuareg continue to have access to servile labour, which performs domestic and herding tasks for their former masters.

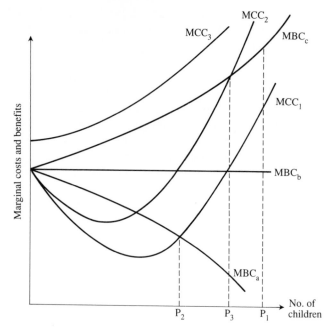

FIG. 12.1. Flow of marginal costs and benefits from child production

income to fluctuation in any one occupation. However, investment in children in Kala is not without risk, as will be seen later. Parents may be unable to establish the degree of control they desire over their child's labour and income. Children are also subject to risk of death or disability and may not attain the level of productivity and income expected of them.

Fig. 12.1 presents alternative forms which the marginal costs and marginal benefits of child-rearing could take. The equilibrium number of children produced depends on the relative shape and position of each curve. For example, where the marginal benefit curve (MBC) always lies above the marginal cost curve (MCC), as for curves MBCc and MCCl, there is no incentive to limit births (except where child-spacing will ensure maximum survival) and fertility levels will reach their natural maximum, as at P1. Where the MCC intersects the MBC from below, as at points P2 and P3, this gives an optimum number of children of OP2 and OP3 respectively. Conversely, where the MCC always lies above the MBC (as with MCC3) one would expect human fertility to fall.

In the case of Kala, it is argued that the MBC always exceeds the MCC, so that no attempt is made to limit fertility below its natural level, an argument supported by the very high levels of fertility found by Randall's (1984) demographic survey of the region.

The rough estimates of costs and returns presented in Table 12.1 also provide evidence for there being substantial net returns on male children, where sons continue to work for the household after achieving adulthood. Their average farm output greatly exceeds their food consumption needs, permitting young male labour to support other less productive members of the household. Maximum benefits are achieved from the labour of unmarried men where they are absent on migration for much of the dry season, thereby reducing the strain on the household's millet stocks and contributing cash earnings to the household budget, while continuing to cultivate the household's fields during the farming season. As will be seen later, the loyalty of young men to their household and their willingness to return from migration to farm each year will depend on the assurance that the household will also fulfil its obligations, by organizing and partially financing the costs of marriage.

RISKS TO CHILD-REARING

The net benefits that may be derived from children have been described above. Next, it must be considered how far these benefits are subject to risk, the sources of these risks and the extent to which different individuals can protect themselves. Two risks are of especial importance here; firstly, the mortality rate of children and secondly, how often and to what extent children fail to fulfil the expectations of their parents. Both of those factors reduce the expected benefit to be gained from the birth of a child and are likely to differ from one household to another, depending on the household's size and economic class.

Table 12.2 presents data on the survival rates for infants and children among the Bambara population sampled. The costs to the household of losing a child will vary according to the age at which the child dies. A baby who dies in the first week of life has brought little or no return but has equally incurred little cost in comparison with a child who dies aged 2 years. Mortality rates for the Bambara sample are high in comparison with demographic data from other developing countries. Particularly high is the death rate among infants in their first month of life and again between 10 and 15 months.

The first peak in infant death rates is due to a mixture of causes, among which childbirth practices and low birth weight resulting from the poor nutritional status of the mother and her heavy work-load are likely to be of major importance. Women in households where they are the only women of working age are liable to have to work harder and thus put their children at greater risk. The smallest households also tend to be those least able to produce enough grain for their annual food needs, so that women in these households are more likely to suffer from poor nutrition. Childbirth practices do not vary systematically across households, these being under the control of a group of elderly women who are responsible for looking after births in a cluster of neighbouring families. There is no traditional midwife.

The second peak in child mortality arises as children are being introduced to supplementary foods during the weaning process. Children are at risk from a variety of gastric complaints resulting from the change in diet and reliance on the low value–high bulk millet porridge. While children usually have preferential access to what cow's and goat's milk is available, for much of the year this is in short supply. Women with their own goats are in a better position as these animals provide some milk in the dry season, when the supply of milk from cows will have dried up.

Child mortality remains quite high even up to the age of five, with 17 per cent of all children dying between the ages of 18 months and 5 years (Hill *et al.*, 1983). This gives an average child survival rate up to 5 years of age of around 58 per cent. The main causes of death in this age-group, in common with other sahelian communities, are probably meningitis, measles, and malaria, the first two illnesses appearing in epidemic form, particularly in the dry season, while malaria is a persistent and recurrent ailment, causing weakness of the system and occasional liver failure. Traditional medicine is used to combat these diseases, western medicine being largely unobtainable.

The villagers of Kala aim to minimize mortality amongst infants by spacing births over at least two years, by this means reducing the physical strain on the mother and giving each child a longer period at the breast before it is weaned. The health of the small child is held to be at risk if the mother becomes pregnant before it leaves the breast; indeed, it is asserted that the quality of the breast milk changes with the new pregnancy in such a way as to harm the small child's digestion.[2] That child-spacing is relatively successful owes little to contraception or sexual abstinence, but is probably due to the suppression of ovulation in women by prolonged and regular lactation. Contraceptive practice relies on the use of charms and occasional abortifacients, both of which are acknowledged by villagers to be less than completely effective.

Table 12.3 presents data on child-mortality rates for women in Kala and the larger Bambara sample surveyed by Randall (1984), and shows that women in Kala seem to experience a higher level of child-loss than those in the sample population. As noted earlier, this may be due to the heavy work-load borne by women and the short time off work given them around childbirth. However, many other villages have hard-working women, especially those where water supplies are poor. Alternatively,

---

[2] Clinical evidence confirms that the milk of a pregnant woman does change, containing high levels of progesterone and oestrogen, both of which may upset the infant's stomach (Short, 1984).

TABLE 12.3. *Proportion of deaths among children ever born for Kala women and the Bambara sample*

Age-group of women (years)	Proportion of deaths among children ever born	
	Kala women	Bambara sample
15–19	0.17	0.17
20–24	0.31	0.30
25–29	0.52	0.34
30–34	0.52	0.38
35–39	0.60	0.40
40–44	0.44	0.41
45–49	0.46	0.43
TOTAL BIRTHS	(448)	(7,089)

Source: Randall, personal communication.

the high reported child-mortality rates for Kala may be due to the permanent presence there of the researchers. This could have affected responses by assuring better recall of deaths than elsewhere because women were familiar with regular interviews. A third alternative is that there was some disease outbreak in the past which badly hit the children of women currently in the 25 to 40 year age-group. A bad measles attack, said to have taken place 10 to 12 years ago, could possibly account for some of these deaths.

Child survival and economic class

Research from South Asia and other parts of Africa has shown a clear relationship between the economic class of a household and the survival rate among children, based on better access by the rich to food, education, and medical care. For example, Lipton (1983) quotes several studies from India which show that low-status groups depending on agricultural wage-labour have higher rates of infant mortality than do higher-status tenant farmers or landowners. Urban residents also have lower death rates among children than rural households in India, given the greater availability of medical care. Hill (1981) finds a similar gap between urban and rural child-mortality rates in Africa, although much of this seems to be attributed to higher levels of education among urban mothers, a factor of great importance in reducing mortality rates in all surveys carried out. The strength of this negative relationship will depend on the characteristics of the population sampled, its social composition, the kind of

Managing the Family

TABLE 12.4. *Fertility and mortality rates by household size, Kala, 1981*

Age-group of women (years)	No. of women	Children ever born	Fertility rate	Proportion dead of children ever born
Small household size (<16 persons) (n = 18)				
15–19	8	0	0.0	0.00
20–24	9	17	1.9	0.41
25–29	10	28	2.8	0.46
30–34	3	12	4.0	0.67
35–39	6	35	5.8	0.60
40–44	0	0	0.0	0.00
45–49	3	27	9.0	0.37
Large household size (>15 persons) (n = 11)				
15–19	12	6	0.3	0.17
20–24	16	25	1.6	0.20
25–29	20	67	3.4	0.51
30–34	6	29	4.8	0.45
35–39	10	50	5.0	0.56
40–44	8	65	8.1	0.51
45–49	8	74	9.3	0.49

Source: Randall, personal communication.

diseases to which it is vulnerable and the ease of access to effective forms of medical care.[3]

Table 12.4 presents data on fertility and child-mortality rates for women in households of different size in Kala. Given the very small numbers involved no firm conclusions can be drawn about differential mortality rates in households of different size or economic status. One would expect child mortality to be higher in smaller households for two reasons: while women in all households face a relatively uniform pattern of activity, in larger households the presence of other women permits

[3] Several interesting cases of the converse have demonstrated that higher economic status does not always ensure a lower child-mortality rate. For example, wet-nursing of infants from richer households in 17th- and 18th-century England produced a high death rate in the first year of life (Stone, 1977). Similarly, Randall's (1984) work among 'noble' Tuareg women of east and central Mali shows that the infants of rich Tuareg women suffer substantially higher mortality than those of their Bella servants. The former do not engage in the care and provision of food and water for their children, as these are managed by the Bella, consequently 'noble' children receive little attention and die from causes related to their neglect.

some sharing of the work-load; households vary in their vulnerability to crop failure, depending on their access to productive resources. In general, large households produce a more regular surplus, so that food shortages are less frequent. However, the almost total inaccessibility of effective medical care means richer households cannot easily reduce the vulnerability of their members to illness and death through lack of medical care.

Child-failure rates

Children may fail to fulfil the expectations of their parents in a number of ways, either through some disability, such as being mentally retarded or physically crippled, (there are 11 children who are either mentally or physically damaged out of a population in Kala of some 250 children under 18) or due to differences in energy, motivation, and willingness to remain under their parents' authority. There is a range in the degree of control that parents can exert over the product of their child's labour. At one end, parents gain nothing from their children's labour where the child leaves the parental home early and contributes nothing to household income. At the other end of the range, parental control is high where children (usually males) remain within the household of their birth, up to and after their parents' death and where they spend a very high proportion of their labour time on activities that contribute to the joint estate. The common tendency for male children to remain within the household of their birth has already been noted for villages like Kala, a household having a sense of permanence transcending the personalities of the individuals of which it is composed at any one moment. On the death of aged parents, men continue living together with their brothers, cousins, and nephews in a group that can persist for several generations.

The main threat from child-failure stems not from the child establishing an independent unit on marriage, as is common in many other peasant and herding communities; rather, the young man may absent himself for several years on migration to the city, depriving the household of his labour on the farm, the remittances sent being usually a poor substitute for this lost labour. From their late teens, young men start to spend several months of the dry season away from the village: weaving at Ségou, harvesting rice in the Office du Niger, digging wells in the Ivory Coast. Most return as the rainy season approaches to be in time for the first sowing operations and they bring back cash earnings, some part of which goes to the head of household, some to the young man's father and mother, and some remains as pocket-money for the next few months.

Occasionally, young men stay away from the village for the whole of the rainy season, and though a brother will be sent down to fetch them he may fail to find them or persuade them to return home. Only rarely does

TABLE 12.5. *Male absentees from Kala households*

Those absent for more than 2 years	Household	Household status	Comments
Almami	1A	Large/rich	Islamic *marabout*
Non	1A	Large/rich	Returned 1982
Ba	1B	Large/rich	Lunatic
Mengoro	4B	Small/poor	Away >5 years
Bugadeli	4B	Small/poor	Occasional visits
Monson	20	Small/poor	Works as servant

a young man decide to stay away permanently, finding a woman to marry in town (see Table 12.5). However, as noted earlier, the most productive years of a man's life are considered to be those of his late teens and twenties while he is still unmarried. Passing one or several rainy seasons away from the village at this stage deprives his household of a source of farm labour. The effects of the young man's absence will be particularly harsh on the smallest households and the receipt of remittances is considered a poor substitute for the young man's contribution to filling the family granary. It is rare for a migrant to return with more than 25,000 FCFA after a period of six months or more away. In contrast, the average farm output per working adult male lay between 1,000 and 1,500 kg of millet in 1980 and 1981, worth two to four times the size of this remittance. Those young men who do absent themselves usually return after several years, being coaxed back to the farm by the preparations for their marriage and being tired of their marginal economic and social position in the city (see Table 12.5).

Girls may also fail their parents by unconventional behaviour. For instance, it is not uncommon for girls to become pregnant before their marriage, with the father in many cases not the prospective husband. Of the 26 girls who married into or out of the village in 1980–2, 10 had had premarital pregnancies, with the husband-to-be not the father in most cases. Such pregnancies delay the marriage ceremony and reflect badly on the girl's household. However, no case was known in which premarital pregnancy caused the prospective husband to refuse the girl, nor is the size of bride-wealth reduced as a consequence, most of this having been paid by the time the wedding approaches.

Recently married women also sometimes run away from their new homes, thereby threatening the pattern of alliance and woman-exchange set up by their fathers. Women are usually sent back in such cases, having been browbeaten by their family and shown the alternative path of abandonment by all their kin, an unattractive option for a young woman in a society in which independence is difficult if not impossible for a single individual.

Child-failure: Incidence by household

Child-failure rates in Kala are relatively low in comparison with neighbouring villages, from which young men are often absent over many farming seasons. Households in Kala take pride in the regular return of their sons at the start of the rains, though elderly men acknowledge that such loyalty is due to the relative wealth of the community and in particular the large cattle holdings of certain households. It might be expected that failure among sons would be higher among poor than rich households, as the latter could use the attraction of an early marriage and access to household assets and wealth to exert control over its youth. By contrast, a poor asset-less household would not have an effective instrument with which to maintain control over its sons' labour. The extent to which this relationship holds in the case of Kala is examined below.

Table 12.5 presents material on the six adult men who had been absent from Kala for more than two years during the time of the research. These six represent only 4.8 per cent of those men of working age, from a total population of 125 men in the 16–55 years age-group. Three of these came from the two richest households in the village while the other three came from amongst the poorest. Of the former three, one has become an Islamic holy man, or *marabout*, against the wishes of his parents and makes occasional visits on his travels; his younger brother, having been absent for more than five years, subsequently returned in 1982 from Bamako with a wife he had married there. The third absentee from a wealthy household is said to be mad and to have disappeared more than ten years ago, since when nothing has been seen or heard of him.

Of the latter three in Table 12.5, two come from a household of four unmarried brothers in their twenties and thirties. Their father having died some 15 years ago, little has been done to arrange marriages for these men. The household's poverty and notoriety for disagreement between the brothers have made it difficult to initiate marriage proceedings. One of the two absent brothers visits the village occasionally; a third brother went on migration in 1983 and was still absent in October 1984, contributing further to the uncertain future of the household. The last case of absenteeism concerns a young man from one of the poorest households who has been away for nearly five years. He is said to be working as servant to a doctor in a distant town, but his father has had no news of him for several years.

A number of young men from the larger, richer households have had a period of several years away, often following a disagreement, before coming back to settle as the following case illustrates:

Sungo spent four years travelling and working in Bamako and western Mali. He was originally prompted to leave in his early twenties by the persistent quarrels between himself and the household head, his dead father's younger brother. He discovered a taste for wandering and picking up languages and said he would have been quite ready to carry on in this way for several more years. However, the youngest of his uncles set out in search of him and eventually found and persuaded him to come back home. This uncle was himself looking forward to retirement but had to wait for Sungo to return and take charge of the large young work-force. In this case, the size and wealth of the household seems to have made the migrant less worried about returning home since his presence was not vital to the household's ability to feed itself.

With the few cases involved, there is no conclusive evidence for there being a differential pattern of absenteeism across households according to their wealth, although with the exception of Non from 1A, the other two absentees from rich households were rather special cases. Young men who have been absent for several years may subsequently return and settle, while others normally resident in the village maintain strong links with urban areas to which they return for a few months each dry season. Both the general poverty of the Malian national economy and the relatively high productivity of agriculture in Kala encourage young men to go back home after a few years away. Poorer villages in the neighbourhood have much higher rates of out-migration to Ségou and Bamako, with a number of men establishing themselves there permanently. The existence of close relatives promotes further emigration from these villages as risks are reduced and the prospects of finding employment and shelter increased.

The overall distribution of risk among households

While no conclusive evidence has been found for higher risks to child-rearing in smaller poorer households than in larger and more wealthy units, there is likely to be some effect of this kind on child-mortality rates and on child-failure rates, respectively, due to the lesser work-load for women in larger households and their greater ability to build up a private source of income and wealth in the form of sheep and goats, and the earlier age of marriage for men from richer households and the assurance of a more comfortable future in comparison with those from small, asset-less households. Factors working against such a relationship include the very limited access of all village households to effective forms of medical care, due to the village's distance from a clinic, and the relative economic and social insecurity faced by migrants from Kala when working in urban areas, which means that even those from very poor village households see a more secure and familiar future in the village in comparison with remaining in town.

MODIFYING THE ECONOMIC ARGUMENT FOR HIGH FERTILITY

The previous discussion has shown that the high rates of fertility found in Bambara communities such as Kala can be explained by the large positive economic benefits derived from children. However, there are several qualifying points which should be made. Firstly, children also play an important political and religious role in Bambara society; secondly, to talk about fertility decisions in the absence of any effective form of explicit contraception is perhaps to introduce too precise a notion of decision-making, although prolonged breast-feeding may provide some level of contraception; and thirdly the rearing of children is not seen as valuable in itself, rather these must be the legitimate offspring of a particular lineage.

The political and religious role of children   By tradition, the strength of a household head, a village chief, or a local war-lord depended on the number of people under his control, since these people provided the military strength that guaranteed both the security of the community and the acquisition, through raiding, of cattle, slaves, and grain.

While the size of different households within the village still remains important in determining their relative political power, this is in part a reflection of the relative economic strength of different households in the community. Political and economic power are closely related. Large household size tends to ensure a greater level and stability of economic production, which reduces dependence on other households. It also encourages household members to remain within the unit. Some of the smaller households must rely on the loan of an ox or on other help from larger neighbours which puts them in a weaker position within the local community. However, the political strength of different households also rests on their length of settlement within the village. The three founding lineages continue to wield preponderant power; later arrivals, despite their large size, remain politically marginal and heads of these households speak rarely at village meetings.

Children also play an important ideological role. The lineage or clan is a central feature of Bambara social structure. Both men and women owe their position and name to the lineage within which they were born, their *jamu*; this then defines the nature of their relations with other lineages throughout the community. Male children are essential if the lineage is to continue to exist in the future; individuals are beads on a continuous thread, each character or personality after their death being reborn in the form of a new member of the lineage. Thus, a man can die in peace if there are male children in the household to perpetuate the line of his ancestors. The death of such a man is described by saying *a sayara*, that he has died, or passed on, *a da bora nyola*, he no longer eats millet, and so on. By contrast, a man leaving no male descendants, when he dies is said to have ended, *a banna, a shi tununa*, his line has finished or been lost. Female children are no substitute for male children in this respect, since they cannot produce descendants for their own or their father's lineage, but can only bear offspring for their husband's lineage. A man with no male heir is full of anguish and despair, as the following case illustrates. By the time this man had reached his late fifties, neither he nor his four brothers had produced a son, although a large number of daughters had been born. His family had to confiscate his knife and keep a close eye on him after several attempts at suicide. Fortunately, patience was rewarded and several sons were subsequently born to this man and to his brothers.

Fertility control in the absence of contraception   In discussions about fertility and the number of children that couples choose to have, it is usually assumed that there is some means by which that choice can be translated into action. Contraception can take a number of forms, ranging from chemical or mechanical aids, through taboos and abstinence, to the manipulation of marriage and the woman's pattern of residence in order to increase or reduce the likelihood of conception. The information available in Kala indicated the absence of any effective form of direct contraception. Certain charms are used to guard against pregnancy in a woman who has newly given birth but as noted before, the main contraceptive is probably the suppression of ovulation from regular breast-feeding of the infant for 12–18 months.

Children versus descendants   The production of children is not seen as valuable unless they are legitimate descendants of a particular lineage. Bambara households belong to large clan groups bearing a common family name. Legitimate children take the name of their father, expanding the size of the household and providing it with another descendant bearing that same name. Illegitimate children are an anomaly, as they do not belong fully to any lineage. These children are potentially just as valuable as workers in the household field yet the circumstances of their birth mean that they can never be so valuable as descendants to either of their parent's lineages. They sometimes take the name of their father and sometimes that of the mother, depending on whether the former has accepted responsibility for the child. Even if the father does accept responsibility and takes the child into his house, the child's position is still problematic, especially if male. An illegitimate man will be forced to leave his father's household on his marriage, when he sets up an independent unit. This is because his half-brothers will find it unacceptable that he remain and possibly become, through priority of age, the family head. The position of many illegitimate girls is not so different from their legitimate sisters, being given in marriage aged 16 to 18. However, the girl's illegitimate status does affect her position in her husband's household and her lack of a solid lineage behind her reduces her access to aid in times of need. In addition, some illegitimate girls are given as wives to men who themselves are illegitimate. The latter will have been forced out of the household in which they were brought up and must establish an independent production unit. In such cases, by being married into such a small, insecure household, an illegitimate girl's lack of parentage condemns her to as weak a position as does a man's.

An indication of the lesser value placed on illegitimate children is seen from the fact that nearly 40 per cent of the girls who married into or out of Kala over 1980–2 had premarital pregnancies. However, a considerable number of the children born subsequently died, usually in the first few months of life. Illegitimate children are reputed to be particularly weak. While child mortality is likely to be high amongst first children, particularly where their mothers are very young, these children are also often neglected as they are considered less than full members of Bambara society. Thus, the 'problem' posed for the family, by an illegitimate child being born, is frequently 'solved' by the baby's death, although no active measures are taken to provoke this.

13

MARRIAGE

Marriage can be viewed in economic terms as an investment, an outlay of capital by the man's family before and at the time of the wedding yielding returns over the forthcoming years. These returns take a variety of forms and vary in importance within and between different societies, depending on the kind of union entered into. Rights which may pass on marriage include those over a woman's child-bearing power, rights of sexual access, and rights to control the woman's labour and assets. However, marriage means different things in different contexts. For example, in matrilineal societies, men do not acquire descendants through marriage, a woman's offspring being her brother's, not her husband's, heirs. In other cases, women may retain a large measure of economic independence, having separate incomes and wealth over which their husbands have no rights of disposal.

The payment of bride-wealth by the man to his bride's family is a feature common to many African societies. However, bride-wealth varies considerably both over time and between societies; such variations are usually attributed to differences in the nature and value of rights transferred on marriage (Goody, 1976). Kitching (1980) notes that in Kenya bride-wealth traditionally covered several elements including compensation to the girl's family for the loss of her labour, as well as the transfer to the man's family of her child-bearing capacity and sexual favours. In addition, the payment of bride-wealth is seen as contributing towards the union's stability, for the girl's family will have a strong incentive to keep the marriage going as they will otherwise have to repay part, if not all, of the bride-wealth received earlier. Kitching shows how the size of bride-wealth has grown over the first half of this century and attributes the substantial increase in these costs to the large increase in value to the man's family represented by the woman's labour in farm production. Guyer (1981) also stresses the need to take the value of female labour into account in understanding changing patterns of marriage and bride-wealth and notes that much of the discussion in the anthropological literature has tended to neglect this aspect of the marriage transaction, focusing instead on the reproductive services gained by the man's family when acquiring a wife.

In the case of Kala, it will be seen that control over the woman's child-bearing powers is only one of the rights which pass on marriage. Other rights of considerable importance relate to her labour power, both in the field and in domestic tasks, to the income and resources to which she has access through her own activities, and to the links of help and support maintained between her and her natal household.

THE INSTITUTION OF BAMBARA MARRIAGE

An understanding of how the Bambara view marriage comes from looking at the Bambara verb *furuke*, 'to marry'. Men are taken as the active partner with respect to this verb (*a ye muso furu*, 'he has married a woman') whereas a woman can only become married and always takes the passive voice (*muso furulen don*, 'that's a married woman', *a furula sango*, 'she was married last year'). Women don't marry men but are married by men.

The Bambara consider marriage to be a fundamental and necessary state in which all adults should be. It is thought very strange that elsewhere men or women might want to remain single throughout their lives. This is a reflection both of the high value placed on producing legitimate children for economic, emotional, and ideological reasons and of the nearly impossible position in which single men or women would find themselves if they lived entirely on their own, given the labour requirements, the specialization of male and female labour, and the high production and demographic risks in this society. The married state is considered so essential that even quite elderly widows are courted by men in their seventies and eighties and pressured into accepting one of their suits. Very few old women have managed to remain unmarried after the death of their husband. In such cases, elderly men are looking for an additional wife to increase their prestige, and to gain access to the considerable income and assets owned by retired women.

Fig. 13.1 presents the incidence of marriage by age for men and women, based on a demographic survey of the Bambara population of this region (Randall, 1984). From this diagram may be seen that girls marry from the age of 15 or 16, with virtually all married by the age of 20. Men marry much later and there is a much wider spread of ages over which this takes place, the mean age at first marriage for men being 28 to 30 years. The large difference in the age at which men first marry is attributable to the resources available to the man's natal household. In general, men from poor households marry later than their better-off peers, which means poor men have less time to generate and establish their descent, contributing to the higher production and demographic risks faced by such households. Rates of remarriage are high. A married man of 65 will have had an average of 2.5 marriages, 80 per cent of men of this age having been married more than once. Married women of the same age will have had an average of 1.5 marriages, and 45 per cent will

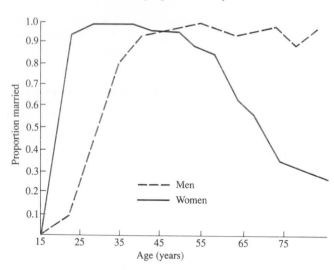

FIG. 13.1. Incidence of marriage by age for men and women. (From Randall, 1984)

have been married more than once (Randall, personal communication). The relatively high rate of remarriage for both men and women is due to three factors: first, the practice of polygyny which allows a man to have more than one wife; secondly, the practice of the 'levirate', an institution found in many West African societies through which women are passed on the death of their husband to the latter's younger brother;[1] and thirdly, the short life expectancy among both men and women that means that many marriages will end in the death of one of the partners. (Figures on life expectancy are presented later in this chapter.)

A man's household has the obligation to provide him with a woman in marriage. She should be a *furumuso*, that is a woman specifically intended for him rather than a wife inherited from another. Only in the better-off households are men provided with a second arranged marriage. However, many men acquire second and third wives as a result of the death of an older brother.

Table 13.1 shows the average number of wives per married man for households in Kala and it demonstrates the general tendency for larger

---

[1] Where there are two widows to be inherited, one will be given to each of the dead man's younger brothers. Where there are no younger brothers to inherit her, the woman either leaves the household or is taken by a man in the following generation, such as a nephew of the dead man. This practice is frowned upon, as he is in effect marrying one of his 'mothers'. Several cases of this inheritance of an 'uncle's' wife had taken place in Kala, and were the subject of some gossip. The social rules do not permit an elder brother to inherit the wife of a younger brother and no case of this was known.

TABLE 13.1. *Number of women per married man by household size*

	Household Size		
	15 people or less	>15 people	Village mean
No. of women per married man	1.12	1.90	1.42
	(0.798)	(0.625)	
No. of households	18	11	29

Note: Figures in brackets refer to the standard deviation.

households to acquire and maintain greater control over all resources, including women. This is also seen by the fact that the mean household size of the 11 households in which there had been at least one planned second marriage was 31.3 persons (as compared with the village mean of 18.2 persons) and that nine of these had more than 20 members.

Marriage is still a business to be conducted between two families, and while the man takes the active voice as far as the verb *furuke*, 'to marry', is concerned, the arrangements for the marriage will have been made without him being consulted. Men and women within the same household are married strictly according to age, a man never marrying before his older brother.

Households are joined together by long-standing links created by former marriages between two families. These links are called *furusiraw*, or 'marriage paths', that connect households over a wide area and down which women have travelled over generations. Because of the strong links maintained between a woman and her natal household, these marriage paths also act as channels down which women receive help in times of need. A woman's father and brothers are the first to whom she will turn when food stocks are short in her husband's household.

The costs and returns from marriage and their variability between households are examined below. While the purpose and content of marriage are discussed here in material terms, this is not to deny that marriage and the production of children serve important emotional, cultural, and ideological functions within Bambara as in any society. Men and women may not choose their partners, but love and respect frequently grow between them.

Costs of marriage

A household must devote a considerable sum over a period of years to acquire wives for its members. Some of these costs are the formal payments of bride-wealth and labour services while others are provided for the wedding festivities (see Table 13.2). Only the girl's household benefits from the former while wedding-day costs are consumed by the community at large. Some variation in these costs exists, depending on the wealth of the man's household and the nature of the marriage being entered into. In addition, the customs surrounding marriage vary from one village to another so that marriage costs will also vary depending on where the woman comes from.

Formal bride-wealth payments   Marriage transactions are initiated by an intermediary, often a blacksmith, who enquires into whether a girl is already engaged, and if not whether the suit of a particular family would be welcomed. Following the gift of certain goods the engagement is formalized and from that time onwards the man's family will make regular gifts of money and goods to the girl's family. Both families and the intermediary keep account of the amount of money that has been given and once this has reached 10,000–15,000 FCFA, this is taken as enough. Some of this money goes to the girl's mother who uses it to buy gold and goods for her child to take on marriage, some goes to the household head who may use it to pay his taxes and some is used to buy cloth, shoes, and a head-scarf in the year preceding the marriage. The formal bride-wealth payment of 10,000–15,000 FCFA does not vary much between households or villages unlike many of the associated wedding costs, although all expenses have been steadily rising over the past few years.

Labour services   A man's household must allocate one or two young men for several months to weave cotton for the girl's family. Most of the thread woven by these young men will come from the cotton bought by the girl's household from the *kwoorisongo* money paid by the groom's family (see below). Given an opportunity cost of labour during the dry season of 5,000–7,500 FCFA per month (as described in Chapter 8), an input of three months' weaving is a significant expense in forgone earnings to the man's household. Where labour is lost during the farming season, the opportunity cost could exceed 50,000 FCFA in forgone agricultural production.

Other pre-wedding expenses   The price of one or two sacks of cotton, *kwoorisongo* (5,000–12,500 FCFA), must be paid to the girl's family in the year before the wedding. Women in the girl's household will spin the cotton before it is woven into the many blankets and shirt-lengths that are displayed on the wedding day and subsequently divided up amongst close relatives of the bride and groom. Another major cost arises in certain cases. Some days or weeks before the wedding is to take place, the couple are supposed to go before the Malian administration to fulfil the civil requirements for a legally binding marriage. This is demanded of all marriages, but it is usually done only in those cases involving girls whose families are resident in or near the district headquarters, or *chef-lieu d'Arrondissement*. In the countryside, fulfilment of traditional rites alone is thought to be sufficient. While the actual ceremony at the administrative headquarters costs very little, certain customs have built up around it which makes it very expensive. As part of the ceremony, the girl is asked whether or not she agrees to being married to the man in question, something most Bambara men consider a dangerous and absurd precedent. The most effective way to bribe the girl into saying 'yes' in front of the magistrate is to take her, her mother, and her best friend shopping the day before. The man is expected to buy them a considerable quantity of cloth, jewellery, shoes, perfume, and so on, and is frowned upon if he bargains too hotly with the market traders. In addition, the man must hire a motor-scooter on which the couple arrive at the magistrate's office. All this can cost up to 50,000–75,000 FCFA, a far larger sum than for any of the traditional marriage payments. The attitude of the girl seems to be that this is the last time she will get anything out of her husband, so she might as well get all she can while she still holds some power. These high costs apply only to marriages involving girls from particular villages close to larger towns from which these customs presumably derive. Some men noted that as a consequence they would find it very difficult to finance a marriage with households from such areas. Girls from these villages also were considered to be a riskier prospect, being possibly unwilling to work as hard as girls brought up in the bush.

Wedding costs For the man's family the main expense comes from feeding a large number of people over several days. This means killing a number of sheep and goats, buying sauce ingredients (such as salt, peppers, fish, and spices), often buying a sack of rice (rice having become the expected luxury needed for a proper wedding breakfast), and cooking plenty of millet to make sure that no one goes away hungry. Other villagers will bring small sums of money, 100 to 250 FCFA as a contribution to expenses which will go towards the cost of kola-nuts and sweets for visitors, to women who will dance, and to those who have carried the wedding gifts from the girl's household. For the household which wants to give a stylish wedding, the costs approach 50,000 FCFA. Smaller and poorer households will get away with 10,000–15,000 FCFA by inviting fewer people and providing less meat. While people complain about the rising costs of marriage, they also vie with each other over how well a marriage is celebrated, the singers invited, and the amount of good food prepared.

While the man's family will meet the main costs of the wedding, in the day or two before the girl leaves her natal home a number of relatives will gather there to sing and dance through the night. These relatives and other visitors will need to be fed and meat provided for them. One or two households said they would postpone their daughter's marriage from the end of the dry season until after the harvest because their millet stocks would be unable to stand the strain. The girl will also receive certain goods from her own family. The richest families will allocate her one of their young male cattle. This animal acts as a sign of the wealth of her natal family and of the strength of feeling towards this daughter of theirs, which should ensure the girl more respectful treatment by her in-laws. Girls will also receive other goods from her household, such as a string of calabashes and a metal cooking pot, worth a total of 7,500–10,000 FCFA. The girl's mother and female relatives are largely responsible for providing these goods.

Total costs of marriage

Table 13.2 summarizes the costs of marriage to the man's family and range of variation in these from one household to another. The lower end of the range lies at around 40,000 FCFA while more expensive weddings can cost up to 200,000 FCFA. Relatively little of this expenditure is redistributive in nature, the girl's family receiving only a small cash sum over a period of years.[2]

One household head reckoned that the total cost of each of the four marriages which his household had recently conducted came to the equivalent of two mature oxen, a sum approaching 125,000 FCFA. While some spend more than this sum, there are also cheaper ways in which to find a woman, although as explained below, there are likely to be higher risks associated with low-cost marriages.

There are two cheaper forms that marriage can take, the first involving exchange marriages and the second where wives are sought from among widows or separated women.

Exchange marriages   One of the poorest households in Kala was involved in a marriage involving the exchange of women, a girl from their household having been given two years back for a girl due to arrive in 1982. These exchanges take place over a short period of time, not exceeding two or three years, and thus require a matching of girls of much the same age. The advantages of such an exchange are that many of the costs of bride-wealth are reduced. Certain problems arise with exchange marriages, most notably that in the event of a breakdown in one of the

---

[2] This is in contrast to a number of pastoral societies where bride-wealth received for a girl provides the capital needed by her brothers to conduct their own marriages (Gulliver, 1955).

TABLE 13.2. *Costs of marriage* (in FCFA)

Type of cost	Variation in cost (FCFA)	Comments
Engagement: cash, kola nut, chickens, and millet	2,500	Initiation of marriage process 10–15 years before the wedding
Formal bride-wealth payments: cash	10,000–12,500	Annual payments over a period of years until total sum reached
Weaving labour: 3–4 months' work by young men	15,000–50,000	Cost of young man's labour depends on season of weaving. If during farming season opportunity cost will be very high
Cotton price: 1 or 2 sacks of cotton for girl's family to spin	5,000–12,500	Escalation from 1 to 2 sacks among richer households
Pre-wedding costs: gifts, hire of *mobylette*	50,000–75,000	'Bribery' of girls from *Chef-lieus d'Arrondissement*, before civil ceremony
Wedding costs: grain, meat, sauce, entertainment	10,000–50,000	Varies considerably from one household to another. Richer households can expect to entertain many more guests
TOTAL VARIATION IN COSTS	40,000–200,000	

unions, the other will follow suit. For the above household, the marriage had run into problems because the girl who had already been given in marriage to the other household had subsequently died. Although the girl who was to have been received in exchange was due to come in 1982, she had still not arrived by 1984 and it is very unlikely that the marriage will now take place.

Search for widows and divorcées In a number of cases, a household suddenly faced with a desperate need for a woman to help with cooking and other household tasks (say on the death of the only working woman) was able to find a replacement in the form of a recent widow or a woman who had run away from her husband. A woman married to the youngest brother in a household has no immediate inheritor on his death, since elder brothers do not inherit the widows of their deceased younger brothers. Competition for such widows is often intense, particularly where the woman is young and still capable of bearing more children, and the woman's own family may play an important part in deciding whom she will re-marry. Where the woman is older, she will have greater choice and will decide which man to take on the basis of her own preferences, the sum he is prepared to pay, and the economic status of his household. Many marriages with widows and divorcées are a short-term measure, the man's household gaining someone to do domestic chores while waiting for an official fiancée to be old enough for marriage. These older women are often childless, one reason why they could be acquired relatively cheaply, and will find themselves socially marginal in their new household, being edged out of their central role in running the kitchen and in their husband's affections as and when the official fiancées enter the family.

Thus, both these cheaper forms of marriage present certain difficulties, the first because of the serious consequences of marriage breakdown and the second because of the lower likelihood of any children being produced from the marriage. The main transaction in the second case is the acquisition of a woman to do household work, which explains the much lower costs involved of around 5,000 FCFA, avoiding the expenses of a wedding, of weaving labour, etc. However, the overall incidence of these marriages is relatively low. Of the 108 married women of working age in Kala in 1981, only six had been acquired in this way and only one of these had been married into a very poor household.

Changing costs and patterns of marriage

The pattern and cost of marriage in Bambara society is changing. So far as marriage patterns are concerned, there is an increasing tendency for households to establish alliances with those outside the village. This is attributed to the greater ease of travel between settlements in the area with pacification at the end of the last century and the subsequent spread of trading links. In addition, villagers note that the village is no longer the solid social unit of former times, when households were closely dependent on each other for their own protection and survival, and when marriage ties between families further tightened this web of alliances and mutual support.

Several men mentioned that they now looked for women in marriage from households in roughly the same economic position as their own, citing several reasons for this. First, girls from richer households may be less willing to work as hard as required of a woman in Kala. However, this difference seems to relate more to girls who come from particular villages rather than from different households within the same village. For example, it is said that many girls from Doura and other district headquarters may have spent some time at school, be used to having a grain-mill in the village and thus be unwilling to devote themselves to farm work and to regular pounding of millet. Secondly, if a man gives his daughter to a household that is much better off than his own, people will say that he sold his daughter to the highest bidder, caring only for his monetary gain. Thirdly, a man will be unwilling to see his daughter married into a very poor household in which she will have a very hard life and face a chronic food deficit. These three considerations tend to mean that like marries like. However, many marriages also continue to take place between households that have been exchanging women over several generations, during which time both sides may have seen substantial swings in their respective economic fortunes.

Costs of marriage are also increasing, both of bride-wealth payments and more particularly the associated cost of the wedding. Villagers attribute this to the fact that wealth is generally rising. They were unclear whether total costs had risen by more or less than the rate of inflation and the rise in the standard of living—that is whether it had become more or less of a burden to find the means to marry. A greater escalation of wedding associated costs as opposed to bride-wealth payments has been noted for a number of other societies (see, for example, Guyer, 1984, for cocoa-producing communities in Cameroon). The differential increase in the two marriage costs is usually attributed to an increased level of differentiation within society (Goody and Tambiah, 1973). Different men and households compete for the available women not through the formal costs of acquiring a wife which are usually fixed by lineage elders over the community as a whole. Instead, competition takes the form of increased expenditures either on other gifts to the girl's family or on hosting an elaborate wedding which both does honour to the girl's family and demonstrates the man's wealth. For poorer households it is probably more difficult to marry now than formerly because of this escalation in wedding-day costs.

It is also said to be harder to obtain a wife except by having a daughter close in age who can be promised in return. This does not mean that there is a rise in the number of direct exchange marriages as described above but that a man who does not have a young girl who can be promised in exchange for the woman he is searching for now will probably have to pay much more than a man from a large family with many potential brides to offer. Acquiring control over young girls to pledge within the network of marriage claims has become more difficult as a result of the breakdown of large lineage–marriage groups into their component households. Formerly, many lineages operated a marriage policy in which widows were inherited by the next man in age, regardless of whether he was in the same household, the redistribution of women from such a policy presumably evening-out in the long run. Credit was also shared for those girls given in marriage to other lineages when it came to going in search of a marriageable girl. For instance, a man from a large lineage but from a small household in which there were no girls to be promised could benefit from the links established by girls given in marriage by other households belonging to his lineage. This remains an important economy of scale for larger households who control a larger number of marriageable girls.

Lineage-wide marriage-groups are in decline due first to the escalation in marriage costs that means that individual households want to keep control over the value represented by an unmarried girl, rather than see her used to enable a more distant relative to marry; and second to the refusal in several instances of the widow concerned, or of other men in the household, to allow her to be inherited by a man from the same lineage as her dead husband but living in a different household.

As far as the change in the legal position of women is concerned, by which their consent is officially demanded before the marriage can take place, the impact of this has been limited to girls from particular villages close to administrative headquarters. Here the man must spend a large sum bribing the girl with gifts to ensure her consent, as described earlier. It is not yet the case that women have any real choice over the man they marry. When questioned about what would happen were girls given the right to choose their husband, men said this would cause many problems, since bride-wealth would already have been paid by another man to the girl's father. However, many men conceded that girls would increasingly demand this right with profound consequences for Bambara patterns of marriage alliance.

RETURNS FROM MARRIAGE

Returns from marriage accrue not only to the husband of the new wife but to the entire household of which he is part. They are composed of the following four elements: the woman's labour services, her sexual favours, her reproductive power, and the assets she owns.

Female labour

A married woman has labour obligations towards both the household into which she is married and to her husband in particular, consisting of domestic chores, work in the field, and providing for her husband's needs. Outside the hours required for this work women are free to pursue their own interests and some gain significant incomes.

Domestic work The main contribution made by women's labour to the Bambara household lies in it freeing the rest of the work-force to pursue other activities. Domestic work takes up a considerable amount of time and energy; women spend three or four hours a day fetching water, pounding grain, cooking food, sweeping, and washing. Men gain from women specializing in domestic work, since it frees them to become involved in more productive activities, which also carry greater status than the daily round of household duties, which earns no financial reward and is no sooner done than it must be done again.[3]

The relative importance to the household of acquiring another female worker depends on the size and composition of the household's existing work-force. An incoming wife makes the greatest contribution to those households which lack an adult woman of working age or an unmarried girl to be responsible for the cooking. In such cases as these, the household is not a viable, independent production unit and must either rapidly acquire a woman to do this work or depend on another household for its meals.

In larger households, with more than one adult woman present, an incoming wife will lighten the domestic work-load of other women in the household and enable them to spend longer on other activities. Food preparation is done on a rota basis in households with more than one woman, each taking on the responsibility for a couple of days at a time. Particular women will also benefit greatly from the labour of the new wife. A woman who acquires a co-wife can transfer some of the burden of work in caring for her husband; for instance, it is usually the younger wife who washes the man's clothes. A woman with a co-wife will also be freer to travel and visit kin in other villages, as her husband will not be so insistent on her return. Similarly, a woman who is the sole female of working age will be greatly aided by the arrival of another woman, whether or not she is married to the same man, as this means she can share the burden of housework with another.

For an older woman, the arrival of a new wife in the household means that she can retire from farming and domestic chores and devote her time to private interests, such as her plots of millet, maize, and groundnuts, a small trading business or cloth-dyeing. A woman hopes for her eldest son's early marriage so that she can be free to cultivate and accumulate on her own account.

Women's farming work In the analysis of agricultural production in Chapter 4, the value of women's labour to the household field was taken as 0.6 of an adult man-day's work, a weight of 1.0 being attributed

---

[3] This is an important point made by Sen (1983) in his discussion of status and bargaining power between men and women within the household.

to the value of a male worker aged between 16 and 45 years. This weighting of female labour was based on the average length of time spent by women in the field and their speed of work at the main task, weeding. Differences in the contribution made by women to farming are relatively small and the general pattern of female labour obligations is remarkably similar across households in the village, as was also noted to be the case for the length of time off from work for childbirth allotted to women (see Chapter 12). Their contribution to the household's agricultural labour-force depends, as with domestic work, on the number of other women present and their age, and whether they are heavily pregnant.

As the number of working women in a household grows, the burden of domestic work on each one falls and this should allow them to spend longer in the household field. In practice, however, women in large households rarely spend longer in the household field than do those in smaller households; instead they use the extra time available to them to weed their own plots of grain and pursue their other private interests.

A woman's age affects her work output as does her state of pregnancy. Women bear a heavy work-load and must be strong to survive both the work and the constant stress of child-bearing. Women in their forties complain about the rigours of work and long to be freed from it by the marriage of their sons. On the other hand, older women usually have an unmarried daughter to help them with domestic chores. Pregnancy is not considered a bar to a woman working, but slows them down. Indeed, women exhibit a certain pride in the way that they continue to go to the field, even up to the day their child is born. Several children have been born on the pathway leading back to the village from the field, the mother having spent a long day weeding.

Sexual favours

Women provide their husbands with unpaid sexual favours. Even before the wedding, many young men demand their rights in this respect, although they will often make the girl a gift of money in return. The establishment of early sexual relations by the husband-to-be is also a way in which he tries to ensure that any pre-marital pregnancy of his bride will have been of his own making, sometimes hastening the marriage by this means. Once married, the woman is unlikely to receive further gifts from her husband. If anything, he is more likely to use his cash to pursue his desires elsewhere among the wives of others or unmarried girls. A wife also has certain sexual rights and can demand sex from her husband. Where a man has more than one wife he must spend two successive nights with each in turn: if he fails to do this, his wives can complain and demand that their rights be fulfilled, which consist of their getting a fair share of their husband's attention and the opportunity to bear children for his lineage. There were several cases in Kala where a new young wife's appearance had so distracted the man's commitment to his first wife, that she had had to complain and ask for help in enforcing her rights for him to visit her hut regularly.

Acquisition of descendants

The previous chapter presented an analysis of child-rearing. It was shown that children provide a source of labour both to the household and to their parents, they represent additional members of the man's lineage and allow the lineage to establish and maintain marriage links with others.

The only means by which a man can gain descendants is by marrying a woman and having her bear his children. True descendants differ from other sources of labour in a number of respects. A man's own children owe him a loyalty that he will not get from other children within the same household, even though in theory he can command anyone junior to him. A man or woman without his or her own sons will have no one to care for their individual needs. A household or individual can often get the services of a young boy or girl over a period of several years, the child coming to live and work as part of the family. This child will be borrowed from a relation, and is often a crucially important source of labour for the smallest household. One elderly woman 'borrowed' a child of her brother in 1981, then aged five, to help her look after herself in her declining years. In 1988, she was still there, helping her aged aunt by fetching water, pounding her millet, and generally caring for her. However, children acquired in this way will not remain within the household forever, the girl leaving on her marriage and the young man at some point in his twenties. These children can serve neither as permanent sources of labour, nor as descendants in the political or religious sense, since they do not belong to the same lineage.

Women's wealth

Women have access to sources of income and wealth which may be tapped by the household in times of need. Women often spend much of the dry season elsewhere earning grain by harvesting and winnowing the crop of more favoured villages. They also receive money and millet as gifts from relatives and lovers. As the rains approach, women return with their earnings, contributing in this way to household food needs during the coming farming season. Since a high proportion of wives come from households in other villages, this gives the husband's household a series of channels through which access can be got to grain from the harvests of

TABLE 13.3. *Proportion of men and women with first spouse still living, by age-group, Bambara survey*

Age-group (years)	% of men	% of women
15–24	100.0	97.8
25–34	96.4	90.3
35–44	93.4	74.4
45–54	84.6	52.2
55–64	69.8	36.3
>65	58.7	19.4

Source: Randall, personal communication.

other settlements in the region.[4] Women in Kala own 75 per cent of the village's 700 sheep and goats, which may be sold *in extremis* to provide food for the woman's small nuclear family unit. Some women also have gold that can be sold in case of need; for instance, in a neighbouring village a woman sold her ear-rings to help buy the family a donkey-cart. Thus, a wife from a large and wealthy family is a positive asset to her husband's household, because of the assets she brings on her marriage, and the help to which she has access in times of hardship.

SOURCES OF RISK TO MARRIAGE

The risks to a marriage include the death of the woman, her illness or disability, her sterility, and the risk of her desertion.

Mortality The Bambara population survey carried out by Randall in 1981 found an estimated life expectancy at 15 years of age of 43 years for men, and 45 years for women. Table 13.3 presents data on the proportion of men and women in different age-groups whose first spouse is no longer alive, from which the risks to marriage from death of a spouse can be assessed. For example, 15 per cent of men aged 45–54 (i.e. after 20 years of marriage) and 30 per cent of men aged 55–64 (i.e. after 30 years of marriage) can expect to have lost their first wife through her death. While the overall risk to marriage from the woman's death is relatively low, at less than 1 per cent per annum over a 30 year period, the incidence may be very uneven. For example, over the five years from 1980–4, there were eight deaths among young married women in Kala aged between 18–45 years out of a population of 108, representing an annual death rate of just under 1.5 per cent. This sample is evidently not of sufficient size

---

[4] Kala usually receives a large net inflow of women at harvest time because of its reputation as a relatively productive village.

for results to be statistically significant, but the high rate of deaths among young women during this period indicates the uneven impact in any population of an average figure for mortalities. Deaths among women are due to a number of causes, some related to pregnancy and childbirth, (such as tetanus, toxaemia, peritonitis) while other are the result of more general ailments (such as malaria, pneumonia, fevers). Over this period, one man had the misfortune to lose two of his three wives, one of whom was only 17 and had been married for just a few days.

Illness This reduces the value of the woman to her husband and to his family. Given the almost total absence of medical care, illnesses tend to resolve themselves rapidly in one of two directions, either the woman recovers or else she dies. In a few cases of chronic illness some women seek medical attention, either at Ségou hospital or with an Islamic *marabout*. In Kala, there were numerous cases of illness among women but this rarely stopped them from working for more than a few days. Three women are partially crippled, each one having a leg that has never recovered from an injury.

Sterility According to the demographic survey done by Randall (1984), the rate of primary sterility among women in this sample is similar to the 'natural' rate of sterility found in all human populations. In Kala, of the 143 women sampled, only one had never had a single pregnancy, although 9 had only had a series of miscarriages or stillbirths, giving an overall failure rate of around 7 per cent. A number of women also had difficulty in achieving another pregnancy after the birth of their first child, which suggests the incidence of secondary sterility, probably due to infection. No data were collected on the incidence of venereal disease but, with a large proportion of young men going on urban migration each year, it is probable that various infections are present; several women themselves described symptoms similar to those of gonorrhoea. A study from Burkina Faso (Retel-Laurentin, 1979) links the low rate of fertility in a particular village to the high incidence of venereal disease present and this association has long been made for populations in Central Africa, particularly Gabon. It is thus possible that the problems that some women in Kala face in conceiving are due to these ailments, though as was seen in Chapter 12 the overall level of fertility is very high, at more than eight births per woman.

Marital breakdown Marriages break up either through desertion by the woman or as a result of her husband's repudiation of her. Official divorce among the Bambara is very low and people when asked will say that it hardly ever occurs. More common are cases of desertion which over a period of years become *de facto* divorce, the woman marrying another husband. In such cases, the new husband is supposed to provide her former husband with compensation for the bride-wealth his family has expended. In the case of official divorce, bride-wealth is only repaid if the woman is shown to have been at fault. Over the two years 1980–2, there were ten cases out of 108 married women of working age in which a wife left her husband's home with the apparent intention of never returning. Of these ten cases, seven subsequently came back after several months had elapsed but three were still absent in 1984. In the former cases, fleeing the man's household is a strategy used by women to demonstrate their anger or resentment at a particular event such as their having been beaten but if the source of conflict is dealt with they are usually willing to return. Cases of longer-term desertion involved women who had been unable to produce living children for their husband. Having no children of their own, these women are in a socially marginal position, especially if their husband takes another wife by whom he gains his own children. Repudiation of a wife by her husband occurs where a man is dissatisfied with the woman's character and working ability in addition to her sterility. No cases of repudiation were known where the woman had already borne children. The two cases noted for Kala involved two very fragile, thin women from village families who had been married into neighbouring villages for ten or more years without bearing children. They had subsequently returned to Kala and remarried within the village, but in neither case had this remarriage been blessed with children.

CONTROLLING RISKS TO MARRIAGE

There are significant risks to marriage from a woman's death, sterility, or desertion. Little is done to counter the risks due to the illness or death of the woman due to the considerable distance of villagers from a medical centre and the high cost of medicines once treatment has started. The man's family hopes to minimize the other risks that it faces by careful choice of a woman from a family they know well, ensuring that the girl will be used to the kind of life and duties expected of her. Where close ties of kinship exist between the two families, it is hoped that any disputes arising during the course of the marriage will be ironed out, each family having a stake in continued good relations persisting between them. As far as sterility is concerned, both traditional and modern medicine are called in to cope with a woman's barrenness. Three women from this and neighbouring villages were known to have recently undergone a course of medical treatment in Bamako for sterility, with success in one case.

Consequences of unsuccessful marriage investment

Investment of resources in marriage promises to yield returns in a variety of forms of which the two main ones are the labour contribution of the woman to her husband's household and the descendants which she will bear for her husband and his lineage. These benefits will be reduced where the woman becomes ill, dies, is sterile, or deserts her husband. A common cause of marriage failure stems from the woman's death. The death rate among men is also high but, with the operation of the levirate by which women are inherited on the death of a man by his next younger brother, the death of a man does not involve the departure of the woman from her dead husband's household, unless there is no younger man available to inherit the widow. Even where the deceased has no younger brother to inherit the woman, it is not unknown for another man in the household to take the woman, even if he is technically part of the next generation, that is a 'son' (i.e. nephew) of the dead man. This creates a slight scandal since the young man is marrying a woman who is of a higher generation and thus one of his 'mothers'. But little account is taken of the judgements of others if the alternative is for a reasonably young woman to leave the household and be taken in marriage by a man elsewhere.[5] From the point of view of the man's family, the man's death represents less of a risk to the marriage investment than does the death of the woman, who has been effectively acquired by the entire household rather than by any individual within it.

The consequence of marriage failure due to the death of the woman depends on the characteristics of the household of which she was part. The most profound effects occur where the dead woman was the only woman of working age present. In such a case, the loss of this female labour puts the whole household's production system at risk. For a short period of time the household may be able to borrow the daughter of another family to help them with domestic tasks but the household must rapidly try to find a replacement to do this work as they cannot count on the indefinite loan of a female worker. In such straits, the success of a household in getting a woman to replace the one that has died depends on their resources and their capacity to attract a woman who happens to be free at that moment. Typically, these will be women who have left their husbands, those recently widowed in a household where there is no obvious successor to take them in marriage or women who have been repudiated by their husbands. Where the household is relatively well off, it can offer the woman or her parents a sum such as 5,000 FCFA. The woman will also be predisposed to join a household that is reasonably comfortable.

The example of Household Z illustrates the grave difficulties faced by a poor household which loses its only working female. This household has found it impossible to get any woman to join them, due to the chronic

---

[5] There were three cases of a man having married his 'mother' in Kala to prevent the woman passing to a man in a different household, see note on page 236.

grain deficit which they face every year, the absence of any assets, and the social status of the head of household who, as an illegitimate man, gains little respect or hearing in the affairs either of his village or within his own family. This household has tried unsuccessfully to attract a woman to help them ever since the man's wife died some ten years ago. Following this death, the man's elderly mother returned to live with him and although already in her seventies, she did much of the cooking and fetching water for her son and grandsons. She died in 1982, after which the household has been absorbed for eating purposes by its household of origin, from which the illegitimate man had been expelled some twenty years earlier. Grain is provided by Z and added to that cooked by the parent household. The prospects for Z do not look good in the medium term future. The man's three sons are aged 14 to 18 and the eldest must wait several years before he will be able to marry. The fiancée of the eldest son died in 1983, aged five years old, setting back further their chances of acquiring a woman to take care of the housework. The consequences for this household of not having a female under their control who can do domestic chores is a loss of independence *vis-à-vis* other households, because Z is unable to function as a fully independent unit. They must rely on the goodwill of others who cook their food and wash their clothes. This means that they are forced to swallow any teasing or insults they face as a result of their difficult circumstances, which involves a loss of pride. This dependence on another household also means that they cannot refuse to do whatever is asked of them, such as helping to water the cattle of the household which aids them in the dry season. Were Household Z not to receive help from elsewhere, either the household head or one of his sons would have to do the cooking and washing which would not only take labour from farm work but would also be deeply shaming.

The above case presents an example of the problems faced by a household when they lose the female labour they need to remain a viable unit. The circumstances are even more severe where the household has been unable to generate descendants for itself. One case like this had occurred in the recent past in Kala, involving a couple who had only managed to produce three daughters. The man himself was fairly isolated in kin terms, having arrived to settle in the village in his youth, an ex-Maure slave by descent. The poverty of the man precluded his acquiring another wife with whom he might have managed to produce male descendants. In their old age, the couple attached themselves to another household, also of ex-Maure slave descent, with whom they ran a combined farming operation until the death of the old couple. The old man's descent line has died out, a fact that the villagers of Kala are reluctant to discuss. In this case, while the household was able to continue as a production unit by joining forces with another household, it was unable to secure itself descendants, its female children not being able to perform this function.

This chapter has presented material on the costs, returns, and risks associated with marriage in the village of Kala. High variations in marriage costs are due to a variety of factors, such as: the wealth of the man's household; whether a woman is being acquired as a full *furumuso*, where the man's household is gaining rights over her labour and off-spring; or whether, as in the case of older women, the transaction essentially involves the acquisition of domestic labour. Over the period 1980–2, there were eight households involved in celebrating at least one marriage, all of them containing more than twenty persons. In all but one case the wedding was a large and costly business, absorbing from 30,000–50,000 FCFA. In the one case, the household's relative poverty forced it to have less expensive festivities, estimated by the household head to have taken no more than 20,000 FCFA.

Highest returns from acquiring a woman worker through marriage will accrue to small households where she is the sole woman of working age. The marginal benefits to the household estate will decline with an increase in the number of married women in the household. However, women in larger households share domestic duties and thereby gain more free time to pursue their own interests. For example, all women in households where they were not the sole woman of working age had private plots of grain, whereas those in single woman households rarely found sufficient time to have a field of their own. These plots of land and other activities mean that women in large households gain substantial sources of income, described in Chapter 3, which raise the returns from marriage to these households.

There are considerable risks to marital investments from mortality, sterility, and desertion. These risks have particularly severe consequences for households containing only a single woman; her death causes the household to become no longer viable as an independent unit, while her sterility puts in jeopardy the future survival of the domestic group. However, there is no evidence for higher rates of desertion from poor households. Instances from Kala of women leaving their husbands spanned all kinds of household and tended to occur mainly among women who had not managed to bear children for their husband.

Marriage involves a considerable outlay of resources which could have been used for other purposes and it often takes priority over other investments, as the following cases show. The head of one small household has postponed digging a well in order to conserve the few head of cattle for meeting his forthcoming marriage costs. Three other households have sold all but their work-oxen cattle holdings in order to finance second marriages for their members. One household head described how he had forgone purchasing a donkey-cart as all available resources were needed for his younger brother's wedding, while another explained that all his millet surplus would be sold to meet his son's marriage costs rather than be invested in buying breeding stock, as in previous years. By granting marriage such high priority, households hope to ensure themselves a supply of domestically controlled labour over the longer term. This labour is crucial for the long-term security of current household members and for the continued productivity of farm and investment activities. In addition, by putting marriage above other potential uses of funds, household heads try to maintain control over their junior male members, by enabling the latter to achieve the higher status of married man (or *musotigi*, 'one who possesses a woman') with all that implies in terms of establishing a line of descent and having access to the woman's labour and other services.

14

BAMBARA HOUSEHOLD ORGANIZATION

The Bambara household was described in Chapter 2 as that unit which farms a common field and consumes most of its meals together. Table 2.1 showed that households in Kala have an average size of 18.2 persons. These are extremely large domestic groups in comparison with those found elsewhere in West Africa or other parts of the developing world. For example, P. Hill (1972) found an average household size of 7.2 persons for her Hausa study and Watts (1983) found one of 6.7 persons per household. Both writers, however, note the existence of larger complex households among the rich in their samples. Studies elsewhere in Mali amongst the Bambara show that the large households found in Kala are in no way exceptional for this ethnic group. Becker's (1989) study of a farming community to the south-east of Mali's capital, Bamako, presents average household size of 19.6 people, with complex households averaging 31.1 and simple households 10.0 people.

This chapter examines the factors which encourage the persistence of these large domestic groups, focusing first on the advantages reaped in the fields of production, investment, and protection from demographic risk, and second on the vulnerability of the individual or small kin group to many forms of risk if it is not part of a larger domestic group. The potential drawbacks to individuals from belonging to a large group, such as loss of control over their own resources, are minimized by defining the specific duties of each individual to the household and the benefits to be received in exchange. Flexibility in these contracts between a household and its members permits the household to respond to changes in internal and external circumstances that threaten its continued unity. The five cases of household division that have taken place in Kala over the last 30 years are discussed at the end of the chapter and are used to illustrate the risks faced by those who separate themselves from a larger domestic group.

THE SIGNIFICANCE OF HOUSEHOLD SIZE AND STRUCTURE

The size and structure of the household at any one point in time is the product of several forces. Fertility and mortality rates are important determining variables partly under the control and manipulation of household members and likely to vary systematically between those of different socio-economic class. Household size is also partly determined by the relative strengths of opposing forces leading either to the formation and cohesion of a large extended group or to its division into several separate units. While certain benefits arise from being part of a large group, problems are also likely to develop over the management of labour and other resources and over the distribution of benefits from the household enterprise. Binswanger and McIntire (1984) note that the upper limit on household size will be reached where the marginal benefits of increased size (in particular those stemming from greater insurance cover) are outweighed by the marginal costs of further growth, seen by these writers as being mainly the result of incentive dilution as household size grows. The continued viability of the large domestic group in Kala is achieved, despite mounting numbers, by adjusting the internal balance of rights and obligations between members and the joint-household estate. Typically, this is done by granting its members greater autonomy over the accumulation and disposal of individual sources of wealth as household size grows.

Modelling relations within the household

Attempts to model the behaviour of households have followed similar lines to the theory of the firm. While some neoclassical work continues to take the firm as a single-minded enterprise whose sole aim is profit maximization, most writers accept the complex but more realistic picture painted by managerial theories of the firm (Cyert and March, 1963; Marris, 1964). These latter theories identify the differing interests of those within the firm and analyse firm behaviour in terms of the relative power exercised by these interest groups. In like manner, while the work of writers like Becker (1981) continues to take the household as a single, well-defined unit with common interests and a clearly identified utility function, many other writers have begun to examine the nature of relations within the household. Sen (1983), for example, describes the household as a nexus of co-operative conflict. In certain areas the interests of household members converge while in others they are diametrically opposed. There are potential gains to all household members from their organization in a joint unit, but the actual distribution of these benefits depends on the power held by each member and the consequent strength of their bargaining positions (examined later in this chapter). A similar approach is taken by Ben-Porath (1980), who sees the household as composed of members tied by a series of contingent contracts. These contracts specify the rights and obligations of different members, such as the degree of protection from risk that the individual can expect to receive and the return contribution he or she must make to the common estate.

Advantages of large household size: co-operation

There are several benefits from the organization of labour and resources within a large household in communities like Kala. Larger households are better able to generate and maintain a surplus and to ensure their reproduction in the longer term because they:

(i) are able to diversify income sources,
(ii) enjoy reduced vulnerability to demographic risk,
(iii) benefit from economies of scale in agricultural production, and
(iv) are better able to acquire and maintain productive assets.

Diversification of income sources   A major advantage of large household size is the capacity to diversify income sources. This is a way to reduce risk since variability in different incomes is unlikely to be perfectly correlated. Examples in the literature include mixed cropping (Norman *et al.*, 1979) and of pastoralists herding a variety of different species of livestock (Dahl and Hjort, 1979; Swift, 1979). In Kala, while some diversification takes place within the farming sector, by the cultivation of two millet varieties of different cycle length, diversification is more important for activities outside crop production. Research work in Hausaland (P. Hill, 1972; Sutter, 1982; Watts, 1983) and East Africa (Kitching, 1977) has come to a similar finding that the wealth of rural households is positively correlated with the pursuit by one of its members of a lucrative off-farm activity, of which trade is especially important. In such cases, a profitable off-farm income and household wealth tend to be mutually reinforcing, surplus generated in one area being used to raise productivity and expand production in the other. In Kala, diversification of incomes takes place both in the rainy and dry seasons.

In the rainy season, women in larger households have time to plant a small plot of maize and millet that provides a supplement to household food stocks and a source of private income for the woman. In none of the five smallest households in Kala, did any woman of working age have a private grain-field of her own, whereas all women in other households had their own private fields. In the last five years, several households have detached one member to engage full-time in petty trade during the farming season, a period when village traders have a near monopoly on the supply of goods in the village. Out of the six permanent trading businesses, five are in the largest and richest households for whom it represents an additional source of income and avenue for accumulation. The sixth case is a man of seventy from a poor household who, while trading full-time, has very low stocks and deals mainly in low-quality fish and peppers, rather than the more profitable kola-nuts, kerosene, sugar, etc. In four of the largest households, an older man was regularly sent off hunting for meat, contributing to the labour-force's productivity by giving them better food rather than remaining with them in the field. In addition, several emergencies may arise that demand that a household member be absent for a few days, even during the rainy season. Examples of this are being sent in search of strayed or stolen cattle, or to the funeral of a relative in a neighbouring village to which households must send representatives.

Opportunities for income diversification in the dry season last from the end of the grain threshing in January until the first sowing in June and during this time household members pursue a wide range of activities. Some of these are essential to the household's farming and livestock activities—such as clearing new land and watering stock—while others represent an opportunity for the household and individual to supplement income from other sources. Advantages from large household size arise because the labour-force can be divided among these different activities, examples of which are given below.

- Women in households where they are not the sole woman in charge of the cooking share the housework, leaving time free to devote to cotton-spinning, collecting bush produce, dressing other women's hair, petty trade, or visiting relatives in neighbouring villages.
- In the larger households several young men can migrate to town, leaving a few of their peers behind to water cattle and prepare for the next farming season. Earnings from migration reduce the pressure for sales of grain or livestock to meet tax, marriage, and other expenses. The exodus of young men to town is especially crucial in years of poor harvest, as this reduces the burden of people to feed during the dry season and also widens the range of possible income sources by which means people will hope to struggle through the following farming season.

Vulnerability to demographic risk   Larger households are more robust in the face of demographic risks in the following ways:

- vulnerability of farm production to the illness or death of a working member will be greater where there are few workers.
- a balanced sex ratio will be more likely where there are several couples producing children.
- a larger household is more likely to contain a greater spread of labour categories, each with its own part to play in household production and organization, from the five-year old given the infants to guard to the retired man or woman left to care for the sheep and goats while those of working age are away in the field.

- a domestic group containing a number of couples of different ages can be expected to exhibit a less marked cycle in its consumer to worker ratio than a nuclear family.

Table 14.1 presents data on consumer:worker ratios for households according to their size. As may be seen from this table, larger households have a slightly higher dependency ratio, though not significantly so. The coefficient of variation is similar for both classes of household. This is in contrast to the expectations noted earlier that large complex domestic groups would see a less variable pattern of changing dependency rates over time, since the cycle of individual nuclear families within the larger group would be expected to moderate each other. However, if one particular household (with a very high dependency ratio of 2.491) is excluded from this class, the coefficient of variation among large households falls to only 9.1 per cent. This is only slightly over half the value for the small household class and would confirm that in general larger households experience less variation in their dependency ratios.[1]

Economies of scale in agriculture   It would be expected that there will be some economies of scale in agricultural production given the number of duties and operations that must be performed during the short rainy season: care of sheep, goats, the donkey, and so on. The data for Kala show no overall tendency for yields of grain per worker to increase with household size; although yields are lowest in the smallest households, this is due to their lower holdings of productive assets, such as wells and plough teams, rather than diseconomies of farm production. To the extent that economies of scale do exist, they probably are obtained at a fairly low level, in moving from a nuclear household to one containing two or more men and their wives. Having access to a variety of different types of labour is more important for farm production than absolute numbers alone. However, even if there are no significant economies of scale to be gained in farm production above a certain minimum household size, larger households are able to accumulate an absolutely larger surplus that can finance regular farm investments, such as oxen and ploughs. Returns to such investments also tend to increase with increasing household size, (as shown in Chapters 8, 9, and 10) as larger households have access to more labour and can cultivate larger areas of land.

Acquisition and maintenance of productive assets   Household size is relevant to two assets in particular, wells and cattle. As was seen in

---

[1] Household 6, containing 26 people, has recently suffered the deaths of several adult men, leading to a large imbalance in the proportion of men to women and children. The household head is well aware of the heavy burden this imposes on grain stocks, but smiles as he accuses the horde of small children of being like vultures, as he knows that they will soon provide him with a steadily expanding work-force.

TABLE 14.1. *Dependency ratios for households in Kala*

	Household size		
	15 people or less	>15 people	Excluding household 6
No. of households	18	11	10
Mean household size	9.9	33.5	34.3
Mean ratio of consumers to workers	1.55	1.75	1.68
Standard deviation	(0.27)	(0.28)	(0.15)
Coefficient of variation	17.7%	16.3%	9.1%

Note: The dependency ratio of consumers to workers is based on the following weights:

Category of person	Consumer index	Worker index
Male/female, retired, inactive	0.6	0.0
Male, retired, active	0.8	0.5
Female, retired, active	0.7	0.5
Male, over 45 years, works in household field	1.0	0.8
Male 15–45 years	1.0	1.0
Female, works in household field, 16–45 years	0.9	0.6
Male/female workers 12–15 years	0.8	0.7
Male/female 6–12 years	0.7	0.3
Male/female 0–5 years	0.4	0.0

Chapter 8, the only households still without a well in 1982 were the smallest, poorest ones. Those households with the labour available have dug their own wells, while sale of assets has allowed the smaller, better-off household to finance this investment. Those with neither labour nor assets to invest in well-digging have been unable to benefit from the high yields resulting from the extension of manured land under short-cycle millet. In the case of cattle, both plough oxen and breeding animals require the presence throughout the dry season of at least one male worker to form part of the joint water-drawing team. In smaller households, there is often only one young male worker; his obligation to water stock throughout the dry season imposes a heavy cost on the household since it limits his freedom to go on dry-season migration and earn cash to finance taxes and other needs.

The consequences of the above advantages of large household size are demonstrated by the following differences in household performance:

- In both 1980 and 1981, 15 households out of the 29 in the village ran out of millet early, i.e. before the October harvest of village-field millet. The average size of these 15 households was 12.7 persons, as compared with the village mean of 18.2.

- This greater ability to ensure sufficient food supplies for household members in the larger domestic groups is reflected in the greater ability of individuals (particularly women) to establish a private holding of sheep and goats. In poor households these animals must be regularly sold to finance grain purchases when the household granary is empty.
- The four households with the largest holding of sheep and goats contained an average of 41.8 persons and had an average of 2.15 animals per person. This contrasts with the mean household size for the village of 18.2 persons and a holding of 1.27 animals per person.

These data confirm the positive association between household size, livestock wealth, ownership of other assets, and ability to produce enough food for the household.

Problems of increasing household size: Conflict

Against the advantages of large household size outlined above, there are certain problems that arise as the production unit grows due to labour management, monitoring of others' efforts, distributional issues, and the reduced family feeling that exists between more distantly related kin. The labour-incentive problem has been widely discussed in several models of farm households, usually within the context of either formulating the correct shadow price of labour (Sen, 1975) or investigating the efficient use of labour and other resources under alternative contractual forms, such as share-cropping (Stiglitz, 1974; Newbery, 1977) or collective farming (Sen, 1966; Putterman, 1981).

The labour-incentive problem   The essence of the labour-incentive problem is that where a labourer does not receive his/her full product, because part is shared within the family or taken by the landlord, it is expected that they will work less hard than where the entire product is paid to the labourer. In both the share-cropping and the shadow price of labour models, the solution to attaining the optimal level of labour effort is reached either by assuming that the desired level of labour effort can be costlessly monitored and enforced (Cheung, 1969) or by assuming that the individual attaches equal weight to income accruing to others as that which he gains himself (Sen, 1975).

The labour-incentive problem in Kala is met by defining a certain sphere within which individuals owe all their time and labour to the joint enterprise of the domestic group, the product of which provides them with their basic food needs. The power to exact this labour effort is backed up by incentive and force. Incentives include the approbation and compliments of others on being a hard-working cultivator, while disincentives include the loss of access to food to those who do not join the common work-group, as food is cooked and served only to this group. Force is used against women and children, in the form of a beating, should they refuse to go to work. Young men who do not work risk ridicule and a beating, and also imperil the return obligation of the household to provide them with a wife.

Group-work both in the field and in domestic chores allows for continual monitoring of each others' work and provides the encouragement and pressure of example. For example, weeding the field is done 'by taking a small area within which each worker is given a ridge to hoe; those reaching the end of their ridge first, turn to help the slower workers finish, before all move onto the next patch. The exacting demands of the household on its members do not cause revolt for three reasons. First, everyone depends on millet grown in the short rainy season for food over the rest of the year and there is consequently a great desire to throw as much energy as possible into farming during this period. Second, the demands made on the individual apply only for a certain period of time and individuals are free to pursue their private interests once this work is done. Third, as will be shown later, individuals face a very risky future if they are not part of a larger household.

Distribution issues   A major area of conflict within the household concerns the allocation of resources between communal and individual activities, such as the amount of time which the individual must devote to joint as opposed to private production. This has been discussed earlier in Chapter 4, where it was noted that labour obligations to joint production are clearly defined and broadly similar across different households within the village. Questions remain though over the control and use of other resources, in particular, women and livestock. Typically, disputes arise over the use of a communal resource for individual benefit or its converse, the attempt to appropriate for household use an asset that belongs to an individual. Examples of such conflicts are given below.

- Women will use their own stores of grain to feed their own children and husband in times of need but object strongly to these being used to feed those outside the immediate nuclear family unit.
- Cattle ownership is often unequally spread within the household. Many of the costs of a man's marriage will be financed from the assets owned by the subgroup of which he is part. Those men belonging to a wealthier fraction within the household may not allow their livestock to be used to pay for another man's wedding. None the less, it is normal for widows to pass on the death of their

husband, to the next man in age within the household, regardless of whether he belongs to the same subgroup as the deceased. Occasionally this causes controversy as some men object to the passage of a widow to a man whose assets had played no part in acquiring her in the first place.

- Similarly, livestock owned by an individual are not available to finance communal needs. In one case, an old woman's ox had been sold and the proceeds used to buy grain for the joint-household's needs. This was acknowledged to have been wrong and the household had to compensate her by giving her another animal.
- Household assets should not be used to enrich the individual, when the household itself has need of these resources. In one case, a retired man secretly arranged with a herder for the latter to water his flock of sheep and goats at the household well, but to paddock the flock at night on the old man's private field. Here the objection was that the individual should not have free access to a valuable resource—dung—of value to the communal farm enterprise. The herder in question was subsequently moved onto one of the household's jointly cultivated plots.

Game-theory and household organization

The above discussion has shown the strong advantages that can be gained by large domestic groups in the production of food, earning of supplementary incomes, the size of investment returns, and the pooling of health and demographic risks. It should also be recognized that individuals face a very weak position if they become isolated in this society. Sen (1983) presents a game-theory approach to understanding different patterns of household organization. He calls the alternatives open to different household members their 'fall-back' positions, and notes that these will determine the bargaining power of different individuals within the household. Where the alternatives open to an individual are favourable, he or she is in a strong position to negotiate the terms they desire from others, whereas someone who faces a very unattractive and insecure alternative will be forced to accept less favourable terms. This is illustrated by Fig. 14.1.

Take two individuals—x and y—whose benefits are measured along the horizontal and vertical axes respectively. Point F represents the distribution of benefits for x and y in the absence of any co-operative agreement between the two parties and is called the 'fall-back' position. The locus ABCD represents the various combinations of solutions possible through co-operation between x and y, among which AB is the locus of undominated outcomes preferred to point F by both parties. The problem of the game is to determine which point on AB will be reached. For x, a

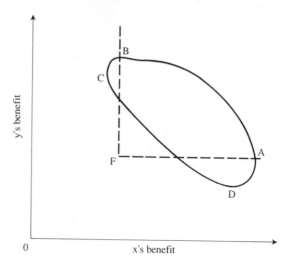

F<small>IG</small>. 14.1. The domestic arrangement as bargaining problem. (From Sen, 1983)

position close to A will be preferred whereas y will want to be close to B. Both x and y have a strong incentive to co-operate since they reap potential gains by moving from point F to AB, but the choice of position on AB is a situation of pure conflict, any gain to x being a loss to y. Sen (1983) considers that several factors will be critical in deciding the final distribution of benefits from co-operation, which include: the economic and physical power available to different individuals; the relative weaknesses of their fall-back position; and the role of ideology in being able to justify a particular distribution of benefits within the society.

The fall-back position for men in Kala   If a man does not want to stay in the household of his birth, he can establish himself in the village as a separate unit, either on his own or with several of his brothers, or he may wish to leave the village and set himself up in another village or town. Each of these decisions is not irrevocable however and men may return to their natal household after 20 years away in the city.

   A single man would find it very difficult to survive on his own as a production unit in a community like Kala, because of the demands of farming as well as food preparation and other household chores and the need for security in the event of illness and old age.[2] Once married, his position is eased somewhat, as his wife takes care of domestic tasks, leaving the man free to farm. For a man with certain assets, such as cattle, a plough, and a well, the nuclear family can be a viable produc-

---

[2] Cooked food cannot be bought in Kala and neighbouring settlements, unlike in many Hausa villages where numerous snacks and meals are made for sale.

tion unit although it faces certain disadvantages, due primarily to its vulnerability in the event of illness or death. Viability is strengthened where the household can borrow specific categories of labour from other relatives during its early years, like a young boy to care for and lead the work-oxen. This relatively favourable fall-back position depends on the man having already acquired a wife and having access to the productive assets needed for successful farming. An unmarried man with several brothers, an elderly mother, and unmarried sisters is also in a relatively strong position, in comparison with a single man, as their separation as a group from the larger household will create a viable production unit.

The relative strength of different men within the household depends therefore on two factors: firstly, the number of people they can potentially take with them in the event of the household dividing—be they brothers, wives, children, sisters, or mothers—and secondly, the assets accruing to that group of individuals, both from the personal wealth of each person and from the share of assets owned at the household level. On the first issue, a man has closest ties of confidence and support with his full brothers and sisters, that is those born of the same father and mother. The position of a man with few close kin in a large household will be weaker than that of a man with several full brothers and sisters. So far as the share of assets is concerned, an individual has rights to that wealth which is identifiably his, such as animals that have been bought from his private income, and to some part of the wealth that is owned at the communal level. In the event of household division, communal assets are generally divided among the different parties according to the relative number of people in each party at that time.

One case was cited from a neighbouring village in which the estate of a pair of brothers was divided, the elder brother having a single grandson while the younger brother had many sons and grandsons. In this case, most of the livestock wealth went to the younger brother, as he had the most male kin. Similarly, in Kala, in 1976, a household divided and the cattle wealth was divided between two parties. At the time, one had several sons in their teens while the other was led by a young man with two brothers aged under ten. Consequently, the first party took the major part of the cattle herd in the name of himself and his sons.

A man's fall-back position must be considered not only in terms of his current productive strength but also his ability to ensure his future security, through the production of legitimate children. This depends on his ability to establish and exploit alliances with other lineages through which marriageable women may be exchanged. Since these alliances are set up and controlled by the elders of each lineage, a young man who has broken away from the control of his elders will find it difficult to negotiate and finance his own marriage, at least if he hopes for a woman from traditional sources.

Another factor that limits the strength of individual men and restricts their mobility from the household of their birth is the ideological power of lineage as an organizational force within the society. This makes it effectively impossible for a man from one lineage to be adopted and fully absorbed into a household belonging to a different lineage and therefore prevents some households being able to acquire more members by poaching them from others.

The fall-back position for women Women are rarely in a position to make a positive choice as to where and with whom they will live, as their marriages are arranged for them by their fathers and brothers. In the final resort they can run away to the city, to parents or other relatives, or to another man. It is rare, however, for women from Kala to go to the city. Only one woman from Kala is resident in Bamako, to which she fled as a young girl some 15 years ago, where she works as a prostitute, completely cut off from her family except for one of her brothers who sought her out and visited her there. Few women visit Ségou on a regular basis, going at most once a year to the market in the company of their husband or brother-in-law. Young men have much greater knowledge about big cities which many visit each year to look for work over the dry season.

A woman who is unhappy with her husband can return to her parents and try to persuade them that she should not be forced to go back to him. This is usually not successful, as the girl's father knows that the stability of the unions into which he and his brothers have entered into would be upset by his taking the side of his daughter in this case. In addition, where a marriage breaks down soon after the wedding, the husband may try to get back part of the money he has given to the girl's family. This will be difficult for the bride's father to return, since money will have been paid over a number of years and spent as it was received. Women who have fled are usually sent straight back to their husbands unless there is evidence of gross abuse, such as where the man continually beats the woman or abuses the name of her father's family. In the latter case, the woman may get the help of her family in getting a divorce, and will have strong grounds for refusing to repay the bride-wealth.

Alternatively, a woman can try to improve her situation by becoming another man's wife. This raises certain problems for the family of the new husband who will find relations with the family of the former husband damaged as a consequence. In addition, financial compensation will normally have to be paid to the woman's former husband.

Thus, for a woman who dislikes her present situation there are few alternatives open. She will usually stay in her husband's household if she has children of her own, as her own future is closely tied to theirs, at least until they are old enough to be independent of her, by which time she may increasingly need their help and the security with which they provide her.

The weak position that women find themselves in is reinforced by the occasional beating from their husbands and by Bambara ideology. Farming is considered to be the most valuable form of work, to which men can devote more of their time than women who are also responsible for domestic tasks. Women, half-jokingly, call their position akin to that of slaves as they are bought and sold by men who take and give them in marriage. They play no official role in village politics, having no forum for regular meetings. Women not only take no part in the *komo* secret society's meetings but are actually a target for its attentions, being forced to hide indoors during *komo* festivities, on pain of a dreadful death. While women joke about these threats, they do not dare to tempt the *komo* to demonstrate its power. There are sufficient unexplained deaths within the community for all people to believe in the *komo*'s ability to seek out a victim.

HOUSEHOLD DIVISION

The strong advantages reaped by individuals from being part of a large domestic group and the weak fall-back position of both men and women have been discussed above. While these are recognized by the Bambara as being very important, households do nevertheless occasionally divide. This is not, however, a regular and predictable stage in the household's path which a man can expect to experience at a certain point in his lifetime, such as on the death of his father.

As a household increases in size over time, with the production of many offspring, it can be expected to divide into two or more groups. The size and structure of the resulting households depend on the lines of cleavage within the former large extended group and the conflicts of interest resulting. A simple case of how households divide is provided in Fig. 14.2. This extended household consists of seven adult men, the children of the same father but two different mothers. In the event of a conflict, the household is likely to split into two, with each group of men born of a single mother forming a separate unit. However, there is no definite point in time when this division will occur. While M_1 is still alive, division is very unlikely. However, division is not inevitable within the lifetimes of any of the men M_2 to M_8. Indeed, if there is no basis for conflict, and if demographic growth within the household has been low, their grandsons may still be living and farming together. Most complex households in Kala were composed of men related at much greater distance than those in Fig. 14.2, their common ancestor often being three or four generations in the past.

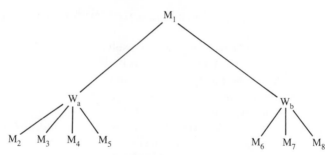

FIG. 14.2. Example of household division. Men M_2 to M_5 are the sons of the household head M_1 by wife W_a, while men M_6 to M_8 are the sons by a second wife W_b

Reasons for household division

There are several reasons given by the Bambara for household division to do with questions of inheritance, conflicts of authority within the household, and personality differences.

Questions of inheritance refer to both women and assets such as live-stock. In the larger households, whereas marriage costs are partially met by the resources of subgroups within the household, widows are usually passed to the man next in age to the deceased, regardless of whether he belongs to the same subgroup which originally used their assets to finance the marriage (see Chapter 13). The dead man's immediate brothers may protest at the passage of the widow to a more distantly related man in the same household and the widow may herself express a preference for another man. Such questions of widow inheritance can provoke a division within the household, although different parties to the dispute will make some accommodation where the desire to remain as a single unit is sufficiently strong. A section within the household may also try to engineer the division of a household and its assets at a time and in such a way as to be to its maximum benefit. This is seen in the case of the division between 15 and 16A, shown in Table 14.2 below and described earlier in this chapter.

Conflicts of authority within the household will inevitably arise as the household grows in size. Two systems of authority exist in Bambara society, the first based on age and the second on generations. Over time, as the age-range of men within the household widens, it becomes increasingly likely that these two systems of authority will come into conflict, as for example when a man's sons are older than his youngest brothers. In general, the generational principle is dominant over that of age, but few if any men would be willing to remain in a household led by someone from a senior generation who was nevertheless younger than them in age.

TABLE 14.2. *Recent cases of household division in Kala, 1950–1980*

Households	Date	Circumstances
1A/1C	early 1960s	Separation of two full brothers from main household. Said to have been personality differences but 1C also a viable unit of several men and women.
1A/21	early 1960s	Illegitimate man forced to establish himself as a separate unit on his marriage.
2A/2B	late 1960s	Separation of three full brothers from main household, both units containing 15–20 people at the time of division, though 2B has subsequently declined in size and fortunes.
4A/4B	mid-1950s	Separation of two full brothers from larger group. Said to have been obstinate and wanted independence.
15/16A	mid-1970s	Separation of man from half-brother's son; former probably engineered split to enable him to take large share of household cattle herd.

Some care is taken to avoid these problems within the smaller households, by a man putting aside plans for remarriage once his own sons approach marriageable age, since this would introduce conflict firstly between himself and his sons over the use of resources needed to take a wife and, secondly, between his sons and his grandsons who could easily find themselves in the situation described above.

Personality differences are held by many to account for the departure of a man and his brothers from the main household. However, although conflicts of personality probably play a role in determining the degree of compromise different men are willing to make in order to keep the household as one unit, individuals are very unlikely to separate themselves off from the larger household unless they can be assured of taking with them a certain number of assets and people. This will depend, as described earlier, on the size of the man's immediate kin-group and their share of household assets.

Table 14.2 presents details of those household divisions which have occurred in Kala over the last 30 years. From this table may be seen the low frequency of such divisions, involving only five cases out of the present 29 households. Over this period, most domestic groups have seen a succession of household heads without this causing division and in none of the above cases was division prompted by the household head's death. In the first, third, and fourth cases, the unit separating itself from the main household had reason to feel confident about their future viability since they took with them a group containing several men, women, and children, as well as an oxen pair. However, in all three cases, the separating group has since become poorer, due to bad harvests, the death of several men and women and the sale of assets, and two of the three (2B, 4B) are now amongst the smallest and poorest in Kala.

That household division is a relatively rare event is due to several factors, some of which have been mentioned earlier in this chapter. First, individuals perceive there to be strong advantages to remaining part of a large domestic group. Second, division of a large household can be postponed by a renegotiation of the terms binding the component elements, typically by granting a greater degree of autonomy to each subgroup over the generation and use of income as household size grows. Third, there is strong ideological value placed on remaining within a single household. Feelings of shame are associated with the division of households since it indicates that the interests of individuals were not able to be accommodated within the larger group. Fourth, while the overall population growth rate is currently estimated to be around 2.5 per cent per annum (Randall, 1984), many households have not seen their numbers grow at this rate. Thus, the anticipated regular division of households due to their growth in size has not taken place.

Given the strong advantages reaped by individuals within larger domestic groups, some explanation must be given for the existence of several very small households which, if they were to join together, would form a more viable socio-economic unit. While it is not unknown for households to co-operate for farming purposes on a temporary basis (as described for two very small households at the end of Chapter 12), the power of the lineage as a social organizing force prevents households from being able to merge fully their identities and to adopt those belonging to a different lineage.

PART V
CONCLUSIONS

15

CONCLUSIONS

The material presented in this book has focused on three interlinked areas of economic and social life for the Bambara farmers of Kala. These areas cover the annual production of the millet crop, the returns from investment of surplus in different farm assets, and the longer-term returns from child-rearing, marriage, and successful household management.

Chapters 4, 5, and 6 presented an analysis of crop production over the two years studied. Despite problems with the definition and measurement of certain variables, this analysis demonstrated, for manuring and plough-team inputs, very considerable differences in levels of factor productivity between crop varieties, between the two cropping seasons, and between different farmers. In many cases, the size of such productivity differentials was such as to outweigh reservations about the accuracy of certain parameters. This analysis confirms the highly variable returns which farmers may expect due to the vulnerability of crop production in the Sahel to the rainfall received in any particular year. The data also show that performance between farmers varies greatly, with some much better able than others to assure themselves a reasonable yield. This traditional Bambara community and its production system are far from being in some long-term stable equilibrium; rather, farmers are continually reacting to changing climatic and economic circumstances by altering patterns of crop production and investment.

Chapters 7 to 11 investigated how returns to investment in the three key farm assets—wells, oxen plough teams, and breeding cattle—vary between producers, depending on the assumptions made about the household's access to complementary assets and its post-investment strategies. An adequate treatment of investment risk depends on knowing the probability distribution of returns over a certain period. In the absence of such data, several fairly simple 'rules of thumb' have been used by which to assess and compare the performance of the three main farm investments in Kala. This comparison of investment performance between different households indicated the most important factors to be taken into account in explaining why some farmers gain much more from investment than others. It was seen that large households and those with complementary assets reap higher returns from the investments examined, first by enabling the services from the asset to be spread over a larger area, thus maintaining high marginal returns to the input concerned, and second, in the case of livestock investments, by reducing the cost per animal of providing dry-season watering labour. In addition, because of their size, large households are better able to generate the investible surplus needed to acquire these assets. Conversely, small poor households in Kala are disadvantaged by their size, which precludes, for example, the use of household labour in well-digging and imposes high watering costs for livestock as labour has a high opportunity cost in the dry season, when it could be earning cash on migration.

Despite the high returns to digging wells which villagers have been reaping, the longer-term returns to this investment were shown to be vulnerable to several factors such as the continued decline in rainfall and limits to the carrying capacity of local pastures. In the longer term, surplus-producing households will need to find other areas into which to direct their investment and energies. Trade has already become of significance for some in the village and the establishment of a few larger shops, stocking a wider range of goods and run by the largest and wealthiest households, is a likely development over the next few years.

Chapters 12 to 14 investigated the interrelations between economic variables and household size and structure. Success in the maintenance and reproduction of the family group was seen to be closely related to successful economic performance in the following ways. Large rich households are able to provide wives for their sons at an earlier age and to conduct a greater number of planned second marriages. They are also better able to safeguard the investment made in a wife through the inheritance of widows by other men in the household. Not only are larger households more resistant to illness and death because of the larger number of individuals over which these risks are spread, but they are also less vulnerable to the cyclical variation in dependency ratios to which nuclear households are subject. The advantages of large household size also lie in the ability to diversify incomes, to generate an investible surplus, to maintain productive assets, and to reap higher returns from investment. Continued cohesion within the large domestic groups found in Kala, despite their considerable size, is made possible by the flexibility of arrangements linking the individual with the joint-household estate. This flexibility permits the renegotiation of the terms linking household members in response to internal tensions and changing external circumstances.

The link between successful demographic and economic performance partly explains the high priority accorded to investment of resources in marriage. The household hopes by such investment to provide itself with a supply of domestically controlled labour for the future and to ensure its older members a relatively secure old age. This priority must be understood in the light of the very difficult position faced by those households whose marital investments have failed and who consequently are unable either to operate as a viable production unit or to ensure their own succession through the production of male heirs.

DATA COLLECTION AND ANALYSIS

The data presented in this book were derived mainly from a two year period of field-work in a group of Bambara villages in central Mali. The methods used for collecting data on the main quantified parameters were described in Chapter 1 and their limitations discussed further there and in subsequent chapters. As was seen, the main problem that arose with the analysis concerned the definition and the measurement of the labour input into crop production, due to the need to aggregate different types of labour, the use of man-days of work, rather than measuring inputs by hour, and difficulties in accounting for different intensities of work input within and between households. The explanation of differences in crop yields by variation in labour input was poor and this is probably due to errors of measurement in all variables used in the analysis, as discussed in Chapter 5. The study would have benefited from an analysis of factor productivity carried out on a sample of small plots, of say 1 ha each, as performed by Bliss and Stern (1982) in their study of an Indian village. Such an analysis would have provided a closely observed set of input–output relationships from which more precise factor productivity coefficients could have been obtained. However, this was not done nor would it have been a substitute for analysis of production at the household level, which was necessary for understanding how overall levels of productivity are related to access to different resources.

In deciding the methods and spread of data to be collected in an exercise such as this, a number of factors must be taken into account. Greater accuracy in the data has to be set against the greater cost involved in acquiring and monitoring the variables being measured. This cost consists not only of the extra input of time from researchers but also, very importantly, the degree of intrusion into the community's life deemed acceptable by both the researchers and the researched. This series of trade-offs must be kept in mind when assessing the results of all data-collection exercises; some material can be treated with confidence while other material is inevitably flawed by the method of acquiring the data and its subsequent aggregation. The significance of differing degrees of accuracy and confidence depends on the uses to which each kind of material is to be put.

DIFFERENTIATION BETWEEN HOUSEHOLDS IN KALA

During the field-work, one question we were interested in answering was whether certain households in Kala were getting richer and others poorer, or whether over the long term temporary differences in wealth balanced out. A variety of models have been developed to help understand and predict the pattern of change in rural society and its response to various forces. The model of cyclical differentiation, developed by Chayanov (1966) is particularly valuable here for its analysis of the links between economic mobility and changes in the household's size and composition. This model presents a picture in which 'polygyny and partible inheritance are the major mechanisms preventing the consolidation' of temporary differences in households' economic status (Guyer, 1981: 44). Richer households tend to conduct a larger number of more expensive marriages than poorer ones and produce more children, so that household wealth becomes fragmented among a larger number of heirs. In this manner 'much differentiation is structurally insignificant . . . People's fortunes rise and fall, either over the life-cycle or over an inter-generational cycle of accumulation and dispersal' (ibid. 44).

The case of Kala also demonstrates strong links between the household's demographic and economic performance. However, these links differ in a number of crucial respects so that, in Kala, the interplay of economic and demographic forces, instead of leading to cyclical differentiation and only temporary differences in economic status, leads to the polarization of domestic groups in terms of their access to labour and their ability to accumulate wealth.

Factors increasing differentiation between households

The Chayanov model takes the nuclear household as its unit of analysis. This goes through a regular sequence of creation, growth, and dissolution as a couple marry, produce children, and die. The timing of these different events and the resulting changes in dependency ratios are crucial in explaining the economic mobility of domestic groups over time. For example, Cain's (1978) study of a Bangladesh village found that poverty is strongly associated with orphanhood, with late age at marriage for men, and with production of few male children late in life. P. Hill's (1972) research in Hausaland similarly attributes the poverty of many men whose fathers had been relatively well off to the early death of the latter, so that the young son loses control over his father's property and lacks his father's support in establishing a viable household and farm of his own.

In Kala, any regular pattern of cyclical differentiation is modified substantially by the presence of large, complex domestic groups containing several nuclear units, as shown in Table 2.1. Members of the household continue to live and work together regardless of the deaths of succeeding family heads. There is no standard pattern of division of household personnel and property on a regular basis and the number of members within the domestic group can build up over several generations before inner conflicts cause the group to split. Thus, economic differentiation between households in Kala due to differences in rates of marriage, the dispersal of property among heirs and changing dependency ratios does not operate in a clear and predictable manner. Only for the smallest households, containing a single nuclear family, are questions of the timing of marriage and child production crucial.

Households differ in their ability to take advantage of new and profitable opportunities as they arise as a result of their differential access to labour and other assets. Households with a large labour-force and assets they can sell are better placed to adopt new technologies than are the smallest, poorest producers and are also able to bear the greater risk associated with adoption of a new technology early in its cycle. This differential rate and speed of adoption between producers tends to accentuate differences in wealth leading to greater polarization.

Several households in Kala account for their currently favourable position, with regards to livestock wealth, by their early take-up of groundnut cultivation in the 1950s, their adoption of ploughs, and the pursuit of a trading business. Their success has depended on a favourable conjunction of circumstances and their having sufficient assets and labour to exploit new opportunities. Access to labour has been as crucial in building up wealth as ownership of saleable assets, since labour can either be invested directly, as in well-digging, or be used indirectly to provide funds for investment, as when migrants' earnings are used to purchase a plough team. Consequently, households with sufficient labour were able in the 1950s and 1960s to achieve considerable wealth creation. This continues to be the case with regard to well-digging, since investment of labour in a well should ensure a regular surplus of grain in future years.

In Chayanov's model, the amount of work put into crop production is determined on the one hand by the diminishing marginal utility of income to the household, once the minimum level of subsistence has been reached, and on the other by the rising marginal disutility attached to work. Chayanov recognized that peasant households were involved in markets to a certain extent and that having access to new consumption goods would raise the marginal utility attached to acquiring extra income. In the case of Kala, producers attach a high marginal utility to income even once their basic subsistence needs have been met, and have always been dependent on trade for certain of their consumption needs. This dependence has been rapidly growing over the past few decades, with markets providing both traditional commodities—salt, kola-nuts, tobacco, and indigo, and new consumer items—bicycles, radios, and watches. People from Kala admit to a substantial improvement in their standard of living over the last 30–40 years, in terms of the number and variety of goods available to them, as well as in their levels of wealth. They attribute this improvement to increased marketing of crops, made possible by the introduction of groundnuts, adoption of oxen-drawn ploughs, and the growth in harvests of manured village-field millet. Since the end of the 1960s, with the decline in groundnut yields, millet has become the main cash and subsistence crop. Farmers sell millet surplus to household consumption needs and either purchase other consumption goods or invest this in livestock (providing a future source of liquidity) or in household expansion.

Accumulation of surplus and its investment in livestock and domestic capital then provide the basis for differentiation, with temporarily richer households able to convert this surplus crop production into a more permanent form of wealth.

Factors reducing differentiation between households

The above factors tend to polarize producers into large, rich households on the one hand and small, poor ones on the other. However, certain environmental and social factors operate to limit the extent and form taken by this polarization and help most poorer households to survive.

Kala lies in a region with abundant cultivable land and low population density. Land is not a scarce factor, control over which can be used to support a position of economic and political power within the Bambara community. All village households have the right to cut a field anywhere within the village's territory. The widespread availability of land also gives everyone access to essential commodities like firewood. In addition, grain-deficit households can supplement their food supplies with bush products, such as baobab fruit, wild rice, and *bere* (*Boscia senegalensis*). These provide a less costly way of coping with grain shortage than many alternatives, such as the sale of assets and labour, or begging of millet from neighbours.

The minimum size of investment needed by farmers to start cultivation has until recently been very low, consisting of hoes, food for the work-force until harvest, and seed grain. Capital is not required either to buy land or to make major improvements, except for a rudimentary clearing. This has meant that it is relatively easy for households to establish themselves as independent producing units. However, for the production of a regular surplus, farmers must now make substantial investments in the form of oxen plough teams and wells.

Households are subject to production, investment, and demographic risks, against which they can protect themselves only imperfectly. The more successful forms of insurance against risk tend to be those in the hands of the larger and more wealthy households, such as income diversification, storage of surplus in saleable assets, and spreading of demographic risk across a larger group of people. Thus, the operation of risk and insurance policies tends to work in favour of larger, richer producers, leading to greater polarization. Nevertheless, such forms of insurance can fail, reducing a once large, cohesive, and well-off household to a dispirited and asset-less collection of individuals. Such a decline in household fortunes may be due to bad luck alone, but is more commonly associated with poor management by the household head and internal disputes between family members.

In the face of considerable risk to harvests, Bambara society has evolved a variety of redistributive mechanisms which have a levelling effect. Examples of these mechanisms include the distribution of grain from harvests and the ideology of egalitarianism which exists within Bambara society.[1] The possession of such an ideology does not prevent inequality developing within this society, but it does help to reinforce levelling processes and minimize the establishment of relations of dependence between Bambara households.

ENVIRONMENTAL DEGRADATION IN THE SAHEL: LESSONS FROM KALA

The sahelian region of West Africa is perceived by some as an area of increasing hopelessness, suffering from environmental deterioration, rising population pressures and a collapse in the region's ability to feed itself. Thirty years of independence and development assistance seem to have brought few appreciable benefits to people living in the more marginal farming and livestock-rearing areas, and overall standards of living throughout the Sahel are estimated to be lower now than in the 1960s.

Problems of environmental degradation are particularly acute in densely settled farming areas where an increase in area cultivated and reduced fallowing periods have led to increased rates of soil erosion and reduced soil fertility (Rochette, 1989). Further north, fields have moved into drier pastoral zones, where farmers practise a very extensive and high-risk farming strategy. Large areas are cleared and sown, leaving the land more greatly exposed to risks of erosion (Bonfils, 1987).

The intensity of resource degradation in any particular place can be explained by several factors, such as human population growth, the introduction of ploughs, and the sedentarization of pastoral groups. However, perhaps the most important factor is the extent to which the community concerned can continue to exercise control over access to the land, water, and other resources within their village territory.

The process of population growth and field expansion is clear to farmers in Kala who have witnessed the results of such growth in the region to the south of their village, where the bush has been gradually filling up with fields, reducing the availability of pasture, game, and bush

---

[1] Details of such mechanisms are provided below in the Appendix.

products. They recognize that this will start to happen in their area sooner or later and are concerned to control this process by, for example, stipulating that only people who settle properly in the village can farm its land. Kala has the advantage of being on the edge of the farming zone, with large expanses of empty bush to the north of the settlement. This means it is still able to maintain a fallowing and manuring system that has been abandoned elsewhere. How long this system can be maintained will depend on population growth, the demand for farmland and the control which Kala can exercise in determining who has access to their lands.

The pressure of demand on given resources and the extent to which local communities can exert some control over them in practice depend in large part on the relative value of these resources. For example, trees close to roads and towns will be sought by woodcutters in preference to those further away, and local people may find it hard to preserve their own trees and supplies of wood from such competition. The village of Kala benefits in this respect from its distance from major markets and roads, and having no resources of especial value to attract outsiders. Woodcutters from Niono and Ségou have areas of woodland at closer hand than the large bushlands surrounding Kala. The main external source of pressure on land comes from farmers from villages close to the bird-infested Canal du Sahel irrigation channels, wanting to cut new fields far from the risk of attack by birds. Fulani herders also want to settle and farm in the region without their rights to do so being dependent on the good grace of a Bambara village. As noted earlier, the Fulani have only been granted rights to settle and farm around Kala for so long as they work as hired herders for village-owned cattle. Maintaining this control puts the Bambara in a strong bargaining position with the Fulani when it comes to the terms of the herding contract. Bambara power is occasionally brought into question, as described in Chapter 11, where a Fulani tried to get a government ruling that he be allowed to settle and dig a well within the village's territory. However, substantial bribes were paid by the villagers to ensure that this decision was overturned by the administration in Bamako.

Apart from farmland, Kala also disposes of good supplies of water, grazing, and game. Water and grazing are sought in particular by pastoralists who must conclude an agreement with a well owner in Kala before being allowed to pasture and water their stock in the dry season. A herder cannot water his animals more than once at the village's wells unless such an agreement has been made (discussed in more detail in Chapter 8). Given the absence of ponds or rivers, herds must be brought to the village's wells if they are to have access to the extensive dry-season pastures available. Hence, by controlling access to water, the villagers can also control access to grazing.

As for game, traditionally hunters from elsewhere were required to ask formally for the permission of the chief of the hunters' society before being allowed to hunt. Adherence to this rule still persists, to a large extent, since it is generally agreed that the chief of the hunters has especially great powers. Should he discover that someone has not asked for his permission, the latter may fear an accident, such as his gun blowing up in his face or his becoming lost in the bush. Nevertheless, such controls have not prevented the gradual disappearance throughout the region of formerly common wildlife, such as lion, antelope, and wild boar. More often than not, hunters now come back empty-handed or with a brace of guinea-fowl at best. The regular hunting festivals continue, with drumming, dancing, and loosing-off of guns, but the paraphernalia associated with hunting is becoming increasingly ceremonial.

The vulnerability of sahelian farmers to crop failure stems not only from the highly variable physical environment and increasing pressure on all resources, but also from the weakness of institutions and rules regarding access to and control over these resources. Rising human demands, increased rates of commercialization and the profits to be made from exploiting certain resources have demonstrated the inability of governments to manage and control access to resources fairly and effectively. As noted in Chapter 2, following Independence, the Malian government announced that resources would be open to all those wanting to use them, while the state retained ultimate ownership. Local communities no longer have rights in law to control access by outsiders, local government cannot effectively manage the huge areas given to them, and disputes tend to be regulated on the basis of who can pay the larger sum to the official with responsibility. Where a decision goes against a particular person at one level, the losing party may move to the next level up and pay a larger sum in the hope that the decision will be overturned in their favour. This lack of firm and fair rules is likely to pose a fundamental constraint on longer-term decision-making for farmers and herders, because any incentive to manage resources better and to invest in their future productivity requires some assurance that rights to those improved resources will be respected.

The villagers of Kala currently enjoy the good fortune of maintaining a large measure of control over their resources. This power in association with the production, investment, and household-management strategies described in this book have allowed them to develop a remarkably successful system, which ensures that most households are able to meet their needs in this highly risk-prone environment.

Appendix: *Levelling Mechanisms within Bambara Society*

Examples of redistributive mechanisms within Bambara society include:

(a) At threshing time, the grain is winnowed by a huge crowd of village and visiting women who set aside a substantial proportion of the harvest (estimated at some 10 per cent of the total harvest of 250,000 kg in 1980) for sharing amongst themselves in payment for the winnowing work. Households which have suffered harvest failure can get an important supplement to their stocks from these winnowing earnings and, although they belong to women, they usually end up being used to feed the family where food is in short supply. Both men and women, but particularly the latter, often travel to stay with relatives in other settlements to harvest and winnow the grain, and may remain for many months of the following dry season. Households which have suffered a poor harvest can rid themselves in this way of many of their members for several months, thereby reducing the strain on limited food supplies. At the same time, those who are away are earning grain which will be brought back and used to feed the household over the following cultivation season. The other side of the coin is that households which have had a good harvest are obliged to house and feed visiting relatives through much of the dry season, thereby using up much of their surplus grain. While this obligation is recognized and honoured, hosts are well aware of the cost. One household head, renowned for his generosity, received a large number of visitors over many months in 1981, including a blacksmith couple who stayed for over a year. He calculated this to have cost him between 400 and 600 kg of millet but, while occasionally incensed by his visitors' lack of scruple, he felt quite unable to protest or ask them to leave. Another wryly mentioned that since his new well provided him with a regular grain surplus, he had acquired many new relatives whom he had never known of before. Several others noted how useful it was to convert surplus grain soon after harvest into something less visible and less easily tapped by the inevitable stream of visitors and praise-singers. Exchanging surplus grain for cattle was considered the best way of doing this.

(b) In many rural societies faced by risk, it is common for ties of dependency to grow up between rich and poor households, often based on relations of indebtedness and wage-labour. Some of the points outlined above operate to reduce the likelihood of such ties developing between Bambara households. In addition, the Bambara are aware that such dependencies may develop and have a set of social rules which aims to prevent them emerging. Thus, they maintain a strong ideology of egalitarianism among themselves, of which age-groups in the village *ton* (see Chapter 2) within which each member is the absolute equal of his peers, are but one manifestation. Each household head is also theoretically the equal of all others, regardless of the size and wealth of their respective families. Gifts presented to the village, such as a sack of salt, would always be scrupulously divided into 29 equal shares, one for each of the households in Kala. However, in practice, size and wealth of household as well as the date of their settlement in the village also intervene in affecting the relative political power of the households at village level, as discussed in Chapter 12. Households in the village avoid relations of indebtedness, wage-employment, and cash transactions amongst themselves, claiming that these forms of contract are not right among those of similar noble (*horon*) social status. Grain tends to be given rather than loaned and wage-employment is limited to a few households which, being short of grain in that farming season, must send out one or two of their members to work for others. No household was involved in selling labour in both of the farming seasons studied, which suggests a lack of permanence in relations between those households buying and selling labour. Another factor limiting the emergence of patron–client relations between the Bambara is the presence of other more exploitable forms of labour, particularly that provided by Fulani herders. The Bambara maintain their access to Fulani herding labour by controlling the terms under which outsiders can settle and farm within the village's territory. Between the Bambara and Fulani there are no constraints over the establishment of wage-labour contracts, the giving of credit, or charging for services rendered.

References

ANDERSON, J. R. and JODHA, N. S. (1973), 'On Cobb–Douglas and Related Myths', *Economic and Political Weekly*, 8/26: A65–7.

—— DILLON, J. L., and HARDAKER, J. B. (1977), *Agricultural Decision Analysis* (Ames, Ia.).

BAUMOL, W. J. (1959), *Business Behaviour, Value and Growth* (New York).

BECKER, G. S. (1981), *A Treatise on the Family* (Cambridge, Mass.).

—— and LEWIS, G. H. (1973), 'On the Interaction between the Quantity and Quality of Children', *Journal of Political Economy*, 81/2: 279–88.

BECKER, L. C. (1989), 'Conflict and Complementarity in Bamana Farming: A Case Study of Soro, Mali' (University of London, Ph.D. thesis).

BEN-PORATH, B. (1980), 'The F-connection: Families, Friends and Firms, and the Organisation of Exchange', *Population and Development Review*, 6/1.

BINSWANGER, H. P., EVENSON, R. E., FLORENCIO, C. A., and WHITE, B. N. F. (1980), *Rural Household Studies in Asia* (Singapore).

—— and MCINTIRE, J. (1984), 'Behavioural and Material Determinants of Production Relations in Land-Abundant Tropical Agriculture', Discussion Paper, ARU 17, World Bank (Washington, DC).

BLISS, C. J. and STERN, N. H. (1982), *Palanpur: The Economy of an Indian Village* (Oxford).

BONFILS, M. (1987), *Halte à la désertification au Sahel* (Paris).

BURT, O. R. (1971), 'Effects of Misspecifications of Log-linear Functions when Simple Values are Zero or Negative: Comment', *American Journal of Agricultural Economics*, 53/4: 671–3.

CAIN, M. T. (1978), 'The Household Life-cycle and Economic Mobility in Rural Bangladesh', *Population and Development Review*, 4/3: 421–38.

—— (1980), 'The Economic Activities of Children in a Village in Bangladesh', in H. P. Binswanger, *et al.*: 218–47.

—— (1983), 'Fertility as Adjustment to Risk', *Population and Development Review*, 9/4: 688–702.

CALDWELL, J. C. (1977), 'Towards a Re-statement of Demographic Transition Theory', in J. C. Caldwell (ed.), *The Persistence of High Fertility* (Canberra).

CHAYANOV, A. V. (1966), *The Theory of Peasant Economy* (Homewood, Ill.).

CHENNAREDY, V. (1967), 'Production Efficiency in South Indian Agriculture', *Journal of Farm Economics*, 49/4: 816–20.

CHEUNG, S. N. S. (1969), *The Theory of Share Tenancy* (Chicago, Ill.).

CISSÉ, M. I. and HIERNAUX, P. (1984), 'Impact de la mise en valeur agricole sur les ressources fourragères. Étude de cas: les jachères de Dalonguebougou (Mali central)', Document de Programme, AZ 96, International Livestock Centre for Africa (Bamako, Mali).

COULOMB, J., SERRES, H., and TACHER, G. (1980), *L'Élevage en pays sahéliens* (Paris).

CYERT, R. M. and MARCH, J. G. (1963), *A Behavioural Theory of the Firm*, (Englewood Cliffs, NJ).

DAHL, G. and HJORT, A. (1979), *Having Herds: Pastoral Herd Growth and Household Economy* (Stockholm).

DELGADO, C. (1979), 'An Investigation into the Lack of Mixed Farming in the West Africa Savannah: A Farming Systems Approach', in K. Shapiro (ed.), *Livestock Production and Marketing in the Entente States of West Africa: A Summary Report*, CRED (Ann Arbor, Mich.).

DILLON, J. I. and HARDAKER, J. B. (1980), *Farm Management Research for Small Farmer Development*, FAO (Rome).

FARMER, G. and WIGLEY, T. M. L. (1985), Climatic Trends for Tropical Africa: A Research Report for the Overseas Development Administration, Climatic Research Unit, University of East Anglia (Norwich).

FULTON, D. and TOULMIN, C. (1982), 'A Socio-economic Study of an Agro-pastoral System in Central Mali', Report to the International Livestock Centre for Africa (Addis Ababa, Ethiopia).

GOODY, J. (1976), *Production and Reproduction: A Comparative Study of the Domestic Domain* (Cambridge).

—— and TAMBIAH, S. J. (1973), *Bridewealth and Dowry* (Cambridge).

GRAAF, J. (1984), 'Economic Theory and the Economy of Palanpur', *Oxford Economic Papers*, 36: 327–35.

GROVE, A. T. (1985), 'No Sign of End to Sahel Drought', *The Times*, 8 Apr.

GULLIVER, P. H. (1955), *The Family Herds: A Study of two Pastoral Tribes in East Africa: The Jie and the Turkana* (London).

GUYER, J. (1981), 'Household and Community in African Studies', *African Studies Review*, 24/2 and 3: 83–137.

—— (1984), *Family and Farm in Southern Cameroun* (Boston).

HARRISS, J. (1982) (ed.), *Rural Development. Theories of Peasant Economy and Agrarian Change* (London).

HEADY, E. O. and DILLON, J. L. (1961), *Agricultural Production Functions* (Ames, Ia.).

HESSE, C., TCHIAN, A., FOWLER, C., and SWIFT, J. (1984), 'A Fulani Agro-pastoral Production System in the Malian Gourma', Draft Report, ILCA, Bamako, Mali.

HILL, A. (1981), 'The Demographic Situation in Sub-Saharan Africa', Discussion Paper 81–2, Population and Human Resource Division, World Bank (Washington, DC).

—— (1985) (ed.), *Population, Health and Nutrition in the Sahel: Issues in the Welfare of Selected West African Communities* (London).

—— RANDALL, S. C., and VAN DER EERENBEEMT, M.-L. (1983), 'Infant and Child Mortality in Rural Mali', Working paper 83–5, Centre for Population Studies, London School of Hygiene and Tropical Medicine (London).

HILL, P. (1972), *Rural Hausa: A Village and a Setting* (Cambridge).

HIRSHLEIFER, J. (1970), *Investment, Interest and Capital* (Englewood Cliffs, NJ).

HOPPER, W. D. (1965), 'Allocative Efficiency in "Traditional Indian Agriculture"', *Journal of Farm Economics*, 47: 611–24.

HUNT, D. (1979), 'Chayanov's Model of Peasant Household Resource Allocation', *Journal of Peasant Studies*, 6/3: 247–85.

Intergovernmental Panel on Climatic Change (IPCC) (1990), *Potential Impacts of*

Climate Change, World Meteorological Organisation (Geneva) and United Nations Environment Programme (Nairobi).

KITCHING, G. N. (1977), 'Economic and Social Inequality in East Africa: The Present as a Clue to the Past', Discussion Paper, Centre for Development Studies (Swansea).

—— (1980), *Class and Economic Change in Kenya: The Making of an African Petite Bourgeoisie. 1905–1970* (New Haven, Conn.).

LAMB, P. J. (1982), 'Persistence of Subsaharan Drought', *Nature*, 299, 2 Sept.: 46–8.

LE HOUEROU, H. N. and HOSTE, C. H. (1977), 'Rangeland Production and Annual Rainfall Relations in the Mediterranean and in the African Sahelian and Sudanian Zones', *Journal of Resource Management*, 30: 181–9.

LEWIS, J. (1978), 'Descendants and Crops: Two Poles of Production in a Malian Peasant Village', (Yale University, Ph.D. thesis).

LIPTON, M. (1968), 'The Theory of the Optimizing Peasant', *Journal of Development Studies*, 4/3.

—— (1983), 'Demography and Poverty', Staff Working Paper 623, World Bank (Washington, DC).

MARKOWITZ, H. M. (1959), *Portfolio Selection* (New York).

MARRIS, R. (1964), *Theory of 'Managerial' Capitalism* (London).

MARTIN, M. (1984), 'Food Intake in two Bambara Villages in the Ségou Region of Mali' (unpublished M.Sc. thesis, Department of Human Nutrition, London School of Hygiene and Tropical Medicine, London).

MASSEL, B. F. and JOHNSON, R. W. M. (1968), 'Economics of Small-holder Farming in Rhodesia', *Food Research Institute Studies*, suppl. vol. 8 (Stanford, Calif.).

MEILLASSOUX, C. (1975), *Femmes, greniers et capitaux* (Paris).

NAG, M., WHITE, B. N. F., and PEET, C. R. (1980), 'An Anthropological Approach to the Study of the Economic Value of Children in Java and Nepal, in H. P. Binswanger, *et al.*: 248–71.

NEWBERY, D. M. G. (1977), 'Risk-sharing, Share-cropping and Uncertain Labour Markets', *Review of Economic Studies* 44/138: 585–94.

NORMAN, D. W. (1972), 'An Economic Study of three Villages in Zaria Province, Samaru', Miscellaneous paper 37, Institute for Agricultural Research (Samaru, Nigeria).

—— PRYOR, D. H., and GIBBS, C. J. N. (1979), 'Technical Change and the Small Farmer in Hausaland of Northern Nigeria', African Rural Economy Paper 21 (East Lansing, Mich.).

NOWSHIRVANI, V. F. (1967), 'Allocation Efficiency in Traditional Indian Agriculture: A Comment', *Journal of Farm Economics*, 49/1: 218–21.

POLLET, E. and WINTER, G. (1971), *La société Soninké (Dyahunu, Mali)* (Brussels).

PUTTERMAN, L. (1981), 'Is a Democratic Collective Agriculture Possible? Theoretical Considerations and Evidence from Tanzania', *Journal of Development Economics*, 9: 375–403.

RANDALL, S. (1984), 'The Demography of three Sahelian Populations: Marriage and Childcare as Intermediate Determinants of Fertility and Mortality' (London University, Ph.D. thesis).

Rapports Économiques, 1936, 1937, 1940, Archives Nationales (Bamako, Mali).

RETEL-LAURENTIN, A. (1979), 'Causes de l'infécondité dans la Volta Noire', Travaux et Documents, Cahier 87, CNRS/INED (Paris).

ROCHETTE, R. M. (1989), *Le Sahel en lutte contre la désertification: Leçons d'expériences* (Weikersheim).

ROUMASSET, J. A., BOUSSARD, J. M., and SINGH, I. J. (1979) (eds.), *Risk, Uncertainty and Agricultural Development* (New York).

SCHULTZ, T. (1975), *Transforming Traditional Agriculture* (New Haven, Conn.).

SEN, A. K. (1966), 'Labour Allocation in a Collective Enterprise', *Review of Economic Studies*, 33.

—— (1975), *Employment, Technology, and Development* (Oxford).

—— (1983), 'Co-operative Conflicts: Technology and the Position of Women', mimeo (Oxford).

SHACKLE, G. L. S. (1970), *Expectation, Enterprise and Profit: The Theory of the Firm* (London).

SHORT, R. V. (1984), 'Breast-feeding', *Scientific American*, 250/4: 35–41.

STARK, O. (1981), 'The Asset Demand for Children during Agricultural Modernization', *Population and Development Review*, 7/4: 671–5.

STENNING, D. J. (1958), Household Viability among the Pastoral Fulani, in J. Goody (ed.), *The development cycle in domestic groups* (Cambridge).

STIGLITZ, J. E. (1974), 'Incentives and Risk-sharing in Share-cropping', *Review of Economic Studies*, 41/126: 219–56.

STONE, L. (1977), *The Family, Sex and Marriage in England 1500–1800* (London).

SURET-CANALE, J. (1961), *Histoire de l'Afrique occidentale* (Paris).

SUTTER, J. (1982), 'Peasants, Capital and Rural Differentiation: A Nigerian Case-study' (Cornell University, Ph.D. thesis).

SWIFT, J. J. (1979), 'West African Pastoral Production Systems', Working paper 3, USAID/CRED (Ann Arbor, Mich.).

—— (1985), *Pastoral and Agro-pastoral Production Systems in Central Mali: Three Case Studies*, ILCA (Addis Ababa, Ethiopia).

TIFFEN, M. (1976), *The Enterprising Peasant: Economic Development in Gombe Emirate, North-Eastern State, Nigeria 1900–1968* (London).

TOBIN, J. (1958), 'Liquidity Preference as Behaviour towards Risk', *Review of Economic Studies*, 25.

—— (1965), 'The Theory of Portfolio Selection', in F. Hahn and F. P. Brechling (eds.). *The Theory of Interest Rates* (London).

TRAORÉ, A. and SOUMARÉ, S. (1984), 'Supplementation alimentaire des bœufs de labour du système agro-pastoral du mil à Dalonguebougou: résultat préliminaire', Document de Programme AZ.111, ILCA (Bamako, Mali).

UPTON, M. (1979), 'The Unproductive Production Function', *Journal of Agricultural Economics*, 30/2: 179–91.

VERGOPOULOS, K. (1978), 'Capitalism and Peasant Productivity', *Journal of Peasant Studies*, 5/4: 446–65.

WATTS, M. (1983), *Silent Violence: Food, Famine and Peasantry in Northern Nigeria* (Berkeley and London).

WEIL, P. M. (1970), 'Introduction of the Oxplough in the Gambia', in P. F. Mcloughlin (ed.), *African Food Production Systems: Cases and Theory* (Baltimore).

WILLIAMSON, O. E. (1975), *Markets and Hierarchies. Analysis and Anti-trust Implications: A Study on the Economics of Internal Organization* (New York).

WILSON, R. T., DE LEEUW, P. N., and DE HAAN, C. (1983) (eds.), *Recherches sur les Systèmes des zones arides du Mali: résultats préliminaires*, ILCA (Addis Ababa, Ethiopia).

World Bank (1989), *Sub-Saharan Africa: From Crisis to Sustainable Growth.* (Washington, DC).

Glossary of Bambara and French Terms

Arrondissement	the local level of administration.
Bambara	the largest ethnic group found in Mali, part of the wider Mandé cultural grouping, dependent on farming and some livestock-keeping.
balansan	*Acacia albida* (also known as *Faidherbia albida*), the widely known acacia tree found throughout the sahelian zone which has the merit of losing its leaves during the rainy season, and therefore does not shade the crop, while bearing leaves which provide much-valued shade in the hot dry season.
bere	a shrub, *Boscia senegalensis*, bearing a fruit widely used as a famine food in the dry season and during drought.
Cercle	the district level of administration.
dah	*Hibiscus* species.
dama	reciprocal work-groups, used for weeding of fields.
dasiri	the sacred grove of trees, near the village, where sacrifices are made at the start of the farming season to ensure good harvests.
dege	a fermented millet gruel, containing small balls of flour, and sometimes soured milk, eaten in mid-afternoon.
fama	those with power, typically used to describe the traditional ruler of Ségou from pre-colonial times.
fantan	those without power, used to describe common folk.
fogofogo	a small tree, *Calotropis procera*, of little value, which grows on exhausted land, such as old bush fields.
fonio	an annual grass, *Digitaria exilis*, formerly cultivated by many but now restricted largely to women.
foroba	the 'big field', describing activities which are carried out by the household as a whole, rather than the more restricted nuclear family (cf. *suroforo*).
Fulani	a large ethnic group found throughout the semi-arid West Africa, traditionally the main livestock-keepers, and used by the Bambara as contract herders.
furu	marriage.
furuke	to marry.
furumuso	a bride, used to describe a woman on her first marriage.
gwa	the Bambara household which lives together, farms a common field, and eats from the same pot.
harratin	the slave class amongst Maure nomads.
horon	the noble caste among the Bambara.
jamu	the clan name of a lineage, used in all greetings, and which helps define peoples' relationships with each other.
jon	the slave caste among the Bambara.
juru	a rope, also used to refer to a debt, since a debtor is perceived to be tied by a rope to the creditor.

komalo	a wild rice which grows in ponds.
komo	the village 'fetish', housed in a small hut, to be placated by sacrifices of millet and chickens; the focus of the *komo* secret society, to which only Bambara men may belong.
kwoorisongo	part of the marriage payment to be made by the man's family, literally 'the price of cotton', bought, spun, and woven by those in the girl's family to provide blankets and cloth for her dowry.
marabout	an Islamic holy man.
Maure	people from Mauritania, here used to refer to the trans-humant pastoralists who visit villages like Kala with their herds through the long dry season.
musotigi	a husband, literally the owner or master of a woman.
numu	the blacksmith caste, part of the *nyamakala*.
nyamakala	the artisan caste among the Bambara.
Office du Niger	the large irrigation scheme, planned from the early part of this century and begun in the late 1920s, to divert water from the River Niger at Ségou into a network of dried-up river beds leading northwards. It was hoped that this scheme would enable the irrigation of 1.2 million hectares of cotton, but today there are only an estimated 60,000 hectares irrigated, largely devoted to rice.
paki	a rapid sowing of millet fields done by dropping seeds into a line of holes made by a long-handled hoe, without any other soil preparation.
Région	the largest administrative unit in Mali, of which there were seven during the period of field-work.
sanyo	a longer-cycle variety of bulrush millet, *Pennisetum typhoides*, grown in bush fields.
sounan	a shorter-cycle variety of bulrush millet, *Pennisetum typhoides*, grown in village fields.
suroforo	'night field' referring to the plots of land cultivated by individuals or small groups within the larger household in the evenings, from which they can earn incomes for themselves, rather than income earned and controlled by the larger household, or *foroba*. Now the term is used to refer to all private, or individual forms of activity, whether or not it involves farming.
to	a thick millet porridge eaten with a sauce of baobab leaves, dried fish, or meat.
ton	the traditional village youth association, made up of young men aged between 15 and 35 years of age, hired to work on fields, fabrication of bricks, and other activities.
Tukolor	an ethnic group from the Senegal River valley who, in the nineteenth century, led by El Hadj Umar Tall, conquered a large part of the Western Sudan, until finally defeated at Ségou by the French colonial army in 1890.

wa   a perennial grass, *Andropogon gayanus*, widely appreciated for its fodder qualities and use for making granaries.

wuluku   an annual grass, *Schoenefeldia gracilis* used for making sweeping brushes.

Index